To Establish Justice for All

Praise for
To Establish Justice for All

"This is the definitive history of civil legal aid in the United States. It is comprehensive and beautifully written. It is a story of the elusive quest to ensure that rich and poor alike have access to our legal system. It is a must-read for all who care about justice in this country."

—Erwin Chemerinsky, Dean and Distinguished Professor of
Law, Raymond Pryke Professor of First Amendment Law,
University of California, Irvine School of Law

"Earl Johnson, Jr., who in 1966 became the director of OEO-Legal Services as a 33-year-old attorney, provides the definitive history of civil legal aid in the United States from 1876 to present. It is a story told with fascinating biographical detail about such figures as Lewis Powell, Sargent Shriver, Richard Nixon, Archibald Cox, Donald Rumsfeld, Dick Cheney, Ronald Reagan, Clinton Bamberger, Gary Bellow, Jean Charn, and Hillary Rodham, among others. From the early era of charity-supported legal aid in the late 19th century, to the progressive idealism of Reginald Heber Smith, to a brief period of impact litigation from 1968–1974, to the political compromises that led to the creation of the Legal Services Corporation, this multi-volume effort chronicles the troubled efforts to provide civil justice for all Americans. The book reveals that despite American rhetoric about its commitment to equal justice, the United States falls far short in providing basic representation in civil matters compared to other advanced western democracies. Johnson has written a book that will fascinate and challenge all American lawyers."

—Robert L. Nelson, Director, American Bar Foundation;
MacCrate Research Chair in the Legal Profession; and
Professor of Sociology and Law, Northwestern University

"*To Establish Justice for All*, from the definitive historian of the American legal aid movement, is essential reading for anyone who has ever worked in a legal aid program or served on a board of directors. Each chapter is filled with finely detailed accounts of the key players and moments that have led to today's system of civil justice. Newer advocates, in particular, can gain a rich understanding of the history of the critical movement of which they are a part."

—Don Saunders, Vice President, Civil Legal Services,
National Legal Aid and Defender Association

"This is a magnificent work. Johnson traces not just the history of an institution—Legal Aid—but also of an idea, the right to counsel in civil cases. Beginning in the 19th century with the struggles of German immigrants and reaching across the length and breadth of 20th-century America and beyond, Johnson traces the search for fairness and the determination of its opponents. The fulfillment of this nation's commitment to a right to counsel remains incomplete, but Johnson's three illuminating, readable and powerful volumes may help expedite the day when those rights are fully secured. This is an essential addition to every law library and important reading for those who care about the nation's legal history."

—Jim Newton, *Los Angeles Times* columnist and author of
Justice for All: Earl Warren and the Nation He Made

To Establish Justice for All

The Past and Future of Civil Legal Aid in the United States

Volume 3

Earl Johnson Jr.

 PRAEGER

AN IMPRINT OF ABC-CLIO, LLC
Santa Barbara, California • Denver, Colorado • Oxford, England

Library of Congress Cataloging-in-Publication Data

Johnson, Earl, 1933–
    To establish justice for all : the past and future of civil legal aid in the United States / Earl Johnson Jr.
        pages cm
    Includes bibliographical references and index.
    ISBN 978-0-313-35706-0 (hardcopy : alk. paper) —
ISBN 978-0-313-35707-7 (ebook)   1. Legal aid—United States.
2. Legal assistance to the poor—United States.   I. Title.
    KF336.J64   2013
    362.5'8—dc23   2013016323

ISBN: 978-0-313-35706-0
EISBN: 978-0-313-35707-7

18   17   16   15   14   1   2   3   4   5

This book is also available on the World Wide Web as an eBook. Visit www.abc-clio.com for details.

Praeger
An Imprint of ABC-CLIO, LLC

ABC-CLIO, LLC
130 Cremona Drive, P.O. Box 1911
Santa Barbara, California 93116-1911

This book is printed on acid-free paper ∞

Manufactured in the United States of America

The oral histories used throughout the book were provided courtesy of the National Equal Justice Library Archives.

This book is dedicated to my wife, Barbara Yanow Johnson,
my partner in life, who shares the dream this country
may one day truly provide its people justice for all.

WE THE PEOPLE of the United States, in Order to form a more perfect Union, establish Justice, insure domestic Tranquility, provide for the common defence, promote the general Welfare, and secure the Blessings of Liberty to ourselves and our Posterity, do ordain and establish this Constitution for the United States of America.

Preamble, the United States Constitution

Contents

PART V

Access to Justice Narrows for the Nation's Poor

Chapter 26

Gingrich's "Contract" Cancels Clinton's "Hope"

The first thing we do, let's kill all the lawyers.
> —Dick the Butcher (helping plot a revolution)
> William Shakespeare, *Henry the Sixth* Part 2,
> Act 2, scene 2, 71–78

If I believed even a quarter of the charges leveled against legal services lawyers, I would agree the program should be eliminated.
> —Alexander Forger, President Legal Services Corporation (1993–97)

After 12 years tottering on the brink, legal services supporters were enthusiastic over the election of Bill Clinton as U.S. president. Only a dozen years earlier, Hillary Rodham Clinton had been chair of the Legal Services Corporation and presided over its best years. There was every reason to expect a new day, indeed the best days ever for the LSC and the lawyers it supported. The White House suddenly turned from the opponent it had been during the Reagan years and the sometimes grudging neutrality of the Bush years to the promise of being an out-and-out champion of legal services for the poor.

THE RETURN TO A FULLY SUPPORTIVE LSC BOARD

The choices for LSC board members certainly were encouraging to those in the legal services community. It was soon clear Howard Phillips, the Farm Bureau and the rest of the "Legal Services Reform Coalition" had no seat at the table when these decisions were made. The Clinton administration picked four Republican lawyers for the required five minority seats on the board with the fifth to be a client representative. Those lawyers were *Bill McCalpin,* who had chaired the Carter board for its final two years, *Tom Smegal,* a former LSC board member who had opposed most of the board's policy initiatives the last four years of Reagan's administration, *John Brooks,* a former NLADA president and staunch legal services supporter, and *Nancy*

Hardin Rogers, an Ohio State law professor who had taught and written extensively on access-to-justice issues.

In another positive sign, Clinton asked his fellow Rhodes Scholar, law school roommate, and long-time friend, Douglas Eakeley, then in his mid-40s, to chair the LSC board. This evidenced the president wanted a close personal connection between his administration and the current LSC board. Eakeley, as well as the rest of the Democrats appointed to the board, had proven they supported a broad vision of the "access-to-justice" goal the LSC Act had promised to promote. Those members included *John Broderick,* a New Hampshire lawyer who had chaired Clinton's campaign in that key primary state, *Laveeda Battle,* an African-American lawyer from Alabama, *Hulett "Bucky" Askew,* the long-time OEO-LSP and LSC staff leader, and *Maria Louisa Mercado,* a Texas lawyer. The two clients, one Republican and the other Democrat, were Edna Fairbanks-Williams and Ernestine Watlington, both of whom also strongly supported the notion poor people should have the full range of legal services paying clients enjoyed.[1]

The Clintons sent another signal the administration was ushering in a new day for the LSC and the clients of legal services lawyers. As soon as the Senate confirmed all 11 board members after an easy hearing in November 1993, the president and first lady hosted a private White House reception welcoming the new board. During the reception, John Broderick and Clinton huddled, with Broderick giving the president his thoughts about some political issues the administration was facing.[2]

President Clinton's LSC board of directors. (Courtesy of Legal Services Corporation)

The day after the White House reception the new board members gathered for their first meeting. They quickly elected President Clinton's choice, Doug Eakeley, as chair, and a Republican, Professor Nancy Rogers as vice chair.[3] They then turned to the board's first and most important decision—the choice of the corporation's staff leader, its president.

As the new board took over, Jack O'Hara was still serving as LSC president and lobbied hard to remain in office. The Clinton board was looking for something new and different. Bare survival had been a major achievement while Reagan and Bush occupied the White House. Now the husband of a former LSC board chair ran the White House. More was possible, much more, and they needed a leader who could make the most of that opportunity. The board launched a full-scale talent search knowing it would take several months to complete.

A YEAR OF HIGH HOPES

The NLADA and the Project Advisory Group (PAG) were equally optimistic about a coming golden age of legal services. Indeed, they were so inspired by the reenergized LSC and the expected White House support that they began developing plans to seek a dramatic upsurge in the corporation's budget. The final year of the Bush administration had seen the budget rise to $357 million. This seemed a vast increase over the low point of $241 million suffered from the drastic cutbacks of the early Reagan years. On the surface, it appeared even higher than the "minimum access" budget of $321 million in the last year of the Carter administration, but when adjusted for inflation the FY 1993 budget would have had to reach $510 million to match the $321 million Congress appropriated for 1981. Also, the number of poor people eligible for legal services used to calculate the "minimum access" target of two lawyers for every 10,000 poor people had increased by 30 percent from 1981 to 1993. So it would take a minimum of $637 million to restore LSC to a "minimum access" budget in the coming fiscal year, which would be FY 1995.[4]

In calculating its recommendation to the LSC and Congress, the American Bar Association figure also took account of the fact that legal costs had increased more than the general cost of living and calculated the LSC budget would have to rise to $848 million to provide the same "minimum access" for the current poverty population as $321 million did in FY 1981.[5] Indeed, the ABA had requested a similar ambitious budget figure for FY 1993 when its president testified before Congress in 1992.[6]

The PAG was even more adventuresome. Composed of the executive directors that ran the nation's legal services grantees, PAG's members knew "minimum access"—providing two lawyers for every

10,000 poor people—had been an interim and not an ultimate goal. They also knew from experience that minimum access really meant some access for some poor people but no access for the vast majority. Thus, the PAG board went about putting together a long-term plan aimed at reaching "true access," not just "minimum access," in the foreseeable future.

Shortly after Clinton's victory in the 1992 election, PAG had set up a working group to calculate what it would cost to provide all poor people in the country access to a lawyer when they needed one. The working group chose Gerry Singsen to serve as a consultant and chief draftsman of the report because of his expertise in financial and statistical issues. A tall, rugged man who looked more like a lumberjack or former college football player than a green eye-shaded accountant, Singsen may have seemed an unlikely pick for this role. But it had been his specialty within the legal services community for two decades. A Columbia law graduate, he was a law clerk for a federal appellate judge before joining the second "Reggie" class. After four years at the Westchester county legal services project, he started his management career in legal services as assistant general counsel of New York City's umbrella organization, one of LSC's largest grantees. Not just a "bean counter" but a strategic thinker, he advised PAG and the NLADA during the OEO-LSP era, then served as LSC's vice president for administration during the Ford and Carter years, and when again outside government helped PAG and NLADA on financial and administrative issues.[7]

Now Singsen was being asked to research and draft the most visionary study in his long career—among other things, projecting the cost of a system that would deliver full access, not just minimum access, to the nation's poor. He used more than one approach in arriving at a total. In one, he started with estimates of the percentage of need legal services lawyers already were meeting based on survey research in several states. He then multiplied the present legal services budget by what it would take to make up the difference and satisfy the full need. (If legal services lawyers were able to meet 20 percent of the need at the present time, for instance, the budget would have to be five times higher to meet the full need.) In a more complex approach, he started with the number of legal problems studies showed poor people experienced every year, and adjusted that figure to take account of what other studies showed about the probable percentage of those problems they would take to lawyers. This produced an estimated annual caseload, which he then multiplied by the average per case cost reported by LSC-funded lawyers.[8]

Whichever approach Singsen used to arrive at an estimated cost for full access, the end result fell in the same ballpark. Singsen settled on $3.6 billion ($5.6 billion in 2011 dollars) as the best estimate and thus the ultimate target. This may have seemed a daunting sum compared to the existing LSC budget or even anything most legal services lawyers were seeking. But that $3.6 billion would still have left the U.S. behind several other industrial democracies—England, Scotland, and the Netherlands, among them—in per capita expenditures on civil legal aid.[9]

By the summer of 1993 the PAG working group had developed a consensus about the value of setting a goal of full access and approved a draft paper Singsen prepared with $3.6 billion as the price tag. The report did not call for the federal government to provide all the required funding through LSC. Rather it envisioned increased contributions from other sources—Interest on Lawyers' Trust Accounts (IOLTA), state and local governments, and private donations—would supply part of the $3.6 billion. Nor did the report recommend or expect the full access budget would be reached in FY 1995, but only urged LSC to recognize it as the corporation's ultimate goal and make a good beginning with its recommendation for the coming year's budget.[10]

At an October 1993, meeting the PAG steering committee considered the working group's draft report entitled, "Equal Justice for People in Poverty." Some members argued against setting a long-term target for LSC funding, especially one calling for a total nearly 10 times higher than the corporation's current budget, fearing it might scare their supporters as well as their opponents in Congress and elsewhere. Then one of PAG's most influential members, Denny Ray, who had headed several local legal services agencies over the years, spoke eloquently about the mission of legal services. He argued it was time to inform Congress and voters what it meant and what it would cost if this nation truly wanted to live up to its promise of justice for all.[11] Ray's presentation carried the day and the PAG steering committee approved the report, "Equal Justice for People in Poverty" and its submission as PAG's plan for this year's and future funding of LSC.[12]

At its December 5, 1993, meeting, the LSC board heard from SCLAID chair Brooksley Born, speaking on behalf of the ABA president who couldn't attend. She presented the ABA recommendation LSC should submit an $848 million budget request, and explained how her committee had arrived at that estimate.[13] The PAG representative, Andrew Steinberg, recommended that LSC adopt "Equal Justice for People in Poverty" and its $3.6 billion full access figure as the long-term goal of LSC. When Steinberg seemed defensive about the size of the ultimate target amount, 10 times the current LSC budget, the board chair, Douglas Eakeley, interrupted. "3.6 isn't very high in terms of accomplishing a fundamental purpose of the government. So you don't need to be defensive with this group in using $3.6 billion, even before you . . . suggest that others have a shared responsibility for accomplishing it."[14]

After Steinberg completed his presentation, Eakeley tried to persuade the board to adopt the essence of the PAG report's recommendation—a long-range goal of equal access to justice for all the nation's poor with the ultimate price tag of $3.6 billion, a substantial amount of that to come from the federal government. But he met too much resistance from other board members, mainly concerned about scaring Congress with such a big number. The board finally settled on $848 million as the LSC budget request for FY 1995—the same amount ABA was recommending—with no reference to a specific long-range target figure.[15]

THE LSC BOARD DECIDES TO HIRE AN INTERIM LSC PRESIDENT

Gerry Singsen was on the agenda for an executive session of the board at its December 5 meeting for a different reason. For many years, he had been monitoring LSC's finances and statistical reports for PAG and NLADA. In the course of recent reviews, he had detected a problem with the prior administration's accounting of lease expenses when it moved locations with three years still running on the rent for its former headquarters. What holdover LSC president Jack O'Hara had told the new board was a $2 million surplus it was inheriting from the old board in fact was a $2 million deficit in the management budget, requiring several cutbacks in staffing and other expenses at LSC headquarters.[16] When PAG disclosed this apparent problem to the Clinton board, Singsen was brought aboard and given access to all of the corporation's financial records. This made it possible for him to prepare a report documenting the deficit. This suggested O'Hara was or should have been aware of this serious accounting problem and revealed the true state of LSC finances to the new board.[17]

The board felt the entire affair reflected poorly on Jack O'Hara's management and led it to decide it could not leave him in place during the months required to complete the search for a permanent replacement. Having read Singsen's report several days before the meeting, Eakeley had anticipated the need to find an interim director to replace O'Hara. He knew it had to be someone who could provide the strong leadership the corporation desperately needed over the next critical months and yet willing to take this demanding job on such a short-term basis.

Eakeley had an idea. While an associate for a major New York law firm, he had served on the board of the Legal Aid Society (LAS) in New York (the original legal aid organization featured in Chapter 1) where he developed great respect for Alexander Forger, the lawyer who chaired the board. Now, years later, Eakeley heard Forger, approaching 70, had recently stepped down as managing partner of Milbank, Tweed, one of New York's largest and most venerable law firms. Forger's wife of 47 years had recently passed away and Eakeley knew he was trying to figure out what to do with his life.[18]

Eakeley thought Forger would be a perfect choice as the LSC's interim president. At well over six foot in height, always dressed impeccably, with the manners and bearing of an aristocrat and a Yale Law School education to match, Forger undoubtedly impressed his wealthy clients as one of them. In truth, he was from a working class background but unlike some who rise from poverty or the lower middle class into the upper class, he didn't look down on those who didn't make it.

Forger would also bring a long and deep history in legal aid to the job. When he joined the Milbank, Tweed law firm in 1950, one of the two named partners, Harrison Tweed, had been a national leader in the legal aid movement for three decades and was at the time the president of New York's venerable LAS. The young Alex Forger was delighted to "tag along" with Tweed and soon became a member of the LAS board. Eventually, he was elected the board's president where he remained for more than a decade. While on the LAS board, he experienced the birth of both OEO-LSP and LSC, followed by the Reagan backlash, all from the perspective of a local grantee. "Not all of which was endearing to me particularly the monitoring . . . In the 1980s the corporation was not in hands that sought to have it grow and prosper."[19] In another of his many leadership roles, while president of the New York bar in 1981, Forger was one of those bar leaders who joined then ABA president Reece Smith in the legal profession's "March on Washington" to protest President Reagan's attempt to abolish the Legal Services Corporation.

Eakeley was convinced Forger would bring immediate stature and proven ability, yet because of his age probably would not be seen as a threat to those thinking of applying for the permanent job. Eakeley phoned Forger and asked if he would be willing to come down to Washington for a few months as LSC's interim president, if the board indeed agreed to replace O'Hara. It didn't take Forger long to say yes. "With the change of administration and a Democratic Congress as well," he later said, "it seemed like this would be the dawning of the golden age of legal services with the opportunity to expand because it was still woefully underfunded and to be able to do a lot of innovative things in delivery of legal services."[20]

At the December 5, 2012, executive session, after deciding to replace O'Hara, the board decided to offer the interim director position to Forger. The next morning they made the choice official with an announcement during a brief open meeting.[21] Thus, on December 30, 1993, a month after taking Eakeley's call, Alex Forger completed his move to Washington and took over as LSC's interim president.

Even before Forger left for the nation's capital, Eakeley arranged for Martha Bergmark to travel up and meet him in New York. Bergmark was a former "Reggie" who had returned to her home state of Mississippi in 1973 to serve her fellowship and a few years later became director of Southeast Mississippi legal services. More recently, she had come to Washington as PAG's executive director[22] and was well known and well respected throughout the legal services community. Both Forger and Bergmark realized this meeting had a purpose—a job interview, and one that went very well. Shortly thereafter, Forger chose her as his executive vice president[23]—guaranteeing him immediate credibility with LSC's grantees and a perfect partner for the establishment lawyer from Wall Street.

Recognizing he was an interim president, and not wanting to make too many staffing decisions that would bind the future permanent presid ent, Forger quickly assembled a transition team of consultants, chiefly experienced legal services lawyers and former LSC staff members. Gerry Singsen was one and Forger assigned him the urgent task of preparing LSC's detailed budget request to Congress for FY 1995, a request Congress would be considering early in the spring of 1994.[24]

The budget the LSC board proposed to Congress was rounded off from the $848 million the board had approved at the December 5 meeting to $850 million.[25] That request did not fare well, however, when presented to the House Appropriations Subcommittee at the March 1994 hearings; nor did the ABA's recommendation when its representatives supported a similar figure. The PAG faced the same skepticism when it presented the essence of its "Equal Justice for People in Poverty" with its ultimate goal of $3.6 billion in funding for lawyers serving the poor.[26]

The subcommittee instructed the LSC to go back to the drawing board and return with a different and smaller budget request.[27] A *Washington Post* writer noted "someone at the Legal Services Corporation must have been smoking pot" when they decided to ask Congress to double the LSC budget in a year of fiscal restraint.[28]

All these legal services advocates were disappointed when the Clinton administration failed to join them in urging a dramatic increase in the LSC budget. Clinton had won the election with the slogan, "It's the Economy, stupid!" But the economy had not taken off yet, nor had tax revenues increased. Many domestic programs were slated for budget reductions, and the administration felt generous in allowing the LSC an increase to $440 million in its FY 1995 budget.

Forger had several meetings at the White House on LSC matters, including its budget requests. Among the usual attendees were a number of administration staff members. On occasion, they were joined by Mickey Kantor, then the trade representative and still vitally interested in LSC, Peter Edelman, who was a strong voice in support of LSC, and

Hillary Clinton. But these meetings failed to yield any change in the administration's position on the LSC budget. The First Lady was absorbed with a different domestic priority, leading the administration's full-court press for universal health insurance. The hoped-for White House dedication to the LSC, its grantees, lawyers, and clients did not seem to be materializing and for the time being, at least, the LSC was on its own.[29]

Congress gave the LSC only a $40 million increase in its FY 1995 budget, and not a penny more.[30] It was a disappointment to the organizations working for legal services clients and their lawyers, but at least an increase and not a cut during a difficult budget year. And there was always next year, when economic circumstances and government revenues might be more promising.

Another piece of legislation important to LSC also had to wait for next year, when the administration decided not to press for the corporation's reauthorization in 1994, even though the House had passed a reauthorization bill in 1992[31] and held hearings on a similar bill in 1993.[32]

But next year—at least the kind legal service advocates were counting on—never arrived.

LSC GAINS A PERMANENT PRESIDENT AND A NEW TOP STAFF

Forger brought by far the most impressive professional stature to the LSC presidency since the first president, Tom Ehrlich, a former Stanford Law dean. With his many accomplishments as a lawyer, his impeccable establishment credentials, and his experience running one of the nation's largest private law firms, Forger exceeded expectations as the interim LSC president, not just in image but in his performance. His age proved irrelevant, as he demonstrated the energy and staying power of a much younger man. The board looked far and wide and found some strong candidates, but Forger had set the bar so high that in the end, no one could measure up.

Finally, after considerable discussion, in June 1994 the LSC board decided to give Forger the chance to make his temporary engagement permanent.[33] By this time, Forger realized how much he enjoyed what he was doing. This was a chance to accomplish something truly meaningful. Being LSC president combined interesting, challenging work with the opportunity to advance a goal that had been close to his heart his entire life as a lawyer—equal justice for the nation's poor. With little delay, Forger informed the board he was pleased to accept the offer.[34]

With his new status as permanent LSC president came challenges. At the top of the list was the staff realignment he deemed essential.

Forger realized he couldn't accomplish what he wanted to with most of the staff leaders he inherited. Just as the Reagan board had replaced the division heads who ran the corporation during the Carter years, Forger began replacing those who remained from the Reagan–Bush years. As his vice president Forger chose Martha Bergmark, making her appointment permanent.[35] He also brought in veteran legal services lawyers to replace other current staff in key positions. This gave Forger's senior staff a level of credibility with legal services grantees, their lawyers, and clients the LSC had not known since 1981. And it put at Forger's side people with firsthand knowledge of the many problems faced by organizations and lawyers trying to bring justice to the poor.

Forger soon learned that replacing senior staff members left over from the Reagan years came with a cost, however. Several of them threatened a lawsuit contending their dismissals were unlawful, a threat that hung over LSC for a long time into the future, although it never materialized. Two of those fired employees went further, however.

Kenneth Boehm, formerly assistant to the LSC president, continually attacked LSC and its grantees from the vantage point of a conservative advocacy organization he founded and now chairs—the National Legal and Policy Center. Using that platform he has written articles, given congressional testimony, and bedeviled LSC's leaders and local legal services lawyers alike by asking for an end to federal funding of legal services for the poor.[36] Another displaced employee, Emilia DiSanto, had been the interim LSC president for a short period when the Wittgraf board decided not to extend Terry Wear's term in office. She also had headed LSC's monitoring and compliance division for many years before and after that appointment. After losing her job at LSC, DiSanto joined Senator Charles Grassley's staff, a long-time critic of LSC and legal services for the poor in general. Her arrival in that position did not reduce and may have increased the senator's frequent press releases disparaging LSC and regular requests for GAO investigations of LSC and its grantees.[37]

A CHANGE OF FORTUNE IS SUDDENLY IN THE OFFING

Forger officially became the LSC's permanent president on June 18, 1994. Had he known how much that job would change just a few months later, he might have had second thoughts about accepting the offer. When he took the position, Forger was looking forward to restoring legal services for the poor to where it had been in the Carter years, and to enhance still more the quality and quantity of services the lawyers it funded supplied the poor. Sadly, that was not to remain his mission. Had the LSC grantees, their clients, legal services lawyers, and their supporters known what was in store, they too might have been less disappointed with the modest budget increase they had received from a Democratic presidential administration and a Democratic Congress.

An inkling of the troubles ahead became apparent during what should have been a moment of triumph and hope. In October 1994, the Clintons hosted a White House reception commemorating the 20th anniversary of Richard Nixon's signing the Legal Services Corporation Act of of 1974. Almost 200 people attended, from all over the country—present and past legal services lawyers, present and past ABA and NLADA presidents, former OEO-LSP leaders, and many who had served on past LSC boards, at least those who had been supportive of legal services grantees.

After the reception, the attendees gathered for a program featuring talks by the First Lady Hillary Clinton and the Attorney General Janet Reno. I happened to be seated next to California congressman Howard Berman, someone I had known casually for a couple of decades who also was one of LSC's staunchest supporters on the Hill. We began chatting while waiting for the program to start. Soon he was telling me how concerned he was and why.

"Look around," he said. "Who's missing from this gathering?"

"I don't know, who?"

Alex Forger, LSC president, 1993–1997, with President Clinton. (Courtesy of Alex Forger)

Alex Forger with Hillary Clinton. (Courtesy of Alex Forger)

Hillary Clinton speaking at the White House event commemorating LSC's 20th Anniversary, October 1994. Others on dais are Janet Reno, U.S. Attorney General, LSC board chair Douglas Eakeley, Roberta Ramo (first woman ABA president), and Alex Forger, LSC president. (Courtesy of Alex Forger)

"I am the only congressman or senator here."

"Why aren't some others here?" I asked.

"They're all running scared. Gingrich and his 'Contract with America' is gaining real traction. Lots of Democrats are afraid of losing their seats. And, I'm worried they will, too. If so, the Legal Services Corporation—and many, many other things—are in real trouble."

Why the Legal Services Corporation? Because it was one of the several government programs jeopardized by Gingrich's "Contract with America." Under the guise of ending the government's deficit spending, Gingrich and his supporters planned to close many programs and even whole cabinet departments, such as education, commerce, and energy. Although not mentioned specifically in the initial "Contract with America," it also was likely the Gingrich Congress would target minor budget items such as LSC and the National Foundation for the Humanities for ideological reasons rather than their impact on the deficit.

Gingrich's allies, the Christian Coalition, had its own "Contract with the American Family," which cited LSC specifically as being antifamily because the lawyers it funded often represented poor people seeking to divorce.[38] To have given the other possible reason for Gingrich to choose LSC as a target—that those lawyers also sometimes won cases against major contributors to Republican politicians—might not have been the argument to take to the people, and wasn't mentioned in either "contract."

Howard Berman proved to be right. A few weeks after the White House celebration of the LSC's 20th anniversary, the 1994 midterm elections jump-started Gingrich's Contract with America. Gingrich staged his own event, ranging all Republican legislators across the Capitol steps and having them sign an oversized document containing the full contract.[39] The Republicans picked up 54 seats in the House of Representatives and 8 in the Senate, taking control of both houses of Congress for the first time since 1953.[40]

Newt Gingrich had no particular personal animus against the Legal Services Corporation, other than that it had emerged as part of Lyndon Johnson's "Great Society" and his equally despised "war on poverty"—and was high on the list of government programs the Christian Coalition wanted to eliminate. But Gingrich's chief ally in the Senate, Phil Gramm, had long held a grudge against LSC and the lawyers it financed. Similar to Ronald Reagan, some of his major agribusiness donors had lost to legal services lawyers representing their farmworkers—and didn't like it. So Gramm didn't like those lawyers and the entity that financed them. During the Reagan years, he had tried unsuccessfully to abolish the LSC and relished this new opportunity to try again.

At its first meeting after the 1994 election, January 27, 1995, the LSC board confronted reality, sharing what many of them learned during conversations on the Hill. As Professor Rogers said, "It does seem there is a real desire, on the part of a number of people new in Congress, for change. . . . And it may be—I don't know how strong the force is—an irresistible force."[41]

John Broderick also recognized it was a "very precarious time" and it was "essential that the administration, and the president in particular, publicly support the work of the corporation" and pledged his own efforts in that direction.[42] Other board members then volunteered information about visits they were having with their own senators and congressmen as well as what was happening in their states, mainly what state and local bars were doing.

But then Alex Forger had to remind the board members they would have to fight for LSC's survival with one hand tied behind their backs—and maybe both—because of restrictions Congress had imposed. "It is very important that each of us recognize that while we can speak directly to members of Congress, we must be mindful that we cannot engage in lobbying beyond that or a grassroots call to action."[43]

Similar congressional restrictions also applied to LSC's grantees and their lawyers, although initially the ban didn't extend to their non-LSC funds. No longer could they mount coordinated grassroots campaigns as the legal services community had done so successfully in earlier years. The NLADA did cobble together its own grassroots effort, replacing the experienced executive directors from LSC grantees with leaders of non-LSC-funded legal aid programs, where they existed, and sometimes bar leaders.[44] Whether that substitute network would have supplied enough energy and political power to make a difference in the mid-1990s will never be known. That is because the campaign to resist what some LSC board members saw as an "irresistible force" was about to be joined by a new well-funded ally.

THE ABA SADDLES UP AGAIN

At a meeting of the ABA SCLAID held shortly after the Republican victory in the midterm elections, a committee member, incidentally a Republican, issued a warning and offered a suggestion. Because of who he was and the experience he brought to the table, the other members paid close attention to the speaker, Howard Dana. Now a justice on the Maine Supreme Court, he had been a member of both the first Reagan and first Bush LSC boards.

"If we're going to save the Legal Services Corporation this time, it will take more than the ABA president, this committee, and some other ABA leaders speaking out in its defense," Dana said. "We need a major grassroots effort—getting state and local bar associations involved and getting local lawyers talking to their own senators and congressmen. But that sort of campaign requires central planning and coordination. The ABA can and should play that role."[45]

The rest of the committee soon agreed with Dana's suggestion. They voted to put together a proposal for a "grassroots" program and ask the ABA board of governors to supply funding for the program's staff and expenses out of the association's budget. By early 1995, SCLAID's program was funded and in operation. Over the next months, it enlisted thousands of lawyers who had relationships with their local Congress members and senators.[46]

The ABA campaign to preserve LSC was organized by SCLAID, and overseen by a steering committee that included several SCLAID members and a few others with experience and important political contacts. Among them was Laurie Zelon, then in her mid-40s, a corporate lawyer from Los Angeles who was soon to chair SCLAID. She headed a subcommittee that oversaw the grass roots program's day-to-day operations. They hired Mauricio Vivero as full-time staff coordinator for the grassroots campaign. Born in Havana, Vivero had immigrated to the United States in 1970 with his family, where he graduated from college and law school. Then in his mid-30s, Vivero had been a public interest lawyer and the Director of Leadership Development for the National Council of La Raza and proved an able organizer of the campaign to counter the assault they knew was coming.[47]

Realizing lawyers are not experts in advertising or media relations and knowing those behind the Contract with America were, SCLAID retained a public relations consultant to work with them in developing messages that would resonate with the public and Congress. What lawyers would understand and appreciate did not necessarily equate with what the average citizen or even the average legislator would find persuasive. From this media advisor, lawyers on the ABA team learned how to be as persuasive in the political arena as they had long been in the courtroom. This was vital because over the next months and years, many of them would be called upon to appear on radio and television news and talk shows defending the LSC and explaining why it deserved to survive. SCLAID also had to convey this same guidance to the thousands of lawyers involved in the national effort.[48]

Zelon and the others overseeing the ABA campaign came together regularly for full-day planning meetings, sometimes in Chicago, sometimes in Washington. With Vivero, they identified key senators and House members, mainly moderate Republicans, who might be moved to part company from Gingrich and the other Republican leaders on this one issue. They then recruited local bar leaders and other prominent lawyers who could be influential with those legislators. Committee members also took on other responsibilities. For instance, Zelon, rather than the ABA president, testified before Congress as the ABA's official spokesperson.[49]

If the ABA or other legal supporters needed a sign they weren't wasting time preparing a defense it came early. Shortly after convening, the Gingrich-led Congress rescinded the small budget increase the prior Congress had given LSC for FY 1995.[50] This returned the corporation to the level the Clinton-appointed board had inherited from the Bush-appointed board. That was only a budget nick compared to the deep budget slashes the new Congress would soon be seeking. Yet it posed a challenge for LSC and its grantees board because it came more than halfway through the fiscal year and after the funds had been distributed on the basis $415 million would be available. So the board had to impose retroactive cuts on most grantee agencies, which became the sole topic of a board conference call meeting the evening of April 11, 1995.[51]

THE GINGRICH CONGRESS'S "GLIDE PATH TO OBLIVION" TAKES SHAPE

The opening salvo in the Gingrich Congress's crusade to stamp out the Legal Services Corporation was fired on March 16, 1995, less than three months after the Republicans took control of the Senate and House of Representatives. Congressman John Kasich of Ohio assumed chairmanship of the House Budget Committee as it planned the government's finances for FY 1996. A year earlier, as ranking member Kasich had introduced a resolution to phase out the corporation over a three-year period, a so-called "glide path", reducing LSC's budget by one-third each year until it reached zero. While his proposal failed when he was ranking member of the minority party,[52] this time Kasich was the budget committee's chair and the "glide path to oblivion" passed.[53] Within the House of Representatives, the budget committees set the goal, but the appropriation committees ultimately committed the funds from the federal treasury and could come over or under the budget committee's mark. This meant the battle over LSC funding moved on to the appropriations committee.[54]

Legal services supporters got the message from the budget committee's action. Without waiting to see what the House Appropriations Committee would do, they were soon scrambling to avoid impending disaster in the House if not yet the Senate. The ABA and NLADA leadership recognized their only hope for saving the LSC in the House was to enlist some moderate Republicans willing to take on Gingrich's juggernaut on this one issue—the survival of LSC. This meant legal services supporters had to swallow their pride and look for friends in unfamiliar places. They soon found themselves joining forces with some former opponents who didn't favor abolishing LSC, but were satisfied to just diminish its role. Old opponents, in particular

Congressmen Stenholm and McCollum, were approached and suddenly became new friends. On May 16, 1995, Stenholm told the House Appropriations Committee, "The reforms Bill and I have proposed in the past are now viewed as the leading alternative to either the status quo or chairman Kasich's plans. I am pleased to report that I have already had very positive meetings with the same individuals and organizations who just a few years ago strongly opposed the McCollum–Stenholm reforms as being too draconian."[55]

"PROSECUTORS" DOUBLE AS "JUDGES" AND THE DEFENSE LOSES IN CONGRESSIONAL HEARINGS

The chair of the appropriations subcommittee with jurisdiction over the LSC was Harold Rogers of Kentucky, who had met several times with George Wittgraf while he headed the LSC board. Wittgraf had answered Rogers's concerns at that time, but regretted he never turned the congressman into a supporter of the corporation or the lawyers it funded. Rogers signaled his views on May 24 when he warned LSC officials he wouldn't be able to fund some federal programs within his committee's jurisdiction with a strong hint LSC was one of those in jeopardy.[56]

Over the next few weeks, the House Appropriations Subcommittee held hearings on the future of the Legal Services Corporation and the funding Congress should provide. Those hearings turned into a near bloodbath for LSC and its supporters.

When politicians, Republican or Democrat, have powerful political reasons for favoring a given policy, it is not always clear whether they honestly believe the reasons offered to justify their position. Sometimes it appears they choose to accept and indeed use any story or statistic or whatever—true or not—that will support the viewpoint their own inclinations or their major financial donors favor. How else to account for the continued repetition of anecdotes supposedly showing terrible abuses by legal services lawyers that had been conclusively proven to be untrue. Indeed some of the stories anti-LSC witnesses paraded before the congressional committees in the mid-1990s were the same or similar to the ones the Reagan administration had lodged against California Rural Legal Assistance in 1970, charges three Republican appointed state supreme court justices threw out as totally without merit a quarter century earlier.

As Alex Forger later observed, "If I believed even a quarter of the charges leveled against legal services lawyers, I would agree the program should be eliminated."[57] As fast as congressmen leveled new charges or repeated old ones, Forger and his staff investigated them. Like the three state supreme court justices who examined the Reagan administration charges in 1971, Forger found little truth in the charges his staff investigated in 1995. But that made no difference this time.

Jack Londen learned this lesson first hand, when he appeared before the Senate Judiciary Committee. Londen was a top-flight litigation partner in a thousand-lawyer San Francisco–based corporate law firm, Morrison and Foerster, and was already a major figure in pro bono and access-to-justice activities in California. His mother was chair of the Arizona Republican Party and his father one of the nation's foremost Republican donors, but Jack had long ago strayed from his parent's political path.

Londen chaired and largely financed "Californians for Legal Aid," one of the many state and local organizations the NLADA and the ABA grassroots campaign coordinated in the fight to preserve the LSC.[58] As such, he had requested an opportunity to testify before the Senate subcommittee holding hearings on the future of LSC.

During the flight across country, Londen thoroughly reviewed the file in a piece of litigation—the *Gerawan* case—which had been featured in a previous day's testimony before a House Committee and had become something of a cause célèbre among Republican legislators. In its testimony, the defendant grower had portrayed the CRLA lawyers who brought the case as villains who victimized him with a "trivial and abusive" lawsuit.

When it was time for Londen to take his seat at the witness table, he was fully prepared to address that claim. But first he responded to the "parade of horribles" the preceding witness from the Farm Bureau had cast before the committee.

"The charges are, in many cases overblown; many times they are misleading. They have been studied in great depth. The General Accounting Office, in its study of many programs, examined practices in general, and five specific cases, and found *no* evidence of abuse."

Then Londen shifted to the case he had personally studied in depth.

"The Gerawan case," Londen began, "which was the subject of testimony last week, is from my home State. I read the testimony submitted last week in the House, and I read the court's opinions. There is *no* resemblance between the two. A case that was called "trivial and abusive" is a case in which a Federal judge found that migrant farm workers were confined and housed—100 of them—in facilities built for a maximum of 40. They lived in beds less than 2 feet apart, stacked together. Forty of them lived in a sleeping space 23 feet by 23 feet, with a single toilet of the type of a single family, that backed up. The sanitary facilities were inadequate. The wiring was inadequate. This was an unsafe and indecent accommodation. These are not technical violations. The residents were charged $40 for the mattresses on the cots. They were charged hundreds of dollars, deducted from their pay, for living in these squalid conditions. These are the facts found by the Federal judge.

"They were not paid for all the hours they worked.

"The findings of fact I think leave the unmistakable conclusion that [these were] serious[ly unsafe] and deplorable conditions.

"The large majority of farmers and growers are decent and try to do right—but they are competing with the few who, in a 100 cases we have seen, do not follow the law.

"Now, who will make the playing [field] level? Who will make it safe, competitively safe, to obey the rules?"[59]

Londen concluded his testimony with a plea that Congress not take away "protection and the lawyers and the representation for farm workers, because if they do not get it from these [migrant legal services] programs, they will not get it."[60]

The only response to Londen's plea came from Senator Kassenbaum, who told him after the hearing that when legal services lawyers were no longer available, "It is nice to see poor people would have such able lawyers as you representing them."[61]

LSC lawyers believed the strength or weakness of the cases they brought was never the real issue. They found themselves in trouble when they won, not when they lost. What counted against them was that some of those cases were controversial—at least with major donors to the Republican Party and many Republican lawmakers. LSC supporters believed that for those senators and members of Congress seeking to abolish the Legal Services Corporation, "controversial cases" became the code words for cases their donors didn't like. And "left wing lawyers" and "left wing causes" and "social engineering" were invectives regularly applied to attempts by legal services lawyers to ensure poor people received government benefits to which they were legally entitled or to better the treatment they received as employees, tenants, or consumers.

It was no surprise when on July 19, 1995, the House Appropriations Committee voted out an LSC appropriation consistent with the first phase of the Kasich plan, an almost one-third reduction in the LSC budget—from $400 million to $278 million.[62] Nor was it a surprise when on July 25 the full House not only approved the cut in the LSC budget but also enacted the Stenholm–McCollum restrictions and eliminated funding for all national and state support centers.[63]

WILL THE SENATE PROVIDE A FRIENDLIER OR FAIRER FORUM?

The appropriations issue then shifted to the Senate, where a committed foe of the Legal Services Corporation and the lawyers it funded, Phil Gramm of Texas, chaired the key subcommittee responsible for determining the upper chamber's position on LSC's appropriation. He had his own prescription for LSC's future—immediate elimination of the corporation, to be replaced with $210 million in block grants to the states. This money the states could spend on legal services for the poor, but only if they wanted to—and with as many limitations on what legal services lawyers could do for their clients as those states desired to impose.[64] Senator Gramm gained subcommittee and then full appropriations committee approval for his substitute bill,[65] and on September 29, 1995, his proposal arrived on the Senate floor with the backing of a large bloc of Senate Republicans. As debate began, LSC supporters realized the existence of the corporation hung in the balance.

The search for a champion able to take on Senator Gramm had brought legal services supporters across the country to an old friend of the OEO Legal Services Program from the 1960s and 1970s, John Robb. A partner in New Mexico's largest law firm and a prominent Republican, Robb was a good friend and long-time supporter of Senator Pete Domenici, the state's popular Republican senator. Robb had cultivated Domenici's support for legal services during both the OEO and LSC eras,[66] so it seemed only natural when he called the senator with a special request. Together they developed an alternative to

John Robb, former SCLAID chair and National Advisory Committee member. (Courtesy of John Robb)

Gramm's draconian bill. It called for only a $60 million cut in LSC's FY 1996 appropriation, less than half the reduction the House had voted, but included most of the House restrictions.

Domenici was especially determined to retain the restriction against class actions. As he told Forger during a meeting with the LSC president, "You have to eliminate class actions if you expect the Senate to be supportive of this program. I have to be able to stand up on the floor and say 'no more class actions'. Although I could live with only a partial restriction on class actions, I think I have to give assurance that there to be no more class actions permitted."[67]

The specter of Gramm's death sentence for the LSC was enough to bring even the corporation's most dedicated supporters into line behind Domenici's compromise. During the Senate debate Senator Ted Kennedy, who had spent nearly his entire career defending first OEO-LSP and then LSC, gave grudging support to the most distasteful element of the proposal, the several harsh restrictions on what legal services lawyers could do for their clients: "Some restrictions are necessary to ensure support for the program . . . [T]his bill . . . would correct the harsh injustice of the committee bill [Gramm's proposal] and enable LSC to continue its important work."[68]

The combination of reluctant Democrats and moderate Republicans managed to outvote Gramm's conservative bloc and pass Domenici's compromise by a comfortable margin—60 to 39.[69] This relegated the ultimate decision to a conference committee, which would attempt to reconcile the competing House and Senate versions.

The conference committee's deliberations dragged on, slowed still further by a series of confrontations between Congress and President Clinton over the total budget. At one point the government shut down entirely. Federal employees were not to report for work unless their presence would be considered essential. LSC was not a government agency but rather an independent government-funded corporation and thus not necessarily covered by the shutdown order. But Forger finally decided it wasn't necessary to determine whether the order applied to LSC. "We knew our work was essential to our clients. So we just came to the office and did our job."[70]

THE LSC BOARD READS THE HANDWRITING ON THE WALL—AND REACTS

By December 1995, the LSC board realized it could no longer wait for a final bill from the conference committee. With the Senate having adopted the essence of the House restrictions, sometimes with differences in language, it was inevitable those restrictions would emerge from the conference process. If the LSC board members dragged their feet any longer in demonstrating commitment to implementing the congressional restrictions, the corporation risked further attack from Congressional opponents. Thus, the board began readying a full set of regulations consistent with the restrictions in the House and Senate bills.

By this time, the LSC board had acquired a powerful new weapon—in the form of a new nominee to a board seat. John Brooks, then past 80, had decided not to remain for a second term.[71] This offered the opportunity to recruit someone who could help on the political front. Two Republican board members took former Congressman John Erlenborn to lunch and asked if he would come back on the LSC board, knowing agribusiness had forced his resignation from the Bush board. "And so I decided having been kind of forced off earlier I wanted back on," Erlenborn later recalled. "I was no longer with the law firm and I knew they couldn't pull that trick on me again of getting our clients talking to the firm."[72] This gave the LSC board a member possessing great credibility with Republican congressmen, having spent 20 years in that body, most of it in leadership positions.

Months passed awaiting Erlenborn's confirmation in the Senate. But the week after President Clinton nominated him, Erlenborn attended the October 6, 1995, board meeting and began helping out with the battle in Congress. During the lunch break at the October meeting he spoke with Eakeley. When the board chair asked what Erlenborn thought they could do in "protecting the Legal Services Corporation," the ex-congressman warned, "one thing you want to do is *not* fight the Congress and try to go to court and knock out any of these restrictions that had been enacted by the Congress." Erlenborn was relieved when Eakeley said, "That's exactly our feeling, too."[73]

The LSC board's cooperative attitude toward Congress and its work on regulations implementing the restrictions may have proved the LSC board's good faith to those in Congress. But this stance didn't meet with universal acceptance in the legal services community. Rumors even circulated the LSC had bargained directly with Congress—selling restrictions for continued funding. This charge angered Alex Forger so much he wrote a letter to the editor of a legal newspaper that had published such rumors. "The specter of our corporation sitting at the bargaining table trading off constitutional rights for life is pure fantasy. In fact, we fought both our budgetary cuts and the restrictions in the limited forums to which we were invited."[74]

Forger was right. He, the LSC board, the ABA and other legal services supporters were presented with an ultimatum not an invitation to bargain. Even moderates among Republicans in both houses—the ones needed if LSC were to survive at all—insisted on the bundle of restrictions McCollum and Stenholm had long advocated. Ted Kennedy, who ordinarily would be the last to yield on limiting what legal services lawyers could provide poor people, had conceded there was no choice.

CAN THE "GLIDE PATH" BE DERAILED BEFORE LSC CRASHES—THE STRUGGLE OVER THE FY 1997 LSC APPROPRIATION BEGINS

Surviving 1995 by securing FY 1996 funding did not mean the corporation and its grantees were out of peril. Although Senator Gramm's attempt to abolish the LSC immediately had failed, the "Glide Path to Oblivion" remained a distinct possibility. The funding level LSC achieved—a reduction from $400 million to $278 million—was consistent with the first installment of the "Glide Path"—the congressional leadership's plan to phase out LSC over a three-year period.

Continuing that plan, Congressman Kasich and his House Budget Committee slated LSC for the second installment of the corporation's glide path. This meant a budget mark of $141 million for FY 1997—a reduction of $137 million from the $278 million Congress appropriated for FY 1996.[75]

Fully realizing the FY 1997 appropriation would be the battleground for LSC's long-term—or even medium-term—survival, the ABA had begun gearing up once again, without waiting for the budget committee to produce its inevitable budget mark of $141 million for FY 1997 en route to zero in FY 1998. The ABA president at the time was Roberta Cooper Ramo, the first woman chosen for that position in the association's 120-year history. In January 1996, she asked a staff member to survey state bar presidents about their impressions of the ABA's campaign in 1995, and whether they had any recommendations for the coming year. Out of that survey came several useful ideas for the ABA team—"publicizing what LSC means, in real terms, to real people," sharing with all state bars what others were doing, and supplying suggestions for "concrete steps they can take at various stages of the battle."[76]

At its midyear meeting in early February 1996, the ABA board of governors committed an additional $101,000 to support the grassroots effort, beyond the $112,000 already allocated for that purpose. By February 15, Vivero had developed a proposed plan and was ready to discuss it on a conference call with the steering group. Among other things, the plan called for developing a national "message," testing that message with focus groups, expanding the national network to 1,000 advocates, holding regional and state events to bring together those involved at the state and local level and finalize the lobbying plans for reaching the key congressmen within those areas.[77]

By March 12, the process was far enough along that Vivero could send out a package to the entire list of national, state, and local advocates outlining the 1996 LSC campaign, The package included a target list of 104 Republicans and 43 Democrats (most from Southern states) who were considered "neither strongly in support n or strongly against LSC." It also provided the memberships of the key House and Senate Committees, and talking points on why "legal services must be preserved." As further ammunition for lawyers making the case with their legislators was a document providing examples of good things legal services lawyers had done for their clients—saving some 250,000 family farmers from foreclosure, increasing the supply of safe and affordable housing, fighting home equity fraud that targeted elderly homeowners, helping to stop the cycle of domestic violence, and improving working conditions for miners and migrants.[78]

SHOULD LEGAL SERVICES ADVOCATES SUE FOR RELIEF FROM THE CONGRESSIONAL RESTRICTIONS?

Parallel with the ABA campaign to maintain LSC's funding level at the FY 1996 level, an ad hoc group of legal services supporters was considering whether to challenge the FY 1996 congressional restrictions in court. Laurie Zelon, the SCLAID chair and the leader of the ABA LSC steering committee was one of those. Others included Jack Londen, who was Zelon's partner at Morrison and Forester, Steve and Marcia Berzon, top-notch labor lawyers, and Alan Houseman, who was masterminding the "save LSC" campaign for NLADA and PAG. Most of the legal work—the research and drafting of a complaint—was being done by the ACLU under the supervision of its national director, Steve Shapiro. But the decision whether to file a lawsuit seeking to strike down the congressional restrictions involved more than the question of whether the suit would succeed. In a February 28, 1996, memorandum to the executive directors of all LSC grantees, Houseman explained:

> While there is a general consensus among the members of the group that has been engaged in these discussions that a legal challenge to the restrictions on non-LSC funds may be successful, there is also a realization that success in the courts entails risks and might only succeed in clarifying the right of recipients to establish affiliated organizations to undertake restricted activities. It could also provoke an adverse political reaction against the federal legal services program.
>
> * * * * *
>
> [I]n considering whether or not to bring a lawsuit, we need to consider litigation not as an end in itself, but as a potential tool to use as part of the broader strategy.
>
> * * * * *
>
> While we think that litigation challenging the restrictions on non-LSC funds may be successful, we fear that it may ultimately represent a pyrrhic victory if the result is that Congress decides that it is unwilling to fund the legal services program unless the restrictions apply to all of a recipient's resources.[79]

The ACLU lawyers continued preparing drafts of a complaint for such a lawsuit,[80] but the political concerns remained hovering overhead as the legislative battle over the FY 1997 appropriation approached and LSC's survival hung in the balance.

THE TWO SIDES ORGANIZE FOR THE UPCOMING CONFRONTATION IN THE HOUSE OF REPRESENTATIVES

On March 20, 1996, even before the FY 1996 appropriation had become law, 15 conservative congressmen, members of the "Conservative Action Team" sent a letter to majority leader Dick Armey (Republican, Texas) urging completion of the three-year schedule for phasing out the Legal Services Corporation.

> After lengthy negotiations last year, we reached an agreement to fund the LSC at no more than $278 million for Fiscal year 1996, $141 million for Fiscal Year 1997, and $0 for Fiscal Year 1998. . . . Every additional dollar that we appropriate is another dollar that the LSC has to continue engaging in politically motivated litigations, such as challenging the constitutionality of welfare reform and blocking public housing developments from evicting drug dealers. . . . Experience has shown that legal services lawyers will exploit the smallest of loopholes to flout the will of Congress and pursue their radical agenda.[81]

This was followed on April 10 by a missive from Congressman Robert Dornan (Republican, California), one of the signers of the Armey letter, sent to his fellow Republicans. He attached his own version of David Letterman's "top ten" list. Dornan called his, "Top Ten Reasons to Defund the Legal Services Corporation." It could have been written by Howard Phillips or Lewis Uhler—and maybe was.

Clinton did not finally sign the FY 1996 Omnibus Spending bill until April 26, 1996,[82] ending the cycle of vetoes, government shutdowns, and continuing resolutions that had preoccupied Washington and the media for many months. But during the Spring, the LSC board had been pushing forward with the drafting and completion of 15 emergency interim regulations to implement the congressional mandated changes, including the package of restrictions. In fact, they already had addressed one of Congress's priorities by approving a competitive bidding system at the board's February 1996 at meeting.[83] By March, LSC could even report there were competing applicants in a few jurisdictions.[84] At its February meeting, LSC also finished drafting a regulation banning representation of accused drug dealers facing eviction from public housing.[85] Before LSC could complete drafting the remaining restrictions, however, the board had to wait until the Senate and House ironed out differences between the two versions they had passed. But what the board had done already allowed LSC's advocates to reassure Congress its wishes were being followed. LSC would guarantee federally funded legal services grantees no longer were filing class actions, representing aliens, lobbying for legislation, or anything else the FY 1996 appropriation bill banned.

With the House leadership and Conservative Action Teams lining up to continue the "glide path to oblivion," LSC's survival depended on finding a group of Republican Congress members with political courage as well as commitment to LSC willing to take on their party's leadership and disappoint the majority of their party's members. Key to that effort was finding one member willing to assume a leadership role as Senator Domenici had done the previous year in the Senate.

This time the connection was not a friend and political supporter, as John Robb had been with Senator Domenici, but an even closer relationship. Larry Fox, now in his late 40s, was a "Reggie" in the early 1970s, and by 1996 was a litigation partner in one of Philadelphia's largest corporate law firms, Drinker, Biddle & Reath. He also was active in the ABA, recently voted chair-elect of the Litigation Section, the ABA's largest and most powerful.[86] As such, he was one of many former legal services lawyers who remained loyal to the LSC and dedicated to its survival. But this particular former "Reggie" was special. He had a brother, Jon Fox, who was a Republican congressman from Pennsylvania. When Larry Fox asked, Jon Fox agreed, and became point man for resistance to his own party's campaign to phase out the Legal Services Corporation.[87]

THE LITIGATION TEAM MAKES AN UNPOPULAR DECISION ABOUT PURSING A LAWSUIT AGAINST THE RESTRICTIONS

It was about this time Houseman and others became worried the filing of the lawsuit he and others on the litigation team had been planning might upset their delicate negotiations with Republican moderates. In an April 30 memorandum to those heading the ABA, NLADA, and PAG legislative campaigns, he set up a conference call for May 6.

> The fundamental issue that we need to discuss and decide is whether to proceed with this litigation. The litigation team believes that the most successful case would be one brought before August 1st and would challenge on its face a number of the restrictions. . . . We have been in touch with programs in California, Alaska, Oregon and Hawaii who have indicated some preliminary interest in suing.
>
> The litigation team will be guided by our views. They view us as the client for these purposes. Of course, if we recommend not proceeding,

we may not be able to curtail litigation brought by programs or staff who are unwilling to adhere to our views. That is a risk we run.

There is little doubt in our minds that most of you are extremely concerned about affirmative litigation brought this summer. However, we believe that to proceed in the most thoughtful manner requires us to fully discuss this issue and frankly air our view and perspectives.[88]

As a result of the May 6 conference call, the litigation team halted planning for the lawsuit. This set off a heated debate within the legal services community. Many who were not involved in the negotiations bridled at the notion they might be hogtied by limitations a court would find unconstitutional if it had a chance. But others worried the fragile deal with moderate Republicans they hoped would save not only LSC but also their own funding might fall apart the moment one of their number filed a lawsuit seeking to strike any of those restrictions.

One of the legal services lawyers most offended by the restrictions was Jonathan Weiss, the executive director of Legal Services for the Elderly (LSE) in New York City. A 30-year veteran who started in 1964 as a neighborhood lawyer in Washington and later joined the Welfare Law Center where he participated in the landmark welfare residency requirement litigation, Weiss had headed LSE since 1970.[89] He was convinced those fighting to save LSC in Congress had made a bad and unnecessary deal in accepting the restrictions, especially the ban on class actions. On May 24, he circulated an angry internet message to the entire LSC grantee community headlined "Let's Litigate against Legal Services Restrictions."

Many of us believe that these provisions are unconstitutional as well as unethical, violative of the free speech of both client and counsel, their freedom of association, the free speech of the non-LSC funders, equal access to the Court, due process and equal protection. Many of us had also hoped that there would have been lobbying against the provisions and if that failed, litigation raising these objections.

These hopes were wrong.

All the groups that claim to speak for legal services or their clients have let us down. . . . Moreover, they have stymied those of us who are willing to advocate for what is right rather than abandon our clients, our obligations, our careers.

We are ready now to fight fully—hopefully to win completely.

After describing all he and his staff had done to prepare for that fight, Weiss pleaded with other grantees and their lawyers to join in and described the many ways they could. He ended with a clarion call.

We are all lawyers. We fight oppression. We fight injustice. We should now do our best for the noble ideals of our profession against the worst unethical restrictions of all our careers. Now is the moment. We must do all we can. Please join us. Please answer. Please help.[90]

Although Weiss's emotional plea failed to produce the nationwide wave of lawsuits he hoped for, it did begin the dialogue, as several grantees started weighing the pros and cons of filing court challenges on their own. In a May 28 memo Houseman forwarded the Weiss message to the rest of the litigation team and warned:

> We have begun to talk with legal services folks who disagree with our decision about proceeding with litigation at this time. As we anticipated, there is talk about proceeding with a lawsuit, although we do not know of any lawsuit that is about to be filed. . . . The political situation has not changed from our last conversation. It is clear that the House will attempt to reduce funding to $141 million for FY97 and eliminate LSC funding for FY98.[91]

The litigation team's abandonment of the lawsuit option in May 1996 may not have forestalled a future legal attack on the congressional restrictions by some legal services lawyers, but it did avoid the risk an explosive lawsuit would shatter the current delicate negotiations over LSC's FY 97 appropriation. At the least, Houseman, Zelon, and others at the front lines of those negotiations could not be accused of personally double-dealing—agreeing to the restrictions in exchange for LSC's survival when talking face-to-face with congressmen, then behind the lawmakers' backs asking the courts to kill those same provisions. If those LSC negotiators had their way, there would be no lawsuits brought by anyone in the legal services community.

BUILDING TOWARD A CLIMAX ON THE HOUSE FLOOR

Making good on his commitment, Congressman Fox led an effort to recruit as many Republican members as possible to sign a letter to Congressman Rogers and his appropriations subcommittee "urg[ing] you to support funding for a restructured LSC for FY 97 at no less than $278 million."[92] Vivero sent a memo on behalf of the ABA team to "key LSC contacts" asking them to reach congressmen on the target list and convince them to "sign on to this letter."[93]

Meantime, John Erlenborn, now the LSC board's vice chair, was also meeting with moderate congressmen, many of whom he knew personally. He gave them a reassuring message. "When I joined the LSC board I could not tell who was a Democrat and who was a Republican and who was liberal and who was conservative. We were all working together. And . . . when I told them what they ought to do is implement the restrictions Doug [Eakeley] said, 'oh, we already have the regulations drafted. All we have to do is enact them after the Congress does pass the bill with the restrictions in it.'"[94]

Yet despite all these entreaties, including the letter from Congressman Fox and his allies, Congressman Rogers stuck with the budget committee's target. The appropriations committee set LSC's FY 1997 budget at $141 million.[95] This meant that the next test whether LSC was to remain on the planned guide path would come on the floor of the House of Representatives during the summer of 1996.

With Congressman Alan Mollohan, a relatively conservative Democrat from West Virginia, Fox fashioned an amendment that maintained the FY 1997 budget level near the existing $278 million figure, but also retained the restrictions from the FY 1996 appropriation. Rather than the existing $278 million level or the $141 million the House Appropriations Committee recommended, the two congressmen had settled on $250 million, knowing the Senate already had voted to give LSC $300 million and the two houses would probably meet somewhere near the middle.[96] They worked the phones and collared fellow members in the hallways, managing to sign up a number of Republicans and conservative Democrats who expressed a willingness to vote for the Mollohan–Fox amendment.

On July 19, 1996, Fox and Mollohan, along with four other congressmen, circulated a "Dear Colleague" letter to the House membership calling on them to "support the Mollohan–Fox amendment on legal services."[97] Even then, with so few announced supporters of their amendment, the outcome remained very much in doubt when debate started on the House floor on July 23, 1996. Because a vote to adopt the second leg of the three-step "glide path" would certainly doom the LSC, the stakes couldn't have been higher for legal services lawyers and their clients. This set up what was an epic debate over the fate of federally funded legal aid in the United States.

AN HISTORIC DEBATE IN THE U.S. HOUSE OF REPRESENTATIVES[98]

Congressman Mollohan was the floor manager for the amendment and Congressman Charles Taylor (Republican, North Carolina) for the opposition, with one hour allotted for debate. Mollohan immediately yielded 12 minutes of his 30 minutes to Congressman Fox, "the coauthor of this amendment" with permission to control that time. Before the debate was over, over 30 members of the House, many of them Republicans, would have spoken in favor and 9 against the Mollohan–Fox amendment.

Mollohan struck a reassuring tone in his opening speech. He first conceded "that in the past the Legal Services Corporation has not been without its share of problems, . . . But over the last year, the Legal Services Corporation has undergone major changes." After listing many of those changes, including several of the key restrictions, he noted "the Mollohan–Fox amendment does not change in any way a single one of these restrictions. The Mollohan–Fox amendment simply increases funding for grants to the basic field programs by $109 million, raising the total funding for legal services for FY 1997 to $250 million."

Mollohan then identified the "offsets," that is, a set of minor reductions in funding for other programs that would allow this $109 addition to LSC funding to be revenue neutral—including $45 million from the Bureau of Prisons, $34 million from the Patent Office, and $12 million from the federal courts, among others. He then turned "to the issue of what happens if we do not pass this amendment . . . . if funding remains at the level of $141 million. . . . The number of neighborhood offices will decrease from 1,100 in 1995 to 550. . . . The harm will be to the most needy for legal services, and it will be great if our amendment is not adopted."[99]

Congressman Taylor countered Mollohan's reassurance with an accusation. "Part of the [previous year's] deal, part of the agreement that was placed in [sic] legal services was there was to be a reduction, a gradual reduction. Rather than zeroing out legal services, we agreed that it would be taken down to $141 million. Now the gentleman proposes to nearly double that amount, breaking that agreement."

That "broken agreement" refrain was to be repeated by a half-dozen other congressmen arguing against the Mollohan–Fox amendment. Congressman Taylor also sounded two other themes that were repeated by others. First, LSC funding was unnecessary because charitably funded legal aid organizations and pro bono private lawyers could do the job. "In the last 5 years, nonfederal funds for legal services grew by 82 percent. . . . Over 25 States have increased their IOLTA grants by 21 percent. . . . Eighty percent of the [private] bar still is not participating in pro bono activities. There is room, plenty of room with 80 percent of the bar to participate and increase its pro bono service."

Second, Taylor recounted a litany of alleged abuses committed by the lawyers LSC funded, charging LSC "did not help the poor. . . . in fact punished the poor. . . . The Legal Services Corporation supported drug dealers against public housing authorities. It voted to keep illegal immigrants in even while we were paying the Immigration and Naturalization Service (INS) and other federal agencies to try to stem the flow of illegal immigrants. It . . . worked against the prison systems of this country." Taylor then spent a couple of minutes blaming a legal services lawyer for representing an unmarried mother in a family law case because after the court returned the child to her custody, the mother beat the youngster so hard he died. "[T]here are many other cases that we can show where legal services fights federally funded agencies with tax-paid dollars. . . . I urge the House to vote against the Mollohan amendment."[100]

None of the pro-LSC speakers attempted to challenge Congressmen Taylor's statistics, such as by asking how low the nonfederal funding was in 1991 before it began the five-year 82-percent climb he claimed. Even a doubling or tripling of such funding would be insignificant if the starting point was only a few million dollars. Instead they gave anecdotal evidence about the paucity of non-LSC and pro bono resources compared to the need for legal services in their own states and communities.

Congressman Fox, the next speaker after Taylor, first established his own credentials to speak in favor of the LSC's survival and then addressed Congressman Taylor's argument that LSC-funded legal services weren't needed because privately funded legal aid and pro bono services could meet the need.

"I can speak with firsthand knowledge of the benefits of these legal services having served on the board of directors of my own local legal aid office in Montgomery county, PA. In every district throughout this country, there are citizens who find need for legal services and assistance at trying times in their lives. While there may be some private resources available in some areas, there is no guarantee that a private lawyer or group will be there to offer pro bono services. The Philadelphia Bar Association raised $100,000 in private donations last year to direct toward legal services. However, this valiant effort cannot even scratch the surface of need that exists among our poor. . . . Even with full funding [of LSC], no one can argue the poor will have equal access to the courts. In offering this amendment, we are merely attempting to ensure that the indigent of our Nation have some access to the courts.

"Properly structured and supervised as it can be," Congressman Fox continued, "this is a fundamentally conservative program, one which facilitates the peaceful resolution of disputes in our society and reinforces the rule of law. Further cuts in funding will constitute a denial of equal justice under the law to millions of low-income citizens who have no other access to the courts. For this reason, I urge members to support legal services and to support the Mollohan–Fox amendment."[101]

Congressman Duncan Hunter (Republican, California) gave "my humble opinion as a guy who used to practice law in the barrio in San Diego . . . in half a barber shop. . . . [W]hat some legal services devolved into was a legal services operation that went for the sexier lawsuits. They liked the class action suits. They like innovating, and they like lawsuits that drew headlines. And they liked to move away from what I call the ham and egg things.

Evidently assuming LSC's current budget was enough to meet the full need, Hunter justified the further reduction in that funding. "I think we have to strike a balance. I think the money that we have in the bill right now is a balance. It does balance the need to have legal services for people who cannot afford them, but it also leaves a little need there so the local bars will step forward and pick up the slack."[102]

Congressman Hunter's rationale brought an immediate response from Congressman David Skaggs (Democrat, Colorado). He first pointed out the current funding level was far from sufficient and the proposed reduction would leave more than a little remaining need and a bit of slack for pro bono lawyers to pick up.

"Mr. Chairman, this amendment would restore just a portion of what is needed for the basic functions of the Legal Services Corporation, and it ought to command the support of every Member of this body. . . . Access to the legal system is more than a matter of equal justice. It is also a key ingredient in maintaining a civil society based on the rule of law. If people are expected to respect the rule of law, they must have some expectation of its protections, as well as of its discipline. Legal Services plays an essential role in that."

Skaggs then turned to Congressman Hunter's expectation private lawyers would donate enough pro bono services to "pick up the slack."

"There is simply no rational basis to assert that additional pro bono work by the private bar can make up the difference for Legal Services. That makes as much sense as suggesting we are going to get volunteer doctors to make up for eliminating Medicaid."[103]

One speaker who stood up early was important for who he was more than what he said. That individual was long-time LSC critic Congressman Charles Stenholm (Democrat, Texas) who rose to defend the Mollohan–Fox amendment, thereby implying LSC had changed enough to deserve retaining.

"For over a decade now . . . Representative Bill McCollum and I have worked to reform the Legal Services Corporation. . . . Absent any other well-developed approach to carrying for the people that depend on legal assistance in their daily lives, I am not yet willing to demolish the LSC. . . . For this reason, and in agreement with many of those who will find things that have gone wrong with Legal Services, this is not the place to make that decision. Let us allow the program to continue and allow the full changing in the program to take place in an orderly manner, so that we do not end up doing more harm than good for all the right reasons."[104]

None of those defending the pro-LSC position attempted to directly discredit the opponent's stories of "abuses" LSC-funded lawyers allegedly committed. Even the favorite repeated by six of those opposing the Mollohan–Fox amendment—lawsuits against the eviction of drug dealers from public housing—failed to draw an explanation.

This despite the fact that more often than not the tenant the lawyers represented was not the accused drug dealer but the parents or grandparents who faced eviction because their youthful offspring was the culprit and had a bedroom in their apartment. Instead of getting bogged down in fights over the facts of these cases, however, LSC's supporters on the House floor treated them as no longer relevant, ghosts of legal services past. Typical was the response from Congressman James Ramstad (Republican, Minnesota).

"There has been overheated rhetoric from those who want to kill legal services for the poor. . . . Some of these anecdotal references refer to horror stories in the past. . . . But the following restrictions are in place. No class action suits by LSC, no lobbying, no legal assistance to illegal aliens, no political activities, no prisoner litigation, no redistricting representation, no representation of people evicted from public housing because of drugs. That is all in the past. I plead with Members of this body, do not gut the words etched on the Supreme Court building, 'Equal justice under law'. Support fairness and equality under the law. Support the Mollohan–Fox amendment to restore legal services funding. Let us do the right thing."[105]

Another Republican congressman, Steven Schiff (Republican, New Mexico), took a different tack on the issue of abuses by legal services lawyers. "I want to address the fact that it has been brought to attention that a number of unpopular individuals have brought unpopular lawsuits through the Legal Aid Society. Well, I can top those examples. We use taxpayers' money to defend people accused of murder. We use taxpayers' money to defend people accused of armed robbery and all the horrendous crimes we can think of. . . . And we do so for the exact same philosophy, that people have a right to present their case in court. And lawyers only represent clients, they do not raise them, and they do not go home and live with them usually.

"The fact of the matter," Congressman Schiff continued. "is that the lawyer is providing a mechanism where even the most unpopular individual can present their case in court and have a judge and jury render a decision. It seems to be that is what American justice is all about."[106]

Neither Ramstad's nor Schiff's arguments brought an end to the litany of charges against LSC-funded lawyers, however. When Schiff sat down, Congressman Dave Weldon (Republican, Florida) came to the podium. He had met with legal services lawyers from his congressional district.

"I did hear about some of the good things they do representing people who are being unfairly evicted from their housing, helping out the poor. But I did get them to acknowledge that there are Legal Services Corporation lawyers in some localities, unfortunately it was not in mine, that engage in what I would call public advocacy to basically thwart the will of the people. . . . [T]he people of America want welfare reform, and Legal Services Corporation lawyers are fighting welfare reform in some communities."[107]

No one asked the obvious question: did the poor people LSC-funded lawyers represent want welfare reform—and weren't they the clients whose needs and desires they were supposed to advocate? But Weldon's argument did arouse a response from Congressman Floyd Flake (Democrat, New York) that raised a similar point.

"Mr. Chairman, we need to focus this debate on the people who are involved. They include Zelma Brooks. A 65-year-old grandmother who was only able to overturn an unfair eviction after 6 months of diligent work by LSC. . . . As much as critics try to make this about the liberal activists who support LSC, this is about Zelma Brooks and all of the people like her. This Congress has placed handcuffs on an organization that has been doing great work under already strained finances. Arguments about deficiencies in LSC are nothing more than rhetoric and exaggerations being used to mask the fact that we are trying to lock the doors of the civil courtrooms to a class of people.

"Anyone who wishes to destroy any organization can hold it up to the microscope and exploit imperfections. However, no amount of partisan attacks and criticisms can mask the fact that millions of people who would normally be without courtroom access have received legal representation in gaining benefits which they were denied, overturning illegal evictions and separating from abusive spouses. Can we in good conscience allow the poorest and most defenseless of our communities to be left without any protection against civil injustice

"Emblazoned on the front of the Supreme Court are the words 'Equal Justice Under Law'. Nowhere does it say that Americans can only seek redress of grievances if they have the personal resources to do it by themselves. Let's not say that today."[108]

Later on in the debate, another congressman, Christopher Shays (Republican, Connecticut), raised another defense to the complaints about "abusive lawsuits."

"What I cannot understand is why we blame Legal Services for seeking to enforce the laws we pass and the Constitution of the United States we would die defending. If we do not like the end result of the court decisions, then maybe we have to look at the laws we pass. What Legal Services attempts to do is make sure that all citizens, the poorest, in fact, have the same right to defend themselves in court. I hope and pray, I truly pray, that we have the good sense to pass this amendment."[109]

Congressman Howard Berman (Democrat, California) followed Shays, sharpening his fellow congressman's point and adding a partisan twist.

"Mr. Chairman, first, I think it is fair to say this fight is not about money. It is about implementing an effort by some Members of the other party to eliminate the legal services program.

"We talk about class warfare. Let me suggest, I understand why some apartment owners, some growers, some government officials do not want Legal Services programs, because they do not want to afford the rights that the law gives. The right move is not to eliminate the poor's access to lawyers. The right way is to change the laws that we do not like that accord substantive rights to people. Surely once those rights are accorded, we would agree that everyone should have access to them."[110]

On another issue, Congressman Berman was the first to challenge the claim there had been an agreement in 1995 to cut LSC funding another $141 million for FY 1997. As several had before him, John Doolittle (Republican, California) referred to that agreement once again, saying, "We ought to maintain the agreement we entered into."

"Mr. Chairman," Berman interjected, "I was wondering if the gentleman could tell me, other than the hortatory language in a budget resolution, which does not appropriate funds nor authorizing legislation that has not passed, what agreement is the gentleman talking about that we reached regarding the eventual elimination of the Legal Services Corporation?"

"This was the agreement amongst the Republicans," Congressman Doolittle answered, "with the Republican leadership."

"The appropriations process each year funds that Legal Services Corporation, am I not correct?" Berman persisted.

"Mr. Chairman, the gentleman is correct. And I would observe that we have been on track. In fact, the figure in this bill reflects the agreement. Now it is being changed."

"Mr. Chairman, if the gentleman will continue to yield, is it the same agreement among Republicans that was going to eliminate the Department of Commerce, eliminate cops on the beat, eliminate the advanced technology program. Is that the agreement we are talking about?"

"Different agreement," Congressman Doolittle conceded, "but the same philosophy, the philosophy that returns power to the people and cuts their taxes, not bigger and more expensive government."[111]

This brought Congressman Schiff of New Mexico into the debate on this issue, too. Obviously offended by the constant complaints about reneging on a supposed agreement by Republicans to slice another $141 million from LSC's budget, he minced no words.

"I am a Republican. I never reached any agreement with anybody. If other Republicans did make such an agreement, and they have to honor their agreement, then they should vote against this amendment. But I do not think all of us Republicans were ever asked to reach this agreement. I know I certainly was not."

Temporarily shifting the debate to a new topic, Congressman George Gekas (Republican, Pennsylvania) stepped to the podium. He had chaired the subcommittee that worked on resurrecting the "block grant" alternative Nixon had rejected in favor of the Legal Services Corporation. Congressman Gekas brought forth that proposal as a reason to vote against the Mollohan–Fox amendment. "If indeed this amendment that we are considering right now was one in which we take $250 million and turn it over to the States in a block grant system, . . . I would vote for it."[112]

But Gekas invitation didn't attract attention from either side and the debate continued on other topics. Congressman Elijah Cummings (Democrat, Maryland) rose to speak immediately after the Gekas interlude.

"Prior to my election to Congress, I practiced law for almost 20 years. It is through my experiences with the American legal system that I feel confident and qualified to comment on this amendment. As a lawyer, I represented all types of people in all kinds of situations. And there is one hard fact that I have witnessed and learned throughout my years of practice—our system of justice belongs to the wealthy and the privileged. Rare is the day when indigents or poor citizens receive equitable treatment in their representation. I believe that ours is the best judicial process in the world. But everyday across this country, citizens with meager resources have little or no voice in the process.

"Last year's bill quieted the voices of the needy, this year's bill silences those voices. . . . I urge my colleagues on both sides of the aisle to vote in favor of this amendment."[113]

Returning to the issue of whether pro bono and other nonfederal sources could replace the lost LSC funding, Congressman John Spratt (Democrat, South Carolina) cited his own personal experience in South Carolina and also supplied some hard statistics backing up his position.

"I helped found the Piedmont Legal Services office in my home County of York . . . I did so because I discovered early in my private practice that pro bono work wasn't enough to meet the needs of the poor. I tried to do a lot of it myself, but I quickly reached my limit. Legal Services are necessary for any but the smallest fraction of poor people to have access to legal help. . . . The bar in South Carolina has a successful pro bono program which last year drew over 3,000 volunteers who closed almost 1,000 cases. But the 44 Legal Services attorneys in South Carolina closed over 16,000 cases. And LSC funding of other programs helped close another 2,000 cases for a total of 18,000, the need will not go away.

"If we lose this fight today, and let Legal Services be reduced to irrelevance, the need will not go away. Within several years, I am convinced we will see our mistake, but it will take another generation to re-establish 343 local legal aid programs; to restaff their offices; to rebuild the resource centers; and to do something right for poor people and our legal system that we should never have quit doing in the first place."[114]

By this time, Congressman Taylor was running short of speakers. Other than another round of argument by Taylor himself, the only one to speak for that side the rest of the debate was Robert Dornan (Republican, California). Dornan rehashed the same alleged abuses, without acknowledging they had ended with the new restrictions, while also repeating the same list of nongovernmental and pro bono resources others had included in their speeches as being sufficient to replace the lost LSC funding. In a curious passage, he seemed to ignore the recently enacted restriction barring LSC grantees from using their nonfederal funds to provide services they couldn't with their federal funds.

"Mr. Chairman, Congress and past administrations have already attempted without success to place restrictions on LSC activities and behavior. Because money is fungible in the hands of private groups that have more than one funding source, LSC and its grantees have cleverly avoided these restrictions or any other attempt to make them accountable to the taxpayers that finance their activities."[115]

Congressman Dornan concluded his speech with a plea.

"Mr. Chairman, the Federal Government can no longer afford to maintain this agency, especially when so many resources already exist for the poor to turn to for legal aid when they need it. It's time to defund the left, to defund the failed Legal Services Corporation."[116]

One issue opponents raised early in the debate remained to be addressed as the one hour deadline approached. Congressman Dan Burton of Indiana had complained that "Congress prohibited Legal Services Corporation from doing certain things. Legal services grantees are getting around these restrictions by forming new shell organizations to accept federal grants so that the original groups can continue to pursue their liberal agenda with private funds. For example, the Philadelphia Legal Assistance Center[117] and the Legal Aid Society of Santa Clara, in many cases the two organizations have the same board of directors, many of the same lawyers, and they share office space. They are two separate organizations in name only. They are just getting around the restrictions so they can do whatever they damn well please."[118]

It wasn't until the congressman from the Santa Clara district, Zoe Lofgren (Democrat, California) finally spoke that the situation could be clarified and the separate nature of the two organizations could be determined.

"The gentleman from Indiana said earlier there are shell organizations that have been created, and that there is something illegal or wrong about this. I am sure he spoke sincerely but I am from Santa Clara County . . . His comments were not accurate.

"I . . . have copies here, and I would be happy to share them with Members, of the articles of incorporation of the Legal Aid Society of

Santa Clara County and the Community Legal Services. They are two separate corporations. I have copies of the boards of directors of the Community Legal Services, which is the Legal Services Corp. grantee, and the Legal Aid Society, which is a private corporation that receives not one penny of Legal Services Corp. funding.

"I helped raise money for the Legal Aid Society which receives no Legal Series money, along with our district attorney who is a tough prosecutor and, I would add, also a Republican. However, he believes, our prosecutor does, as do I, that we need to be able to do such things as provide restraining orders to victims of domestic violence without asking for their financial statements. That is one of the many reasons why I support the Mollohan amendment. I am glad to be able to offer facts in support of it."[119]

Only once did the debate expose some of the furious lobbying pressures to which Republican congressmen were subjected by those outside interests seeking to continue sending LSC down the "glide path" to oblivion. That hint came in an emotional outburst from Congressman Alcee Hastings (Democrat, Florida).

"I rise today in support of the Mollohan–Fox amendment, and to express my dismay with the fax that I received from the Christian Coalition urging that I oppose this amendment. Mr. Chairman, I am a Christian and I support this amendment, because following the Christian teachings that I was taught, I believe that helping the poor is a Christian thing to do. Helping the poor access the same legal system to which people with money can access at will is, I believe, a very Christian thing to do.

"I am dismayed that the Christian Coalition intimates that they speak for Christians. Clearly they do not speak for the poor or the charitable, for if they did, they would not urge us to kill this amendment."[120]

Congressman Taylor assigned himself the task of summing up for the opposition side. In an unexpected choice, he started by referring to Clark Durant without using his name.

"Mr. Chairman, a former chairman of the Legal Services Corporation several years ago, seeing the multitude of abuses in the big government Legal Services Corporation tried to reform it. He was sued with taxpayer's money by the Legal Services Corporation and never got through any of those reforms. Today he stands as a strong opponent to the big government Legal Services Corporation that the gentleman wants funded for $250 million."[121]

Taylor then made a final plea to his fellow Republicans.

"I would say most of the people on this side of the aisle [e.g., Republicans] who have spoken to increase the funding amount to $250 million voted for the budget amendment that actually would hold it to $95 million, while we are talking about $141 million today. . . . The myth is these folks think legal services will come to a halt if we do not keep the Federal government, that is, the big government that is hurting the poor more than it is helping, involved. That just is not true." This was followed by the same list of nonfederal and pro bono resources Taylor had featured in his opening statement.

Taylor concluded the case against the Mollohan–Fox amendment with an attack on the offsets proposed in that legislation.

"The gentleman also suggests taking $57 million from our Federal Prison Program and our courts. That will keep more violent criminals on the street. So while he is working for a national program, a big government program, we in fact will be hurting the justice system of this country. I urge Members to vote 'no' on the Mollohan amendment."[122]

After Taylor sat down, a half-dozen supporters of the amendment added their comments to the debate—including Congresswomen Nancy Pelosi (Democrat, California), Juanita Millender-McDonald (Democrat, California), and Cardithia Collins (Democrat, Illinois), along with Congressman Donald Payne (Democrat, New Jersey), who was the chair of the Congressional Black Caucus, and Congressman Jerry Costello (Democrat, Illinois).

Congresswoman Collins gave what could have been a good summation for the pro-LSC forces on the House floor.

"Since its creation in 1974, the Legal Services Corporation has come to represent a chance, not a guarantee, but just a chance to receive fairness in our society and from our judicial system. Unfortunately, that chance is not even a dream without adequate funding. . . . Many of my constituents rely on LSC for a chance at fair treatment in the judicial system. . . . [T]he LSC deserves more, not fewer, resources. It is a well-run corporation that is cost effective and programmatically extraordinarily successful."[123]

But the most powerful plea for an affirmative vote on the amendment may have come from Congressman Chet Edwards (Democrat, Texas) during the middle of the debate.

"Mr. Chairman, each morning Members of this House with hand over heart turn to this flag and give a pledge: One nation under God, indivisible, with liberty and justice for all.

"In a few moments with our votes we will decide whether justice for all is simply words to be recited, or an ideal worth defending. I believe in the Pledge of Allegiance, I believe it is worth reciting, and I believe it is worth defending.

"Vote 'yes' on this amendment."[124]

THE VOTE IN THE HOUSE OF REPRESENTATIVES AND ITS AFTERMATH

Whether the pro-amendment forces had the better of the debate or not, when the vote was taken in the House of Representatives, 56 Republicans broke with Gingrich and Armey to join the vast majority of

Democratic members and support the Mollohan–Fox amendment.[125] The leadership's "glide path" plan was halted by a margin of 68 votes, 247–179,[126] and the Legal Services Corporation had survived another brush with death.

The House leadership was not happy with the 56 moderates who refused to go along with the "glide path." Tom DeLay (Republican, Texas) was typical in his response, "I think it's disgusting. A bunch of them just ran for the hills."[127]

With this epic confrontation on the floor of the House of Representatives in the summer of 1996, the LSC found the power of its fundamental rationale. Gingrich's Contract with America juggernaut had met its match—the commitment to equal justice for all citizens that most people in this country share with enough members of Congress to save LSC. While the House Appropriations Committee and Republican leadership would seek to resurrect the "glide path" in the future, they had taken their best shot in the summer of 1996, and lost.

Any feeling of relief the LSC board, legal services lawyers and their clients may have felt after the 1996 House vote was muted by the price they had paid. The LSC emerged from the ordeal alive, but in the process the legal aid system it funded lost its right arm and much of its brain power. The "right arm" the legal aid lawyers and their clients lost was the ability to file class actions or engage in legislative advocacy.[128] Because of restrictions LSC had to accept in order to recruit moderate Republican support, no LSC grantees were allowed to offer clients these forms of representation with LSC funds or even with money they received from private donations or state and local governments.[129] Nor were legal services clients allowed to accept the legal fees courts sometimes award to winning parties—even though other litigants could.[130] The "brain power" civil legal aid stood to lose was in the national and state support centers that housed the experts in the legal fields most important to the poor—housing, consumer, employment, public benefits, etc., a resource LSC was now prohibited from funding.[131]

Both efficiency and effectiveness were bound to suffer—efficiency because a single class action or legislative change can help hundreds or thousands of people in a single stroke, far cheaper than trying to do it one case at a time, and effectiveness because poor people often face complex legal problems, as well as simple ones, and those problems are best handled with the help of lawyers who have made themselves experts in those fields of the law. Beyond the restrictions, poor people had seen the federal program that provided most of their legal help emerge from the "Contract with America" battle badly crippled, and with much less funding and thus far fewer lawyers to help them.

ANOTHER SOURCE OF LEGAL AID FUNDING IS PLACED IN JEOPARDY

There was another reason for concern among LSC grantees and other civil legal aid organizations in 1996. A right wing public interest group was trying to dismantle the state IOLTA programs, the second-largest source of funding for civil legal services to the poor. This attack was launched in the federal courts rather than Congress or the state legislatures.

In late 1994, about the time the Republicans won control of Congress, the Washington Legal Foundation (WLF) filed a lawsuit in a Texas federal court alleging all IOLTA programs were unconstitutional. The foundation based its case on the theory IOLTA "took" property from bank depositors in the form of the interest paid to civil legal aid programs and other recipients without giving those depositors the "just compensation" to which they were entitled under the Fifth Amendment.

Legal services supporters had breathed a sigh of relief in January 1995 when the federal trial court in Texas ruled against the WLF and found IOLTA to be constitutional. As the trial judge explained in *Washington Legal Foundation v. Texas Equal Access to Justice Foundation*, "Simply put, the Court cannot conclude that the Plaintiffs have a property interest in interest proceeds that, but for the IOLTA Program, would never have been generated. Without such a property interest, the Plaintiffs are unable to state a viable Fifth Amendment pertaining to their ownership of the interest generated by funds placed in IOLTA accounts."[132]

Over a year and a half later, on September 12, 1996, not long after the 1996 congressional battle over LSC's survival ended, the IOLTA programs were under a cloud again. Although in earlier Florida and Massachusetts cases federal appellate courts had upheld IOLTA programs as constitutional,[133] a panel of the Fifth Circuit reversed the Texas District Court and found IOLTA represented an "unconstitutional taking" of the depositors' property. The court explained,

> It has been suggested that the IOLTA program represents a successful, modern-day attempt at alchemy. . . . According to the defendants' theory, the interest proceeds generated by Texas's IOLTA accounts exist solely because of an anomaly in banking regulations and, until the creation of the IOLTA program, that interest belonged to no one. The defendants then contend that Texas used the IOLTA program to stake a legitimate claim to these funds and that the plaintiffs cannot now seek to repossess the fruits of this magic as their own. We, however, view the IOLTA interest proceeds not as the fruit of alchemy, but as the fruit of the clients' principal deposits.

State law defines "property" and the United States Constitution pro-tects private property from government encroachment. Texas observes the traditional rule that interest follows principal, which recognizes that interest earned on a deposit of principal belongs to the owner of the principal. In the light of this rule, it seems obvious that the inter-est earned in the IOLTA accounts is the property of the clients whose money is held in those accounts.[134]

Based on this reasoning, the Fifth Circuit returned the case to the district court to consider whether and how much the depositors should be compensated for this deprivation of their property rights in the interest income IOLTA turned over to legal services programs.

While the Texas trial court was considering whether the Fifth Cir-cuit's ruling meant the state's IOLTA program was unconstitutional and could no longer use the funds to support legal services, the WLF filed another constitutional challenge against the IOLTA program in the state of Washington in January 1997.[135] From then on and well into the early years of the next century, the Texas and Washington cases bounced from court to court and back again, with both sides winning sometimes and losing other times, a saga to be recounted in future chapters. All this would culminate in a final showdown before the na-tion's Supreme Court more than a half decade after the WLF initially filed the Texas case.

HOW THE TWO CAMPS VIEWED THE OUTCOME OF THE MID-1990S FIGHTS OVER LEGAL SERVICES

While LSC, its grantees, their lawyers and clients had every reason to fear the WLF litigation and especially to bemoan the compromise they had been forced to accept in their confrontation with the Gingrich Congress, there was another group of people who should have felt vindicated. After a quarter century of campaigning, Howard Phillips, Bill Harvey, Don Bogard, Clark Durant, Terry Wear, Michael Wallace, the Legal Services Reform Coalition, Congressmen Bill McCollum and Charles Stenholm, along with scores of their allies, had finally seen Congress enact most of the restrictions they had been fighting for two decades to install limiting what legal services lawyers could do for their clients. Although some in their camp were satisfied, for others it wasn't enough. They wanted the Legal Services Corporation abolished and were disappointed the Gingrich Congress had failed to do so.

In an editorial representative of their lament, the *National Review* wrote,

Earlier this year Republicans talked boldly of zeroing out programs. The House Appropriations Committee would simply allocate zero funds for certain noxious government agencies. Since there's no way for the Senate or the White House to spend money without House assent, this would be an easy, effectively veto-proof way to eliminate programs on the conservative hit list. But as it turns out, the dreaded zero-out is getting elbowed aside. . . . The Legal Services Corporation is typical. . . . Unless a last-ditch attempt to zero out the LSC or block-grant its funding to the states wins either on the House floor, or in the Senate through the exertions of Phil Gramm (both unlikely), the LSC can breathe the same words of relief it did after Senator Warren Rudman (R., N.H.) intervened on its behalf in the 1980s: Saved by Republicans.[136]

Alex Forger, who led the LSC during the mid-1990s, gave his own assessment of the experience. Addressing a law school conference after he left office, Forger spoke of what it was like to defend LSC in the Gingrich-led Congress.

> I have become very cynical, as you know, of this process. But seeing it close at hand is something totally different than one would see from the vantage point of a law firm in New York City when dealing with Congress on matters of banking or tax. When you're there representing people who lack influence or clout, the door is generally closed.
>
> In the floor debates, the end justifies the means. If you're against legal services, you say whatever you want; that's okay. You can even make up quotes, as was done by Representative Dornan of California in declaring, on national television no less, that "the President of Legal Services [Forger] is particularly arrogant. Let me tell you what he said: Congress can't tell us what cases we can take." A pure, absolute fabrication. I brought this to his attention. Makes no difference. There is no accountability. You say what you want to say—black is white or red—and you pass around all of the long ago discredited stories. . . . Most of Congress doesn't really know much about legal services, what it does, or the importance of its work, and they take direction from the detractors.
>
> The Farm Bureau is by far the most powerful influence. I think, if Congress dared to do so, they would eliminate permitted representations of migrant workers. The Farm Bureau, in its zeal to discredit LSC, alleges lawyer misconduct such as extortion, blackmail, and the like. It does so because LSC is extremely unpopular [with agribusiness] in its efforts to enforce employment, housing, and environmental requirements to which the growers are subject.[137]

A Wall Street lawyer had come to Washington to help the poor and learned the hard lesson most legal services lawyers already knew. Lawyers representing the poor are often in the right and can win in court. But their clients are never powerful in the political arena. And as Forger found, with the Congress of the mid-1990s, truth was no defense.

REPORT FROM THE FIELD: Doing Well from Doing Good—The
"Reggie" Who Pioneered Class Action Employment-Discrimination
Lawsuits

Many legal services lawyers put the training and expertise they
gained while working in the legal service program to good use after
leaving for private practice. Some of those did more for low-income
people as private attorneys than they ever did as legal aid lawyers.
But few if any accomplished so much—for their low- and moderate-
income clients and for themselves—as Guy Saperstein. In his intrigu-
ing book, *Civil Warrior: Memoirs of a Civil Rights Attorney,*[1] Saperstein tells the story of how he made the transition from "Reggie" to
one of the most successful and wealthiest class action lawyers in rhe
United States.

   If the last name sounds familiar, Guy's uncle was Abe Saperstein,
founder and owner of the famous Harlem Globetrotters basketball
team. Guy was born in Chicago and raised in that city and then in
North Hollywood, where he was a good athlete and brilliant under-
achiever in high school. Yet, despite mediocre grades, when he scored
in the 99th percentile on the SAT, Guy had his choice of colleges.
Saperstein elected to attend the University of California-Berkeley
where he worked his way through school.

   Saperstein's life as a lawyer began in 1969, when as a graduating
senior from the University of California-Berkeley's Law School, he
applied for and received a Reginald Heber Smith Fellowship. Saperstein counted himself lucky to have won a "Reggie" because 5 of the
10 top students in his class also earned those fellowships, while his
came "on the strength of my leadership" in a community assistance
project and "not my grades." The year 1969 was the time of turmoil
for the Reggie class when Terry Lenzner had to make an emergency
visit to the summer training program at Haverford College in order
to settle some grievances. (See chapter 13.) Beyond the controversy,
however, the classes were taught by some of the best lawyers and law
professors in the country. "I was excited in a way that never seemed
possible in law school," Saperstein wrote. "This was an opportunity
to represent the powerless people who get pushed around by society
and had no way to protect their rights. This is why I had become a
lawyer."

   After a month's training in class action litigation among other
skills legal services lawyers needed at that time, Saperstein chose to
spend his two-year tour as a Reggie at the newly created Colorado
Rural Legal Services (CRLS). He devotes a chapter in his memoir to

this experience. Because CRLS was a brand new organization Saperstein helped the executive director, Jonathan "Skip" Chase, set up the four regional law offices before he started helping clients. Both of them sported long hair and full beards so had to steer clear of the cowboy bars where they would be considered "hippies," not a popular group among the patrons of those places.

Because most of their clients would be migrant workers, Chase thought the lawyers should learn what it was like to be one of them. For four days, Saperstein lived in a migrant camp and dug for sugar beets with a short-handled hoe. "At the end of the day," Saperstein wrote, "I found it almost impossible to stand up and I felt like I was ready for a back implant." He found the "living conditions in the migrant camps as bad as the working conditions . . . unheated, uninsulated barracks, no privacy, no hot water" and no toilet facilities at all in the fields. This experience left an indelible impression on Saperstein. For the 30 years he was in private practice, one wall featured a photograph of a migrant worker bent over working with a short-handled hoe to remind him "of the real value of labor" and of those he came to represent.

During the nearly two years Saperstein spent as a CRLS "Reggie" he was assigned to the "class action office" at the program's headquarters with occasional two- and three-week stints working in one or the other of the regional offices handling day-to-day cases of consequence only for the individuals involved. He learned from both types of experiences. The most important victory achieved was a class action opening up public hospitals to poor patients where they had been denied admission in violation of federal law.

Saperstein's legal services experience not only equipped him with class action skills, it also put him on track to his eventual specialty— employment-discrimination class actions. Returning to the Bay area without a job, Saperstein had struggled with a solo practice before forming a partnership with a young Stanford lawyer, Charles Farnsworth, and opening an office in a rundown area of Oakland. Shortly thereafter, he received a call from Steve Ronfeldt and Russ Galloway, lawyers with the Legal Aid Society of Oakland. They had more Title VII employment cases than they could handle and asked if he would be willing to litigate one of them. Saperstein warned them he didn't know Title VII law and had never tried an employment-discrimination case. But they reminded him he had plenty of experience in federal court and with class actions. Saperstein was soon lead counsel in one of the Legal Aid Society's major Title VII cases, a class action for race discrimination against Trans International Airlines. Not satisfied to sue only the airline, Saperstein came up with legal theories allowing him to add as defendants the Federal Aviation Administration and the Port Authority that ran the Oakland airport.

After fighting and winning several pretrial motions and discovery disputes, Saperstein forced the airline into a favorable settlement—cash awards for the named plaintiffs, a court order compelling an increase of minority and female hires by the airline, and a $30,000 attorney award for the plaintiff's lawyers, of which Saperstein received $22,000, the largest fee he had seen at that point in his career. Saperstein was feeling good about that fee, until he found out the firm defending Trans International Airlines had earned $300,000 for their work on the case—10 times more for losing than his side got for winning the case. He had learned his lesson and never accepted such a small fee in the future—the next class action case he handled yielded a $282,500 fee. One judge spotted the real reason Saperstein was asking for substantial fees, "You want to build a war chest to fund future cases, don't you?"

Thanks to that first case referred to him from the Legal Aid Society of Oakland, Saperstein had found his field—employment litigation. Although he also filed and won a number of wrongful termination cases, his specialty within the employment law field was to fight racial, gender, and age discrimination in the workplace. Over the years, his firm sued grocery store chains, restaurants, and clothing manufacturers, among others—leading to several settlements in the $100 million plus range and earning him fees to match. But if Saperstein developed a specialty within a specialty it was insurance companies and their discrimination in the hiring and promotion of agents, soon becoming known as the "Ralph Nader of the Insurance Industry." After wringing generous settlements out of Fireman's Fund and Prudential, Saperstein's firm engaged in a 23-year war over sex discrimination at State Farm. The case finally concluded with a mammoth settlement—monetary awards totaling a quarter of a billion dollars, an agreement for 50 percent of hires to be women for several years, and to provide them the support to become successful agents. The $250 million monetary recovery was the largest ever in an employment-discrimination case and remained the record for the next decade.

Saperstein's firm ended up with $65 million in fees for winning while State Farm paid its outside counsel $110 million for losing. State Farm issued a statement admitting they had been wrong and had been bested by Saperstein and his team. "We were like Robert

Duran in the ring with Sugar Ray Leonard and we said, 'No mas'." The company took the loss to heart in another sense—it revamped its employment practices throughout the country, not just in California. A few years later, a State Farm lawyer conceded to Saperstein that, "you're the guy who brought us into the 20th century of personnel practices. We now are hiring better-quality agents than ever before and the women are selling as well, or better than the men."

In these and scores of other cases, Guy Saperstein, the former "Reggie," indeed did good for many others while doing well for himself.

1. Guy Saperstein, *Civil Warrior: Memoirs of a Civil Rights Attorney* (Berkeley: Berkeley Hills Books, 2003).

Chapter 27

Coping with the Compromise

Resistance, Readjustment, and Reassurance

> The poor have to labor in the face of the majestic equality of the law, which forbids the rich as well as the poor to sleep under bridges, to beg in the streets, and to steal bread.
> —Anatole France *The Red Lily* (1894)

> It must be possible for the humblest to invoke the protection of the law, through proper proceedings in the courts, for any invasion of rights by whomsoever attempted, or freedom and equality vanish into nothingness.
> —Reginald Heber Smith *Justice and the Poor* (1919)

What was happening in Washington during 1995 and 1996 struck a series of body blows to LSC grantees throughout the country. Worst off, of course, were the national and statewide support centers. They lost all their funding and presumably would disappear. Local programs suffered a one-third cut in their LSC grants, which forced them to close offices and discharge lawyers and other staff members, meaning far fewer poor people could be served.

But reduced financing from the federal government was only one problem the legal services community had to face. As a result of new restrictions, LSC-funded legal services lawyers could no longer represent any of the millions of low-income undocumented aliens who too often were denied their legal rights by employers, landlords, and others. These were the very problems faced by those German immigrants to New York City in 1876 that gave birth to the nation's first legal aid organization. Nor could LSC-funded lawyers represent any poor persons with desegregation, abortion, or redistricting cases. Most important for the vast majority of poor people and their problems, LSC-funded lawyers had been stripped of some of their most important and powerful tools as members of the legal profession—the ability to file class actions, to participate fully in administrative rule-making, or to present legislative solutions to their clients' problems. And to compound the problem, any grantee that received even a dollar of LSC

funding was barred from using its non-LSC money for any of the prohibited services.

TO RESIST OR NOT TO RESIST, THAT IS THE QUESTION

Lawyers are fighters by nature, especially against what they perceive
to be unjust policies, so one might expect the first reaction of legal
services attorneys would be to resist these restrictions in the courts,
or at least test their constitutionality. But as revealed in the chapter 26,
as of May 1996, those lobbying to save the LSC from destruction in
Congress had closed down the planning for a lawsuit challenging the
restrictions. This set off an angry debate within the legal services community. Many who were not involved in the negotiations bridled at
the notion they might be hogtied by limitations a court would find unconstitutional if it had a chance. Others worried the fragile deal with
moderate Republicans that saved not only LSC but their own funding
might fall apart the moment one of their number filed a lawsuit seeking to strike down any of those restrictions.

As we saw, one of the legal services lawyers most bothered by the
restrictions was Jonathan Weiss, executive director of Legal Services
for the Elderly (LSE) in New York City. After learning the national
lawsuit was not going to happen, he had immediately sent an e-mail
message, "Let's Litigate against Legal Services Restrictions" to legal
services lawyers around the country.[1]

Although Weiss's call to action failed to produce the nationwide
wave of lawsuits he hoped for, the LSE chief did find a kindred spirit
in New York—Burt Neuborne, a New York University law professor
and former ACLU lawyer who was one of the founders of the Brennan
Center on Justice.[2] When Weiss asked, Neuborne said yes. He then explained why he wanted to help those legal services grantees or clients
who might want to fight the restrictions in court. "This [the imposition
of restrictions] is the end game of the effort by the Republican right to
remove law reform as an option for poor people. The sad thing is legal
services is prepared to surrender a large chunk of what it is for fear of
being put out of business. I'd like to be a good team player, but I so
profoundly believe that they're wrong, I can't let this go."[3]

Neuborne's support for a resistance movement brought an immediate response from Alan Houseman, Laurie Zelon, and others who
had been lead negotiators for the legal services community with Congress. They had abandoned the planned lawsuit in May 1996 for what
they saw as sound reasons—the almost certain loss of support from
moderate Republicans if legal services lawyers sought to strike down
the restrictions Congress had passed, and, if that happened, the certain end of the Legal Services Corporation. Based on that calculation,

"we made a political decision not to file a major lawsuit," Houseman explained.[4]

With the legal services grantees who had been ACLU's clients choosing against filing a lawsuit, the ACLU lawyers felt they had been co-opted and were reluctant to file a constitutional challenge against the wishes of their former clients. But Professor Neuborne, who had been the ACLU's legal director earlier in his career, felt no such inhibition and was poised to test those restrictions in state or federal courts.

Jonathan Weiss and his LSE program filed the first case raising the constitutionality of the restrictions. It arose in the context of one of LSE's ongoing class actions and the requirement it withdraw from the case midstream. LSC's congressional critics had painted an image of LSC grantees as class action machines spending most of their time churning out new waves of such major lawsuits. If that image were accurate, it might have been expected thousands if not scores of thousands of these slow-moving cases would have accumulated over the years and now needed to be closed out or transferred to other lawyers. But out of the millions of cases legal services lawyers had handled in recent years, only 630 were class actions.[5]

When President Clinton signed the appropriation bill containing the restrictions on April 26, 1996, LSC-funded lawyers were given until August 1 to remove themselves from those 630 cases. As that deadline approached, grantees around the country had managed to conclude or transfer all but 20 or 30 of their class actions.[6] Several of the remaining cases were in New York state courts, one of which was *Varshavsky v. Perales*, a class action LSE had brought on behalf of all homebound disabled welfare recipients who were unable to attend fair hearings in welfare offices. Based on both statutory and constitutional provisions, the lawsuit sought an injunction ordering New York welfare officials to hold fair hearings in the homes of disabled people.[7]

The trial judge, Beverly Cohen, was in the midst of considering the briefs and hearing oral arguments on the motion for a preliminary injunction when LSE's lead counsel in the case, Valerie Bogart, made the judge aware of the LSC ban on legal services lawyers continuing to serve in class actions. But Bogart didn't file an unqualified request to withdraw from the case. Instead, with Burt Neuborne and his team as her counsel, she presented the court a "conditional" motion to withdraw.

The motion was "conditional" in the sense it asked the judge to decide whether the class action restriction was constitutional. If so, Bogart and LSE would be compelled to withdraw and the court would have to find substitute counsel to represent the disabled plaintiffs. But if the judge found the class action restriction unconstitutional, the LSE lawyers would continue representing the class and the litigation could move forward without interruption. Neuborne accompanied the motion with a legal memorandum explaining how this particular restriction indeed violated the U.S. Constitution.[8]

In an order issued December 24, 1996, Judge Cohen denied the "conditional" withdrawal motion, and also invalidated the congressional class action restriction and the LSC regulations implementing that restriction to the extent they prevented LSC grantees from using non-LSC funds to support class action representation. The judge accompanied her order with a lengthy decision, surveying the relevant Supreme Court opinions and concluding the class action restriction denied poor people their First Amendment rights.

> The [restrictions on class action representation] are unconstitutional, as they do not allow Legal Services for the Elderly [LSE] to proceed with a class action, a constitutionally protected activity, even when using segregated or transferred non-federal funds. The [restriction on class actions] threatens our most cherished First Amendment freedoms: freedom of association, freedom of speech and freedom to petition the government for redress of grievances. The rhetoric of budget reform is being used to thinly disguise an attack on basic freedoms. The restrictions could effectively bar LSE attorneys, their clients, their private and State donors, and those to whom LSE wishes to donate its non-federal funds from exercising their constitutionally protected right to freedom of association. That Congress may not do this has been explicitly stated in a long line of Supreme Court precedents that derived from attacks on desegregation and unions. At bottom, the legislation weakens the ability of poor people to stand up for their legal rights and to have an impact, when it may be their only effective method to petition the government for redress of grievances.[9]

This was a victory for LSE and its homebound disabled clients, and also an encouraging sign for Weiss and Neuborne and their hopes to strike down many of the congressional restrictions in the courts. But it was only a small sign. There are many levels of courts between a state trial judge and the U.S. Supreme Court. Judge Cohen's order declaring the class action restriction unconstitutional affected only the case before her. It did not set a precedent binding on courts elsewhere in the country—or even elsewhere in New York.

It was apparent Neuborne or anyone else interested in striking down some of the congressional restrictions would have to take the fight to the federal courts. At the request of Weiss and a few other legal services agencies and client organizations in New York, Neuborne and his team began preparing a federal lawsuit seeking to overturn most of the congressional limitations on what LSC-funded lawyers could do for poor people.

Other than the *Varshavsky v. Perales* decision and a few other successful "conditional" withdrawal motions in New York state courts, the litigation front remained quiet throughout 1996. Most grantees and their lawyers were preoccupied with adjusting to the reduced funding from LSC and most also were fearful of congressional reaction should they seek to overturn any of the restrictions in court. Meanwhile during much of 1996, as will be recalled, the LSC itself along with the ABA and its grassroots campaign, the NLADA and other supporters, had been fully engaged in the struggle to halt the "glide path to oblivion" and save LSC from a second one-third cut in its funding, a legislative battle which was recounted in chapter 26.

AN EXERCISE IN REINVENTION: THE NATIONAL AND STATE SUPPORT CENTERS

It was the national and state support centers that faced the ultimate challenge, of course. They had seen their funding eliminated when Clinton signed the FY 1996 legislation in April 1996. Congress didn't even provide these support centers phase-out grants to complete litigation or other activities they already had undertaken.

The loss of LSC funding came with one saving grace, however. These support centers were completely freed from the restrictions that accompanied the corporation's funding. Because LSC grantees, including the support centers, had had to live with restrictions, some quite severe, that predated the Gingrich Congress, this opened up a full array of possibilities for these centers if they could just come up with other sources of financial support.

Typical of the trauma these support centers endured was the Western Center on Law and Poverty, the main state support center for California, its hundreds of legal services lawyers, and some six million poor people. As will be recalled, this was not the first time the Western Center had faced the prospect of losing its LSC funding. In 1983, the center had been able to win a court judgment that reversed LSC president Donald Bogard's attempt to defund the program. But this time there would be no last-minute reprieve for the Western Center and Mary Burdick, who was still it executive director.

When Burdick learned Congress had passed the bill that would terminate LSC funding of all support centers, she had to make some hard decisions. One option was to put the staff on short rations—ask them to take pay cuts or work half-time. This was the course some support centers chose to try. But Burdick recognized it would take several years to replace the $1.2 million in lost LSC financing. This was far too long to expect staff members to remain on a reduced salary or half-time basis, and thus risked losing the entire staff, probably the very best ones first. Better to make the choices herself now rather than letting time and fate decide who would remain. In what she says was "the worst year of my life," Burdick laid off a third of the full-time litigators, most

772 *To Establish Justice for All*

of the administrative and management staff, and cut the number of attorney assistants to the bare minimum. Only the legislative staff in Sacramento emerged unscathed—a testament to the fact both the local LSC grantees and the Western Center litigators told Burdick her highest responsibility was to preserve that unique resource intact.[10]

Burdick then began assembling new or expanded sources of support for the Western Center. The organization already had one annual check that would not be available in most states—California's Interest on Lawyers' Trust Accounts program. The legislation creating that program required 20 percent of IOLTA revenues to be distributed to support centers. Although the Western Center was the primary statewide support center in the state, a number of national support centers also were located in California, or relocated there after Congress cut off their federal funding. As a result, the Western Center had to share that pot of money with several other organizations. But at least its annual IOLTA grant was a start.

Burdick also approached all the local programs and asked them to contribute a small piece of their own non-LSC funds to help the Western Center continue offering them support services. Most programs did so, providing a much needed infusion of cash and moral support.[11]

Because the center no longer received LSC funds, it was free to seek court-awarded fees in major cases it won—something local LSC grantees could no longer do. Largely growing out of one of Western Center's early landmark cases, *Serrano v. Priest*,[12] California had a quite generous system for awarding fees to successful litigants in cases the courts found to advance the public interest.[13] Most of the Western Center's litigation fit that definition. Thus, when the center's lawyers won a victory in court it frequently came with a payoff that could be added to the center's treasury and thus support future litigation.

Burdick also began a campaign to raise money from private law firms, especially from Los Angeles' ample supply of large corporate firms. Until that time, most members of the Western Center board had been directors of local legal services programs (LSPs), some law school professors, with only a smattering of private lawyers. No one on the board was expected to donate money or to raise it from others. Burdick changed that, enlisting influential partners from major corporate law firms and with the expectation they would bring in substantial financial donations to the Western Center's coffers.[14] The center started an annual fundraiser, "the Western Center Garden Party" that brought its financial supporters to the backyard of one of its former board chairs, corporate lawyer John Brinsley. Over time law firm donations soon became a major source of support for the center, especially as the corporate law firm business boomed in the late 1990s and early 2000s.

Burdick also made good use of Western Center's reputation built during more than a quarter century of federal funding. She approached foundations interested in promoting certain policy objectives that squared with the center's goals and the aspirations of the poverty population it served. If a foundation was interested in advancing a certain agenda in the area of health, or welfare, or housing, the center would submit a proposal for a grant to support litigation or legislative activity or policy advocacy to move that agenda forward. Those proposals were successful frequently enough to generate another fairly steady revenue stream to help replace what was lost when Congress turned off the LSC spigot.[15]

But the steadiest and most reliable source of income came from an unexpected place. Shortly after the Gingrich Congress cut off LSC financing of the center, a wealthy lawyer began making anonymous annual donations of $250,000 or more to the center—every year for nearly a decade. In the final year, he donated $450,000 to the Western Center budget. Burdick knows this generous donor's identity, of course, but still protects his anonymity to this very day.[16]

Through a combination of these strategies, in only a few years the Western Center had restored its annual budget to the level it was in 1995, the year before LSC funding ended.[17]

A different mix of non-LSC revenue sources allowed another of the statewide support centers, the Massachusetts Law Reform Institute (MLRI), to survive. For that center, it was an increase in the institute's share of IOLTA and state government support that allowed it to make up for the loss of its LSC grant. The money from those state-based funding sources was distributed by the Massachusetts Legal Assistance Corporation (MLAC) to local legal services agencies around the state.[18] So when the Gingrich Congress axed MLRI's federal financing, that was where the institute looked for a lifeline.

By the mid-1990s MLRI had been operating since 1969 under the leadership of its founder and original executive director, Allan Rodgers.[19] The institute had become an invaluable asset to the other legal services agencies in Massachusetts and Rodgers himself an institution in the state's legal services community. Thus, he had strong support from the frontline legal services grantees when he requested a dramatic raise in MLRI's state funding, even though this increase would come out of the hides of these same local grantees at the very time they were facing their own cuts in federal funding.[20] The willingness of those local grantees to sacrifice a big piece of their own state monies so MLRI could survive was a powerful testament to how critical the lawyers in the local offices considered the legislative advocacy, the expertise, and major litigation help the support center supplied. MLRI also managed to augment the IOLTA and state government funding it received from MLAC with foundation grants and court-awarded fees.

But the willingness of local grantees to part with a substantial share of their MLAC funding is what allowed this state support center to continue at a meaningful level after LSC cut off the federal money.

The first of the national support centers—formally named the "Center on Social Welfare Policy and Law" but widely known as the "Welfare Law Center"—also had the benefit of an experienced and able director when the Gingrich Congress cut off LSC funding. Henry Freedman had been one of the original "Reggies" in 1967 when he was assigned to the center. In 1970, he took over as the center's executive director.[21] Thus, like Allan Rodgers in Massachusetts, he had run the welfare center for a quarter century when he and his program faced their greatest challenge in 1996. While it had a long history of attracting some funding from foundations, corporations, and law firms, the annual LSC grant still provided over 80 percent of the center's support.[22]

Freedman immediately recognized the advantage of being located in New York City, amidst the nation's wealthiest collection of corporate law firms and major foundations. The center already enjoyed a stellar reputation in both those communities, which were reminded of the center's importance and its desperate financial plight when the *Sunday New York Times* ran a front-page article featuring a national conference the center held about the Gingrich Congress's new "welfare reform" legislation. This article reported Congress had defunded all legal services support centers, including the Welfare Law Center.[23]

As he was planning how to reinvent the center, Freedman later said, "We would not have made it through 1996 without foundation support. Most critical was the Ford Foundation, which had notified us earlier that its support [under a previous grant] would end in 1995. I pressed for a reprieve, and after many anxious months the foundation renewed the grant."[24]

With the Ford Foundation having given the center the equivalent of a "bridge loan" allowing it a short-term lease on life, Freedman began cultivating other foundations, most of which he had never approached before. "A number of New York foundations new to us supported us because they understood the critical role that impact litigation could play in turning back Mayor Giuliani's . . . illegal efforts to deny benefits to tens if not hundreds of thousands of eligible families."[25] Another set of foundations made grants because "we were successful in demonstrating that we could collaborate with colleagues in effectively addressing issues that fell within current foundation priorities and were in our core areas of concern."[26]

The early foundation support gave Freedman time to diversify the center's funding base. Until 1996, like the Western Center, the Welfare Law Center's board had been made up of legal services lawyers and client representatives, none in a position to make or raise significant donations. But fortunately the board chair, Stephen Kass, was an exception. A prominent, well-connected private lawyer, he was able to enlist a dozen bar leaders to sign an emergency appeal to hundreds of lawyers in wealthy corporate law firms. Freedman followed this initial request for immediate donations with a longer range strategy—restructuring the board to include a healthy group of big firm lawyers. From this grew an ambitious and successful fund-raising campaign that includes an annual dinner featuring prominent speakers such as Senator Ted Kennedy. Each year the dinner also honors a major corporation such as General Electric or Google, thus attracting generous donations from law firms that already are employed or hoped to be hired by the honoree firm.[27]

Another important source of funding for the Welfare Law Center in the post-LSC era, as was true for most support center, came from the legal fees, sometimes in the hundreds of thousands of dollars, courts occasionally awarded when the center won an important case. The losing party, whether a business or a government agency, could be ordered to pay fees to the center, along with any money or other relief the litigation required the loser to give to the parties the center represented. Because the amounts of these court-awarded fees tend to ebb and flow from year to year, they are not a dependable item in the center's budget. "The board decided to place half of all future fees in a 'stabilization fund'." Freedman said. "With board approval we are able to access the Stabilization Fund when other revenues fall short."[28]

By 2009, the Welfare Law Center could report, "we have rebuilt our program and have a budget larger than when LSC funds were at their height."[29] Other national and state support centers adopted a mix of funding strategies similar to the Western Center on Law and Poverty and the Welfare Law Center, with varying degrees of success—a blend of foundation grants, law firm donations, and court-awarded fees—in some states supplemented by IOLTA and state government appropriations. Undoubtedly to the surprise of many in Congress and others as well, nearly all the support centers survived, a testament to the determination and skill of their leadership and the value of the services they supplied. Sometimes they changed in form and size, usually emerging as smaller organizations. But they lived on, now freed of the restrictions and actively pursuing class actions, pushing legislative reforms, and representing clients LSC-funded programs no longer could.

A NEW CENTER OF RESISTANCE

While the support centers scrambled to survive and the local grantees busied themselves adjusting to the funding cuts and restrictions, a group of legal services directors in the western part of the country remained unconvinced they should abstain from challenging the restrictions in court. It was the most western of those grantees, the Legal Aid Society of Hawaii (LASH), that took the lead. For the better part of three months in 1996, LASH's staff and board debated whether to go against the advice of the legal services community's national leadership and indeed many of their fellow LSC grantees and file a lawsuit seeking to undo the limitations Congress had imposed. The Hawaii program's staff leader, Victor Geminiani, later published an article explaining the competing considerations and justifying the ultimate decision:

> The decision to initiate our lawsuit against LSC, a primary and historical funding source, was the most difficult of my career.[30] . . . We in LASH believed the expansion of restrictions to all program funding finally crossed the line of acceptability and presumed that a legal challenge was being somewhere prepared. In the meantime, the dominant philosophy among programs and our national institutions seemed to be one of compliance and passive acceptance of the consequences.
>
> When no legal challenge developed, we began our own research on the constitutionality of this dramatic expansion of federal control over local program activities. . . . The staff and board of LASH spent over three months considering the implications of securing a federal court ruling on the constitutionality of the federal requirements. . . . In our conversations with others around the nation, the questions that were raised fell roughly into three areas. They involved the possible response from Congress to a successful challenge; the value of maintaining federal funding at least for unrestricted activities; and the impact of a possible elimination of federal funding on programs which are almost exclusively dependent on that funding for their continued existence.
>
> The first point concerning the possible response from Congress was and remains the most difficult to predict. We believe that federal funding for legal services remains a very high priority with the American public. . . . The 1996 congressional election results [which substantially reduced the Republican majorities in congress] also seemed to indicate that the American public strongly wished to see an end to rigid positions controlling our political system. . . . Once again moderates in Congress will control our community's ultimate destiny and hopefully will not be misled by the constant distortions of the critical work that we do.[31]
>
> We rejected the choice between the two bad options of giving up LSC funding or accepting restrictions on non-LSC funds. . . . [O]ur legal research indicated a solution to our dilemma which was clearly in LSC's power. LSC could implement *legal* [that is, constitutional] rules on segregating restricted activities to ensure than no LSC funds be used to conduct these activities. [Our decision to sue] was founded upon a deep belief that our program, with a long and respected reputation, should not be required to face the consequences of a series of bad choices.[32]

In a final appeal to those in the legal services community who opposed any legal challenge to the restrictions, Geminiani concluded:

> We are ultimately considering the very soul of our nation's responsibility to guarantee equal access to justice for all of our citizens. That concept remains the foundation upon which we have built our nation and the social contract that holds us all together.[33]

After the LASH board and staff arrived at a decision to litigate, Geminiani began assembling a lawsuit to be filed in federal court in Hawaii. Although rebuffed by several LSC grantees and lawyers, he managed to persuade a few to join as co-plaintiffs—Legal Services of Northern California headquartered in Sacramento, San Fernando Valley Neighborhood Legal Services and Orange County [California] Legal Aid Society from the greater Los Angeles area, and Alaska Legal Services. A client group joined the suit because their members were the ones being denied services the restrictions prohibited, as did two non-LSC funders whose grants couldn't include forms of representation they felt critically important because the federal restrictions applied to the grants they made as well as LSC's own funds.[34] The litigation directors of the Orange county and Northern California programs put their own names and reputations on the line by joining as individual plaintiffs.[35]

While LASH was preparing its lawsuit to file in a federal court in Hawaii, some 6,000 miles to the east, Burt Neuborne and his team finally were putting the finishing touches on a similar federal lawsuit they planned to file in New York. Thus, in January 1997, within days of each other and just weeks before Alex Forger stepped down as LSC president, legal services lawyers and their allies filed two federal lawsuits at opposite ends of the country challenging the constitutionality of most of the restrictions embodied in the compromise legislation. *Velazquez v. Legal Services Corporation*,[36] was brought in New York City, and *Legal Aid Society of Hawaii v. Legal Services Corporation*[37] in Hawaii.

Forger might have had his own reservations about the constitutionality of some of those restrictions. But he and the LSC board knew they had no choice but to defend each and every clause in the LSC legislation if the corporation was to survive. Thus, in one of his final acts as LSC president he had the disagreeable task of beginning to organize the legal defense to the two lawsuits.

LSC board chair, Doug Eakeley, was quick to reassure the House Appropriations Subcommittee. "We remain firmly committed to implementing the will of Congress, and will decide upon the legal strategy we deem best suited to defend the funding framework Congress has enacted."[38] That legal strategy included lining up major corporate law firms to represent the Legal Services Corporation on a pro bono basis—Covington & Burling in the Hawaii case and Kronish, Lieb, Weiner & Hellman in New York.

The House Subcommittee chair, Harold Rogers, was not easily reassured. He quickly warned Eakeley and the others on the Clinton-
appointed LSC board there would be consequences if they failed to
defend the restrictions vigorously in court.

> Your supporters in Congress are watching you very carefully to see if
> you are not only defending those restrictions but defending them with
> zeal and enthusiasm. Because they want to believe, some of them to be-
> lieve, that you will defend them with one arm tied behind your back,
> all the while winking at the judge. . . . So I guess we want to see how
> intent you are on defending the restrictions, which you probably don't
> like. Well, it is not probably, I know you don't like them, but neverthe-
> less, they are the will of the Congress and written into law. So I guess we
> want you to roll up your sleeves and show us your scar. Are you really
> with us on this?[39]

It would be nearly four years before the U.S. Supreme Court determined the final outcome of these two lawsuits, which turned out to be
a mixed verdict. That story will be covered in this and the next chapter.
But the uproar the filing of these lawsuits caused among legal services
grantees and their lawyers was immediate. Those who brought the
cases found themselves quite unpopular with many of their fellows.
In a typical reaction, when Geminiani and some of the others involved
in the Hawaii case entered a meeting of project directors, they were
serenaded sarcastically with a chorus of, "Here come the cowboys."[40]

A NEW LEADER FOR THE LEGAL
SERVICES CORPORATION

With Alex Forger's departure on February 14, 1997, the Clinton-
appointed board began looking for a replacement. Martha Bergmark,
the interim president and with vast experience in the legal services
community, was a strong contender. But rather than making her appointment permanent the board decided to mount a full-scale talent
hunt headed by board member John Broderick, then a newly appointed associate justice on the New Hampshire Supreme Court. More
than a dozen prospects applied for the position, but one promising
name was submitted by others without his knowledge.

John McKay was a 41-year-old commercial litigator, managing
partner of a medium-sized firm in Seattle and a Republican. He had
been raised as 1 of 12 children by his mother, a nurse, and father, a
physician. Both were active in community affairs and influenced their
offspring to feel an obligation to live life in service to others. A Jesuit education reinforced this sense of obligation. McKay went to the
University of Washington expecting to become a doctor like his father

but instead emerged with a degree in political science. After graduation, he moved to the nation's capital as legislative aide to his state's only Republican congressman, Joel Pritchard. A year later, he entered law school at Creighton, his parents' alma mater. When he graduated, McKay joined a private law firm in Seattle, Lone Powell, and later moved over to Cairncross and Hempelemann, where he was the managing partner.[41]

Over the next several years McKay represented corporations, but satisfied his commitment to serve others by representing poor people for free, becoming well known in the pro bono community for his work. It was natural Washington's legal services supporters would turn to him when the Gingrich revolution threatened LSC's survival. The 1994 election had brought a dramatic turnover in Washington's congressional delegation, from Democratic to Republican, and they needed a Republican champion with good relationships in that party. They asked McKay to take over as chair of the "Equal Justice Coalition," an organization legal services supporters in Washington state had formed to lobby both state and federal legislators for increased legal aid funding.[42]

McKay accepted the offer to head Washington's "Equal Justice Coalition" and began carrying the legal services case to the state's congressional delegation. In an effort to neutralize a prime center of opposition—agribusiness—he sat down with several of the state's major growers. He focused on those with good records for obeying federal and state regulations governing the relations between growers and farmworkers. He made the case growers like them that followed the law had nothing to fear from legal services lawyers representing their workers.

"Why should you help the lawbreakers in your midst by joining their complaints to Congress?" McKay argued. "They're out to gain a competitive advantage over you by avoiding the costs of complying with the law. It's not in your best interests to help them do so by getting rid of the legal services lawyers who are trying to bring them in line."[43]

Soon the state's Access to Justice community also was reaching out to law-abiding growers, putting them on committees and handing out annual awards to them. As a result, Washington senators and Congress members were soon receiving a very different message from agribusinesses than lawmakers from California, Florida, and several other states that were heavy users of migrant labor.

Also in his capacity as chair of Washington's "Equal Justice Coalition," McKay found himself in Washington, testifying before a House Committee about legal services. Julie Clark, the NLADA's lobbyist, had managed to have him added to a panel of Republicans, all LSC opponents, scheduled to appear at hearings in early 1996. McKay prepared for the hearings much as he would for a trial, and thus he was able to refute many of the charges the other witnesses on his panel brought against the LSC and the lawyers it funded. After successfully exposing several specific charges as meritless, McKay testified such complaints were "nearly always baseless. The factual allegations [were] often false—and are typically distorted."[44]

McKay's performance before the House Oversight Committee did not go unnoticed by legal services lawyers in the audience. A few months later, shortly after the search for a new LSC president started, McKay received a call from the search firm that was scouting candidates for LSC president. "We just received an application, fully filled out. It puts you in contention for the presidency of the Legal Services Corporation. Is that O.K. with you?"[45]

McKay was startled by the call. It was not a job he had thought about, nor did it fit with the direction of his career. But he shrugged his shoulders and allowed his application to go forward without thinking he would be offered the position by a board controlled by appointees of a Democratic president—or knowing what he would do if he did receive the offer.

A few weeks later McKay was one of several candidates Justice Broderick and the rest of the search committee brought to Washington for interviews. While the others fidgeted in the waiting room, reviewing their application papers and other materials, McKay was so nonchalant he spent the time reading the sports pages. His interview obviously went well, because a week later McKay was called back for an interview before the full LSC board, along with only one other person, Martha Bergmark.[46]

After his board interview, McKay had the sense he would receive the offer and for the first time confronted the question of what he would do if that happened. He went for a walk on the Mall that stretches between the Capitol and the Lincoln memorial, in order to ponder his future. At first, he was trying to figure out how he would explain why he was saying "no," having gone so far in the selection process. But somewhere during his stroll on the Mall, his parents' lessons and his Jesuit upbringing came to the fore. This was an opportunity, a unique opportunity, to serve others, indeed others who sorely needed that service. By the time he began heading back to the Georgetown hotel where the LSC board was meeting, McKay had decided he wanted the job. Before he arrived there, his cell phone rang. It was LSC chair Doug Eakeley.

"John, I wanted you to know the board has decided it wants you as the next president of the Legal Services Corporation. I hope you will accept the position."

"Of course," McKay replied. "I am very honored."[47]

**John McKay, LSC president 1997–2001, and Senator Ted Kennedy.
(Courtesy of Legal Services Corporation)**

This was the first time an LSC board had picked as the corporation's staff leader a member of a political party different from the chief executive who appointed that board. But the times were also different. A hostile Republican congressional leadership had LSC in its sights, while the Democratic president, although supportive, had his own problems—personal as well as political. LSC's survival depended largely on a bloc of moderate Republicans, a group John McKay had more in common with than Forger or any other Democrat.

The LSC board may have been convinced they had picked the right man for the job, but McKay faced initial skepticism among LSC staff members—and LSC grantees as well. LSC senior staff was in for a surprise at its first meeting with their new boss. The main topic was a letter just received from the House Budget Committee instructing LSC to submit an FY 1998 budget explaining how it would "wind up" the corporation's affairs in two years. Obviously, the House leadership was intent on resurrecting their "glide path to oblivion" for LSC, despite the fact it had collapsed on the House floor in June 1996. The staff began discussing the preparation of such a budget when McKay interrupted. "What are we talking about!" he said angrily. "As long as I'm here, this Legal Services Corporation is not about to tell anyone how to eliminate itself." LSC's senior staff was surprised but not unhappy about McKay's outburst, and word of his reaction soon reached others in the legal services community.[48]

McKay obviously was a far different LSC president than some of the previous Republicans in that position such as Don Bogard and Terry Wear, who were committed to either ending the program or emasculating the grantees and their lawyers. McKay was not only loyal to the Legal Services Corporation, but he was a personable, clean-cut, energetic leader, and an engaging public speaker—the perfect "face" for the corporation in the political climate of the late 1990s. McKay had no illusions about why he had been picked. As he observed later, "I was hired because I spoke 'Republican'. I even looked like a lot of the ninety new Republican congressmen, mostly relatively young, who came in with the Gingrich revolution."[49]

SOLIDIFYING THE MIDDLE

With McKay's appointment, the campaign to reassure Congress the LSC had changed, and so had the grantees it funded, was in full swing. In addition to McKay, the LSC board's vice chair, John Erlenborn, had enlisted in the cause. As a former 20-year Republican congressman living in Washington, he was able to have frequent and warm conversations with former colleagues or friends in many congressional offices.

McKay assumed primary responsibility for working with Congress. In a few months, he sat down with over 180 senators and members of Congress.[50] Mauricio Rivera, who had headed the ABA's grassroots campaign to save LSC in 1995 and 1996, had moved over to head governmental relations for the corporation.[51] Accompanying McKay and Erlenborn to meetings with senators and members of Congress, he witnessed the success both had in convincing wary lawmakers the LSC had changed and deserved their support. McKay used charm and a trustworthy manner; and as Erlenborn said modestly, "I helped by being able to get in to see members having known so many of them that were involved."[52]

When McKay met with hostile congressmen, he did his best to set the record straight, diplomatically, when they brought up stories of supposed abuses by legal services lawyers that had proven false or misleading. He also didn't shrink from coming down hard on LSC grantees or individual lawyers he felt had made mistakes or shown bad judgment.

One of those was a highly publicized case in Texas that had dogged the LSC for years and fired up much of the Republican opposition. In 1994, a large LSC grantee, Texas Rural Legal Assistance (TRLA), had brought a class action challenging an election in a rural county, *Casarez v. Val Verde County*.[53] The county was predominately Mexican-American and poor, and also contained a large military base. Evidently, the local Republican Party had recruited the soldiers and their families, largely Anglo, to register as voters in that county. According to the lawsuit, they also apparently left those soldiers on the rolls and had them vote in the Texas county long after they and their families were reassigned elsewhere in the world. Enough of these military families voted for the Republican candidates to elect an entirely Anglo county government in this Hispanic-majority county.

Because the vast majority of the Hispanic community was composed of poor farm workers, TRLA filed a lawsuit challenging the legitimacy of long-departed military personnel voting in a Texas county and thus determining the outcome of the election. Not surprisingly, this lawsuit angered Texas senator Phil Gramm as well as many other Republicans in Congress and became Exhibit A in the Gingrich revolution's charges against the LSC.[54]

While this lawsuit had gone on for years during LSC's battle for survival, Alex Forger and the LSC board had tried to defend the case as legitimate. McKay, however, took a different tack. He summoned TRLA's executive director, David Hall, to Washington and told him the case should not have been filed, and why.

"Yes, the Democratic majority of the population was poor. And, yes, they lost and maybe the election was stolen by the Republicans illegally. But legal services lawyers have no business trying to overturn an election. That's just too political."[55] McKay also told Hall he was quite willing to say the same thing to TRLA's staff as well. Although it was more than a year before McKay reached that part of Texas, he finally did. As he explained it, unlike so many lawsuits some congressman or the other charged was "political" when they weren't, this one was—true, electoral politics—and not where legal services lawyers belonged.[56]

As a result of McKay's and Erlenborn's efforts, LSC's support within the moderate wing of the Republican Party solidified and some conservative opponents lost their zeal. It also helped when Gingrich had to step down from the speakership shortly after the 1998 November midterm elections,[57] and the energy behind the "Contract with America" dissipated further.

Not that there weren't tough fights in the House after McKay became LSC president in May 1997. When the FY 1999 appropriation reached the House floor on August 5, 1998, the members debated the $300 million LSC appropriation for three hours before it finally passed. Immediately thereafter, the House appropriated more than $20 billion for a collection of other government departments and agencies without debate and by voice vote.[58]

In 1999, McKay had to deal with an issue that jeopardized support even among moderate Republicans in the House of Representatives. A quick check of the case numbers reported by a handful of grantees detected significant discrepancies between the totals reported and the totals that could be verified. Some ambiguity in LSC's definitions contributed to the overcounts, but it became enough of a concern LSC required all grantees to audit their case closing statistics and also asked the corporation's inspector general (IG) to conduct a study of cases closed during 1999.

Reviewing the files in a sample of reported cases from 60 grantees, the IG found on average 13 percent of the sample shouldn't have been counted. The reason wasn't that those were nonexistent "ghost" cases grantees had added to their case reports. Rather it was because of deficiencies in the files of real cases they reported. The most common problems, accounting for four-fifths of the discrepancies, were a failure to include a record of citizenship, or to indicate whether a legal service had been performed, or when a case ended midstream with no result, or when the grantee had represented the same client with the same type of problem twice during the year.[59]

Applying essentially the same standards, the grantees' own self-audits reported their raw statistics should be reduced 11 percent attributable to the same sorts of problems in the files of some cases. Because LSC's own annual report was published after receiving the grantee's correction but before the IG completed his study, it applied the 11-percent correction in announcing the closed cases figure yielding a total of 924,000 for 1999.[60] McKay reassured Congress that LSC would continue to closely monitor its grantees' statistical reports to ensure overcounts did not occur again. Despite his best efforts, and those of the ABA and other supporters, McKay still lost the votes of a few moderate Republicans he had counted on to insure LSC's survival.[61]

THE CONGRESSIONAL RESTRICTIONS ARE TESTED IN THE COURTS

While John McKay was busy in the fight to preserve LSC's appropriation and most LSC grantees and their supporters were absorbed with finding new funding to replace the sudden one-third drop in LSC grants, the New York and Hawaii court cases challenging the restrictions had begun making their way through the federal judiciary.

This was the first time anyone had argued in federal court that congressional restrictions on what LSC-funded lawyers could do for their clients were unconstitutional. Lesser limitations had been in place from the beginning of the corporation's existence but what the Gingrich-led Congress did in the mid-1990s created both the motive and opportunity to mount a constitutional challenge. The motive was that the restrictions were far more onerous than what had come before, and thus very difficult to ignore. The opportunity came because Congress imposed the prohibitions on what grantees and their lawyers could do with money coming from other sources, including IOLTA and state government funding, as well as the LSC grants. This raised the possibility Congress had been guilty of burdening LSC grants with "unconstitutional conditions."

There is no doubt Congress can tell recipients of federal funds what they can do with the money the federal government itself is providing without offending the Constitution. This is true even when Congress tells the grantees what they can or cannot say when performing the functions financed with federal money and even when the recipient would prefer to say something else. That might appear to interfere with recipients' First Amendment right to freedom of speech, but no one is forcing them to take the money with those conditions nor is anyone prohibiting them from saying what they want when not engaged in federally funded work. But what if Congress conditions its grant with a blanket prohibition that tells grantees they may not say something they would like to say if they accept the federal money—not just while doing the federally funded work, but ever. That would be an example of an "unconstitutional condition." The federal government would be asking recipients to forfeit entirely their First Amendment rights to freedom of speech just to receive a federal grant. Imagine if citizens couldn't receive a social security check unless they agreed not to say anything critical of the government. That is the sort of price courts have held people in this country should not be forced to pay.[62]

This was the constitutional battleground on which the legal services lawyers and LSC met. The basic issue was whether Congress went too far when it extended the restrictions to limit what LSC-funded lawyers could do with non-LSC funds. In going that far, had the lawmakers converted the restrictions into "unconstitutional conditions" violating the first amendment rights of the grantees, their lawyers and clients? The New York case also questioned the constitutionality of several of the restrictions on other grounds, even when those restrictions limited what legal services lawyers could do with LSC funds. But, in the end, the only issue that gained some traction in the trial courts was the provision extending those limitations to nonfederal moneys.

Although the two cases had been filed within a week of each other in early January 1997, the Hawaii case moved ahead much faster than the New York case. On February 14, the very day Alex Forger left LSC and three months before John McKay took over, the Chief Judge of the Hawaii federal court, Alan Kay, issued his decision. Judge Kay had been appointed by President Reagan. Nonetheless, in an encouraging beginning for the LSC-funded programs and client groups that had brought the case, Judge Kay granted a preliminary injunction temporarily prohibiting LSC from enforcing 9 of the 12 challenged restrictions. The judge first found nine restrictions infringed on the grantees and their clients' first amendment rights to lobby and to associate for the purpose of petitioning government through litigation. The three exceptions to Judge Kay's injunction were the class action prohibition, the denial of representation to most aliens, and the provision denying LSC-funded lawyers the ability to collect attorney's fees when they won a case. For different reasons Judge Kay found those three restrictions were consistent with the First Amendment.[63]

After finding nine of the restrictions infringed on first amendment rights, Judge Kay then found a serious question existed whether these restrictions represented unconstitutional conditions on the use of a federal benefit, in this case the funding of legal representation for poor people. The reason—the interim LSC regulation implementing the congressional restriction against using nonfederal funds to engage in prohibited activities placed too many obstacles in the path of a grantee wanting to establish a companion program using solely non-LSC funds that would thus be free of the restrictions.[64] This was because those initial regulations told LSC grantees that any funds they transferred to another organization, no matter where those funds came from, arrived with the congressional restrictions intact.[65] This regulation was coupled with a preexisting "interrelated organizations" provision that imposed all the congressional restrictions on any companion organization "controlled" by an LSC grantee. The eight-factor definition of "control" was so broad that it effectively made it impossible for an LSC grantee to start or cooperate in any meaningful way with an organization that was free of the congressional restrictions.[66]

Finally, the judge found the balance of harm favored the local grantee agencies and their clients. They would be harmed far more by enforcement of these potentially unconstitutional limitations while the case was being fully litigated than LSC or the federal government would be hurt by continuing to fund these grantees without being able to enforce 9 of the 12 challenged restrictions. On this basis, the trial judge issued a preliminary injunction against enforcement of the nine restrictions while the litigation proceeded on the question of whether the court should make the injunction permanent.[67]

LSC now had a choice. File an interlocutory appeal seeking to overturn the trial court's preliminary injunction and thus allow nine of the congressional restrictions to be suspended for the year or more it would require the Ninth Circuit to decide whether the district court was right. Or take the trial judge's problems with the LSC regulations seriously, and try to amend them in a way that would cure the problems the judge had identified. The corporation chose the latter course, and the LSC staff started drafting amendments to the restrictions.

On March 8, 1997, while Martha Bergmark was still interim president, and the search for Alex Forger's successor was just underway, the LSC board found it had to respond quickly to Judge Kay's opinion. As Laveeda Battle, chair of the Operations and Regulations Committee explained in introducing a proposed revised interim regulation, "[W]e've had. . . . as all you know, . . . a lawsuit which has raised certain constitutional issues which caused us to take a look back at the constitutional implications of the act we undertook. . . . and the fact the real issue that has come up in this litigation has come from the fact that we went one step beyond what the statute actually required. . . . [W]e made some significant changes to the provisions in 1610. . . . which reflects information. . . . about related organizations and we also have a provision which reflects the standards which were enunciated in *Rust v. Sullivan* which is, I guess the landmark constitutional case establishing what the constitutional requirements are if you have restrictions which may impinge on First Amendment rights."[68]

John Erlenborn, a member of Battle's committee, added the imprimatur of a former Republican congressman in support of the revised regulation. "[I]t was the regulations adopted by this board that unfortunately went beyond the congressional restrictions and therefore I think that we have this opportunity to remedy this without going back to the Congress and asking them to do anything and I think that this is proper, and we should be doing this."[69] The motion to issue the new interim regulation then passed unanimously.[70]

This change made it somewhat easier for an LSC grantee to establish an "affiliate" entity that would be financed entirely with non-LSC funds, and thus would be free to do all the things the parent LSC-funded grantee couldn't. Under the regulation, the "affiliate" could represent prisoners or undocumented aliens, file class actions, and lobby legislators for bills that would benefit its clients. It could even handle abortion, desegregation, and redistricting litigation. But the new regulation stated the "affiliate" could not be "controlled" by the LSC grantee, using language that created some ambiguity about what degree of connection between the two entities would be permissible.[71]

Once the revised and liberalized restriction was in place, LSC's lawyers from the Covington and Burling team returned to the Hawaii district court and argued the congressional restrictions and especially the "all funds" provision no longer imposed "unconstitutional conditions" on the grantees and their clients. They argued that any LSC grantee could choose to establish a free-standing and separately financed corporation that would not be subject to the strings that came with the funding LSC provided.

Judge Kay was persuaded the Covington and Burling lawyers might be right. He filed a second opinion cautiously suggesting the interim revised regulations may have mooted the constitutional problems the LSC grantees and client organizations had raised and that had bothered the court the first time around. On April 9, 1997, he issued an order to show cause why he shouldn't find the issue was moot and dissolve the preliminary injunction he had issued on February 14.[72]

Before the Hawaii court held its hearing on the order to show cause, the New York court caught up and convened its first hearing. The judge, Frederick Block, enjoyed the advantage of having the two Hawaii decisions and LSC's interim revised regulations before him. Judge Block shared Judge Kay's concerns the initial regulations had placed too many obstacles in front of an LSC-funded grantee that wanted to create an "affiliate" organization funded from other sources. The court suggested that denying LSC grantees the viable option of a companion organization would turn the LSC's "all funds" prohibition into an unconstitutional condition.

Judge Block was worried not only about the LSC's initial regulations, however. He wasn't at all certain the interim revised regulations cured the problem. During his questioning of LSC's lawyers, he dropped strong hints about what he saw as possible defects in those interim regulations. Those regulations still retained the original and long-standing "interrelated organizations" provision, even though it was apparently qualified in a confusing way by another new set of criteria defining "affiliate" entities.[73] LSC grantees could collaborate with these "affiliates" but not with organizations they "controlled" or were "controlled by." Yet they were not deemed to "control" or be "controlled by" such entities if they satisfied the definition for being "affiliates" because they met the "program integrity" standards of the "affiliate" category.[74] The "interrelated organizations" regulation seemed superfluous at best and a possible source of future mischief at worst. In this interim regulation, moreover, the "program integrity" standards required the two organizations have "separate facilities," something that also bothered Judge Block.

After expressing his concerns about the interim regulations, Judge Block concluded the hearing with an admonition.

> Maybe as a result of this opportunity for all of us to discuss these issues, there can be some further way in which these matters can be addressed, or there will be an ongoing dialogue between people of good will and good spirit in our great profession. If [this hearing] has possibly facilitated that possibility, I feel that's also a purpose to be served from my end of the spectrum.[75]

It is hard to imagine a stronger message to a litigant to do something more or be prepared to lose.

LSC took the judge's admonition to heart. Staff and board went back to the drawing board once again. At the May 21, 1997, meeting, about the time John McKay was hired as LSC president, the board of directors considered the final revised regulations. For the most part, the final regulation tracked the issues Judge Block had identified in his questioning, and repaired the defects he had noted. Laveeda Battle, on behalf of the Operations and Regulations Committee, explained, "In light of. . . . comments, we made some changes to 1610. One of the things that we did was. . . . take out the provision. . . . which related to interrelated. . . . organizations. And in taking that out, we tried to mirror more specifically the case [*Rust v. Sullivan*], which really addresses that constitutional standard in coming up with a test which we now call the Program Integrity Test."[76]

The final 1610 regulation eliminated the "interrelated organizations" provision entirely and also rewrote the "separate facilities" reference. No longer an absolute requirement, "[t]he degree of separation from the facilities in which restricted activities occur" was one of several discretionary factors, no single one of which was essential, that LSC was to use on a "case-by-case" basis to determine an affiliate's "program integrity."

The action then bounced back to Hawaii. On August 1, 1997, Chief Judge Kay issued his third and final opinion in *Legal Aid Society of Hawaii v Legal Services Corporation*. By this time, the final regulations were in place and, as foreshadowed by his second opinion, the judge found against the plaintiffs. He ruled the restrictions, including the provisions that extended those restrictions to "all funds" an LSC grantee received from any source, were constitutional. In essence, Judge Kay found LSC's revised regulations opened a constitutionally sufficient window which allowed LSC grantees and their clients to exercise First Amendment rights and bring their problems to government through litigation or lobbying.[77]

The Hawaii court's third decision came out in time to essentially decide the New York case, in the view of that court, at least. On December 5, 1997, almost a year after the *Velazquez* case reached his court, Judge Block filed his decision. He discussed the three Hawaii opinions at length, as well as tracing the evolution of the LSC regulations. Although critical of the initial and interim regulations, he found the final versions allowed sufficient latitude to LSC grantees to protect their First Amendment rights and thus avoid the "unconstitutional conditions" problem.[78]

The judge also highlighted what the regulations did not prohibit.

> The statutory restrictions at issue here [as implemented by LSC's regulations] do not prevent LSC-subsidized lawyers from fully advising their clients of their legal rights and practical options; indeed, the regulations do not inhibit lawyers' speech to their clients at all. For example, an LSC lawyer is free to advise potential clients that their case is best

suited for class action treatment, or that they may have a claim that a welfare law is unconstitutional. The lawyer is also permitted to advise potential clients that while the LSC-funded entity cannot take the case, the lawyer knows of other attorneys who can.[79]

Judge Block concluded his opinion by praising both those who challenged the restrictions and LSC for their response which the judge felt cured the original constitutional problem.

> In many ways, the litigation stands as a testament to the continued vibrancy and vitality of the very First Amendment rights at the heart of this lawsuit—access to the courts, free and open public debate, and freedom to associate for the vindication of legal rights. It also reflects the value of advocacy in the judicial setting by protagonists acting at the highest level of the legal profession. In that regard, plaintiffs are commended for bringing and furthering this litigation; defendants are commended for appropriately addressing plaintiffs' concerns.[80]

With both federal trial courts having found LSC's changed regulations satisfied the complaints from the legal services community, once again many in that community questioned whether it was wise to appeal those rulings.

In the end, the lawyers behind the two federal cases disregarded the criticism and filed notices of appeal. It would be over a year before the Ninth Circuit decided the Hawaii case and almost two years before the Second Circuit decided the New York case. Even as the Hawaii and New York cases went forward on appeal, they had improved things for LSC grantees. Those cases and the trial judges who heard them had forced major changes in LSC's regulations. They opened up an avenue—perhaps closer to a bumpy road—for LSC grantees who wanted to offer their low-income communities services such as class actions and legislative advocacy the organizations themselves were no longer allowed to supply.

WILL LSC GRANTEES TAKE ADVANTAGE OF THE JUDICIALLY-MANDATED OPPORTUNITY TO CREATE NON-LSC FUNDED AFFILIATE ORGANIZATIONS?

Over the next few years, several LSC grantees chose to travel that bumpy road, setting up affiliated corporations. In Tennessee, for example, one of the LSC grantee programs chartered a new nonprofit corporation, the Tennessee Justice Center (TJC), housed a floor below in the same office building as the local Knoxville LSC grantee. With its own board drawn from throughout the state and a small staff of experienced litigators, it accepted referrals from LSC lawyers anywhere in Tennessee.[81] The TJC received funding from IOLTA, foundations, and private donors, but nothing from LSC. It could do everything LSC grantees couldn't, including representing undocumented aliens, litigating class actions, and drafting and seeking passage of legislation helpful to the poor.

Meantime, in California, CRLA, so opposed by agribusiness and others in the anti-legal services coalition, didn't have to create a new affiliate organization independent of LSC funding because it already had one. During Governor Reagan's assaults on CRLA during the early 1970s CRLA had started a new entity—the California Rural Legal Assistance Foundation. CRLA supporters began funneling donations from non-LSC sources into the foundation, guaranteeing farm workers a legal voice Reagan couldn't shut down. Twenty years later, the foundation had a different purpose—providing forms of representation CRLA itself could no longer supply, including representation of undocumented aliens and legislative advocacy in Sacramento.[82]

In many places, the same objective—a legal services agency not bound by LSC restrictions—was achieved without the LSC grantee creating an affiliated corporation. In New York, the grandfather of all legal aid organizations—the Legal Aid Society of New York—elected to surrender its LSC funding rather than submit to limitations Congress had imposed. This gave the entire New York area and the LSC grantee agencies there a resource free of LSC restrictions to which they could refer applicants they couldn't serve, such as undocumented aliens, or clients who needed services they weren't allowed to offer, such as class actions or legislative advocacy. John McKay was surprised and disappointed when he learned most New York area LSC grantees failed to take full advantage of that resource and instead persisted in their attempts to overturn the congressional restrictions in the courts.[83]

In the Los Angeles area, several sizeable legal services organizations had grown up in recent years that for different reasons needed no financial support from LSC. In 1970, the Beverly Hills Bar Association started the Beverly Hills Bar Foundation to provide pro bono services donated by Association members. The foundation employed Stan Levy, a former Western Center lawyer and acting director, to supervise the office.[84] A few years later the Beverly Hills bar and Los Angeles County Bar Association combined forces to create a much larger pro bono program named "Public Counsel" that by the mid-1990s had a large paid staff supervising the pro bono work volunteered by thousands of private lawyers. At present, Public Counsel is the largest pro bono program in the country. It is staffed by more than fifty salaried lawyers augmented by the donated services of over 5,000 private attorneys and law students. It has an impact-litigation unit, an appellate unit, and several policy advocacy projects, along with direct service in nearly every area of the law.[85]

Another non-LSC-funded program in Los Angeles, called Bet Tzedek, also started in the 1970s and was available to pick up some of the slack when LSC closed down the support centers in the mid-1990s, while also drastically restricting what other LSC-funded program could do for the low-income community. Again it was Stan Levy, by this time a Rabbi as well as a lawyer, who played an important role in creating a new legal aid resource. In 1974, he recognized a great need for legal help in the Fairfax area of Los Angeles, then a Jewish area of the city, where many of the residents were elderly and poor, a sizeable number of them Holocaust survivors. Levy managed to recruit 18 volunteers—lawyers, social workers, and secretaries—to donate $5 and one night each week. The money was used to rent a small office on Fairfax Avenue and the one night of pro bono service from each volunteer staffed that office. Thus was born Bet Tzedek ("The House of Justice"). From this tiny, part-time, entirely volunteer beginning, by 1996 Bet Tzedek already had grown into a large organization with a dozen full-time paid staff supplemented by hundreds of pro bono lawyers. It also had expanded its mission to include serving poor people of all races and ethnicities, and with an emphasis on impact litigation, and legislative and policy advocacy.[86]

As mentioned earlier, the Western Center on Law on Poverty also had managed to stay alive, despite losing its LSC funding. As a result, three sizable non-LSC-funded agencies were free to represent client populations and offer services the LSC-funded programs in the Los Angeles area could not. Largely for this reason, those LSC-funded programs did not feel compelled to create their own affiliated corporations.

The revised LSC regulations may have opened a small crack through which LSC-funded programs could ensure poor people still enjoyed the full range of legal representation they once could offer, even though they had to go to another office for some of those services. But in many parts of the country, opening a companion corporation was only a theoretical option, and unlike a few fortunate urban areas such as Los Angeles no significant non-LSC funded agencies existed. Except for the largest metropolitan areas, seldom was it possible to raise enough outside funding to afford a second independent corporation to take cases the local LSC-funded organization was prohibited from handling. Moreover, having lost a third of their own federal support, LSC grantees everywhere were struggling just to raise enough money from outside sources to replenish their own coffers. As a result, few affiliated entities arose around the country despite the revised regulations the Hawaii and New York federal courts had influenced LSC to adopt.

IOLTA FUNDING REMAINS IN JEOPARDY

LSC had managed to secure the future of some federal support for civil legal aid, but the one-third cut in that support wreaked havoc for most local LSC-funded grantees and their lawyers. Those funding losses would have been even more disastrous except for the availability of a second source of funding—the IOLTA programs that started in Florida in the early 1980s and by the mid-1990s were operating in every state but Indiana.[87] Now LSC grantees and other civil legal aid agencies were nervous whether this prop might disappear just as it was becoming essential to their survival. IOLTA funding continued to be in jeopardy from the lawsuits the Washington Legal Foundation (WLF) had filed in Texas and Washington.

Having lost before a three-judge panel of the Fifth Circuit in the Texas case, *Washington Legal Foundation v. Phillips,* the IOLTA defendants, which included the Texas Supreme Court, asked for an "en banc" rehearing before all judges of that circuit. The hope was that a majority would agree to rehear the case and overturn the decision by the three-judge panel. On February 14, 1997, the date Alex Forger left office, the full court denied the requested rehearing.[88] Thus, Texas Chief Justice Phillips and his codefendants had no choice but to seek review by the U.S. Supreme Court.

On June 17, 1997, the Supreme Court granted the requested certiorari in order to resolve the conflict between the Fifth Circuit and the Eleventh Circuit (an earlier Florida case that had upheld IOLTA as constitutional).[89] The circuits had split on the issue whether interest earned on funds deposited in an IOLTA account is the property of the clients.[90]

Meanwhile, encouraged by their victory in the Fifth Circuit, the WLF had continued pressing its companion case in Washington's federal courts. On January 30, 1998, the district court for the Western district of Washington, sitting in Seattle, issued its opinion. As the Texas trial court had, the Washington judge granted a summary judgment in favor of IOLTA, resulting in a dismissal of WLF's claim.[91] But the judge chose not to publish his opinion, probably feeling he had nothing significant to add to the debate between the Fifth and Eleventh Circuits, a dispute the U.S. Supreme Court would be resolving in a few months.

The WLF parties appealed the Washington case to the Ninth Circuit. Before that court could hear argument, however, the Supreme Court filed its opinion in the Fifth Circuit case, *Phillips v. Washington Legal Foundation* on June 15, 1998. In a 5–4 opinion authored by Chief Justice Rehnquist, the court affirmed the Fifth Circuit on the narrow issue of whether the interest earned on an IOLTA account was property of the clients whose funds were deposited in that account. Yet in doing so it expressly reserved other issues that remained as obstacles to WLF's attempt to kill the nation's IOLTA programs.[92] As Chief Justice Rehnquist explained:

> In sum, we hold that the interest income generated by funds held in IOLTA accounts is the "private property" of the owner of the principal. We express no view as to whether these funds have been "taken" by the State; nor do we express an opinion as to the amount of "just compensation," if any, due respondents. We leave these issues to be addressed on remand.[93]

With that decision from the Supreme Court, the Texas litigation returned to the starting point—the district court for the Western district of Texas in Dallas. Because the reviewing courts had issued stays preventing immediate enforcement of any injunctions or other relief the WLF parties sought, the Texas IOLTA program remained intact as did those elsewhere in the country, but with an ominous threat remaining.

The final case in the IOLTA odyssey decided during Clinton's presidency was the Texas district court's opinion after remand from the Supreme Court. Although only a trial court, at the bottom of the federal ladder, this litigation attracted an amazing array of legal talent, from Boston and Washington, D.C. as well as Dallas, Houston, and Austin. Most were from large and prestigious corporate law firms who were donating their services pro bono to represent IOLTA defendants.[94] Ironically, the conservative WLF was standing nearly alone, facing a team of outstanding corporate lawyers who spent most of their time defending the same business interests WLF existed to advance.

Finally, after thorough briefing and several lengthy hearings, and a year and a half since the remand from the Supreme Court, Judge James Nowlin filed his opinion on January 28, 2000. Once again, the judge ruled in favor of the Texas IOLTA program. Accepting, as he had to, the Supreme Court's finding the interest accruing in IOLTA accounts was the property of the clients, he concluded that fact didn't affect the outcome—those clients were still not entitled to halt the IOLTA program's collection and distribution of that interest income to legal services agencies.

> The Fifth Amendment provides that "private property" shall not be "taken for public use without just compensation," Judge Nowlin began. "The United States Supreme Court determined that the interest income held in IOLTA accounts is the 'private property' of the owner of the principal. . . . The Fifth Amendment does not proscribe the taking of property; it proscribes taking without just compensation. . . . Regardless of the Court's determination of whether a taking occurred, the crux of this case rests on the issue of just compensation. . . . In determining just compensation, 'the question is what has the owner lost, not what has the taker gained'. . . . The Court will measure any required compensation by

Mr. Summers' loss, not by the government's gain, or in this case the gain enjoyed by the recipients of [IOLTA] funding."[95]

Applying these legal principles, Judge Nowlin engaged in a detailed analysis of the evidence the parties introduced and concluded:

> The Court finds,. . . . that without IOLTA the interest generated by Mr. Summers' principal would possess no economically realizable value. . . . Based upon all the evidence before it, Mr. Summers' loss is zero. . . . In the absence of a compensable loss, the Court finds there has been no taking without compensation in violation of the Fifth Amendment.[96]

This decision gave IOLTA another lease on life—for the time being at least. It proved to be the last word on the constitutionality and hence the survival of IOLTA funding during the 20th century, but only because it would take time for the federal appellate courts to consider and decide the various appeals then pending before them. Until those appeals were resolved, the future of IOLTA and the financial support it provided remained at risk.

JOHN MCKAY'S SECOND ACT—CONSOLIDATION AND COORDINATION

Once McKay got his footing and learned more about the national program he was administering, the new LSC president developed his own vision for what needed to be done. While nearly everyone on the LSC board and within the larger legal services community applauded McKay's successful missionary work with Congress, not all were equally pleased when he began executing his own vision and forcing changes in the nation's delivery system.

McKay quickly realized the resources Congress was willing to appropriate for the legal representation of the poor would remain seriously inadequate for the foreseeable future, a realization shared by the Clinton-appointed LSC board and everyone in the legal services community. But his approach to that problem was not shared by all.

McKay wanted to dramatically increase the raw numbers of poor people legal services lawyers helped. Some in the legal services community viewed this emphasis on numbers as coming at the price of reduced quality and lessened impact. McKay saw what Congress had done in 1995–96 as mandating a focus on "individual representation," with a narrow definition of that term. "Taken as a whole," McKay wrote, "the restrictions on the types of case LSC programs are allowed to handle convey a strong congressional message: federally funded legal services should focus on individual case representation by providing access to justice on a case-by-case basis. Therein lies the key to bipartisan support and the future of federally sponsored legal services."[97]

Meanwhile, at a September 1997 conference marking the opening of the National Equal Justice Library, and many times elsewhere, Alan Houseman was making a different point. Despite the congressional restrictions, LSC-funded lawyers "could still do 98 percent of what they did before Congress acted." Class actions and legislative advocacy were out, but other forms of representation that could bring about broad policies helpful to those who were poor remained lawful.[98]

This suggested that as far as LSC was concerned there was an official interpretation of Congress's action as articulated by McKay, and another, unofficial interpretation put forth by Houseman and some other legal services leaders. The official version read the restrictions broadly and drastically narrowed the "access to justice" LSC-funded lawyers were expected to provide their clients. The unofficial interpretation was the opposite, reading the restrictions narrowly and maintaining a broad reading of the "access to justice" the LSC Act promised. "I have enormous respect for Alan Houseman," McKay said later, "but I can't say he was helpful while I was LSC president."[99]

This difference was more rhetorical than real. In truth, most LSC-funded legal services lawyers had always spent most of their time on "individual representation," that is, cases that only affected the individual involved and often his or her family, but not others "similarly situated" or the "poverty community" in general. But occasionally, closer to rarely, the only way to avoid losing for the individual client and all the other future individual clients disadvantaged by the same law or practice was to seek a change through whatever legal tools remained available to legal services lawyers after the 1995–96 compromise—whether that was 98 percent or half of the legal tools they formerly possessed. The very first legal aid organization in the nation had recognized this in 1903 when New York's Legal Aid Society added "to promote measures for their protection" to its charter. And, Reginald Heber Smith had come to the same conclusion in 1919 when he called on legal aid societies to maintain a "fighting fund" needed to pursue appellate litigation when the outcome of an individual's case would implicate others "similarly situated.[100] That legal services lawyers were only involved in 632 class actions in 1996, out of the millions of cases they handled during the years those actions were proceeding through the courts is evidence of how rarely legal services lawyers found it necessary or appropriate to seek relief beyond the individual client. Now, after 1996, they had fewer tools and thus fewer opportunities to do so, but still occasionally had the need and the ability to make things better for the one and for the many—usually through an appeal or an injunction and using only a small share of the available resources. So McKay's vision and Houseman's vision were not nearly as incompatible as they sounded.

But in any event this difference of opinion wasn't nearly as controversial within the legal services community as another of McKay's initiatives. He sought to decrease the number of grantees through merger and consolidation—as a means of increasing efficiency. LSC had inherited many of those grantees from the OEO Legal Services Program, which in the initial 18-month funding frenzy of 1966–68 had financed virtually any program a community action agency or local bar association put together. That made sense when legal services was part of the War on Poverty's "community action program" built around strengthening low-income neighborhoods, many of them quite small. This pattern was compounded in the late 1970s and early 1980s when the LSC was spreading its "minimum access" funds to virgin areas of the country and often had to yield to Congress's preference for small, existing bar association programs rather than the multicounty or statewide grantees LSC felt were more efficient. In too many areas of the country, these earlier funding policies had led to a hodgepodge of small, sometimes even tiny LSPs, each with its own board and administrative staff. Virginia, for instance, had 17 individual LSC grantees and the San Francisco Bay area had 6.[101] Some were as small as three or four lawyers.

McKay wanted to provide "access to justice" to as many poor people as possible and this disjointed pattern seemed to make no sense to him. Too much money and effort were being spent on administration and maintaining boards of directors for this host of individual agencies. Just as bad, in most places there was no coordination among them. When McKay convened a meeting of the 24 California grantees, he gained the impression, accurate or not, that most of the executive directors didn't know each other, and were shaking hands for the first time.[102]

McKay's position in favor of major consolidations and large programs came in part from his experience in the state of Washington. Legal services leaders in that state had merged all local LSC grantees into a single statewide program, the Northwest Justice Center, with offices throughout the state. At the same time, they had set up another statewide program, Columbia legal services, financed entirely through foundation grants and private donations that was free of the LSC restrictions. Another organization, the Legal Foundation of Washington, administered IOLTA and distributed its revenues to smaller specialized legal services agencies and local pro bono programs throughout the state. Through this statewide network, Washington was able to offer the full range of legal services, not just those Congress approved, and to the full range of possible clients, including undocumented aliens and those involved in abortion cases.[103]

When McKay suggested voluntary consolidations of LSC grantees in various parts of the country, he met resistance nearly everywhere.

The reasons were fairly evident, even if often self-serving. Every time one grantee was merged into another, an executive director lost his or her position and the prerogatives that went with it. At the same time, a board of directors would have to dissolve. A majority of those board members ordinarily would be members of a local bar association, often a small one. Not infrequently, members of those local bar associations looked upon the LSC grantee as an important association project, if not a virtual child of the bar, one they didn't want to lose. A merger into a larger program also could threaten to take resources away from the smaller grantee's area, the closure or downsizing of an office and a loss of staff lawyer positions in that community.

As a result, powerful constituencies were arrayed against McKay in most areas where he hoped to consolidate LSC grantees. But the LSC president was not one easily discouraged. Despite resistance from a minority of the LSC board[104] as well as NLADA and most local grantees, he was prepared to compel mergers and consolidations, at least where he felt they were most needed. He also pressed for state-wide planning and coordination among all grantees with the expectation it would lead to universal geographic coverage and eventually to a comprehensive range of services from a mix of LSC-funded grantees and those funded from other sources not bound by the congressional restrictions.[105]

McKay could have refused to refund grantees that rejected requests to merge or enter into consolidations. But that would have been an unwieldy tool because of the need to hold hearings and justify those refunding refusals. McKay had another and easier way to force compliance: he could open the territory the reluctant grantee presently served to competitive bids, and he also had the power to define service areas.[106] If three or four grantees served adjoining counties, for instance, McKay could combine the counties into a single service area and invite the existing grantees and other new entities to compete for a grant to serve that entire region.

McKay first deployed that approach in the San Francisco Bay area, one made up of seven counties and served by six independent grantees of different sizes and varying quality—from large to tiny, from excellent to poor. At this point, McKay was still feeling his way in trying to consolidate grantees. It began with a need to defund a formerly flourishing but now ineffectual program in Alameda county. Most of its good lawyers had left to work in a public interest law firm, after the congressional restrictions went into effect. After personally telling that grantee it was being terminated, McKay crossed the bay and told the San Francisco grantee, San Francisco Neighborhood Legal Assistance Foundation (SFNLAF), he wanted that program to take over Alameda county—but only for the rest of 1998. For the 1999 grant, LSC would open up Alameda county for competitive bids.[107] And then, McKay dropped the bombshell. For the 2000 grant, he was redefining the service area to include all the counties surrounding the San Francisco harbor, and holding a competition to choose a single grantee to run LSC-funded legal services in that entire region.[108]

The six grantees had only three options if they wanted LSC funding for 2000—bid against each other, merge five into the sixth, or consolidate and form a new organization. In the end, two of them—Marin county's program and San Mateo county's program decided to give up their LSC funding. The rest chose consolidation and began forming a new entity—Bay Area Legal Aid. The largest grantee in the mix, SF-NLAF, drove a hard bargain. Even though San Francisco had a smaller population than most of the other counties, it had the most powerful board, the largest staff, the best management, and the best reputation. If it came down to an open competition among existing grantees, it was the one most likely to be chosen. So SFNLAF's board insisted on being a majority of the Bay Area Legal Aid's board—for the formative first two years of the new organization. The other grantees saw this as a "San Francisco takeover" and initially resisted the proposed consolidation. But over time they came to realize that in five years, after a planned transition from the San Francisco dominated board, it would evolve into one based on population. Another virtue from their perspective: the consolidation involved a redistribution of resources, increasing the number of lawyers in the other counties.[109]

After agreeing to the consolidation, the new board conducted a nationwide competition for an executive director, but ended up choosing Ramon Arias, who had headed SFNLAF's staff for 10 years.[110] His first major action after assuming the new position was to move his headquarters from San Francisco to Oakland, in Alameda county. As Arias hoped and expected, this symbolic gesture completely changed attitudes throughout the region.[111] The specter of a "San Francisco takeover" dissipated into the mists of the bay they all shared.

McKay told Arias this was the first consolidation he had forced through the imposition of a redefined service area and the threat of competition. In most places, it was enough to threaten to invoke these bureaucratic tools, and then allow time for grantees to work out their own mergers and consolidations. But in the Los Angeles area, the voluntary approach only worked half-way. Of five grantees in Los Angeles county, two managed to negotiate an arrangement where the larger program, the Legal Aid Foundation of Los Angeles, absorbed the smaller Long Beach Legal Aid Society but with the Long Beach office and most of its staff retained.[112] The San Fernando Valley grantee and the San Gabriel Valley and Pasadena grantees, on the other hand, were unable to agree on a merger. McKay then redefined the service area to include the territory those grantees served and invited them to submit bids, which they did. He chose the San Fernando

Valley program as the winner of the competition—and the winner it was in all respects. After removing San Fernando Valley from its name, the organization became Neighborhood Legal Services of Los Angeles, and only brought over one lawyer from its former competitors.[113]

It was only a matter of time before an unhappy grantee facing loss of its identity in a merger into a much larger grantee took LSC to court. Ashtabula County Legal Aid Corporation (ACLAC) balked at the prospect of being absorbed into the Cleveland Legal Aid Society. Yet ACLAC's board knew it would lose out to its big neighbor if it tried to compete for the grant in the new expanded service area LSC had put out to bid. So ACLAC first asked LSC to subdivide that service area, carving out the county it had served for years. When LSC turned down that request, ACLAC filed a lawsuit in federal court, challenging LSC's refusal to subdivide service areas during the grant competition process. Once again recruiting a prominent law firm to donate its services pro bono, LSC negotiated a settlement of the ACLAC lawsuit, successfully avoiding the possibility of an adverse court ruling that might halt the consolidation campaign.[114]

It sometimes took longer than a year, as it did in Los Angeles county with its population of nearly 10 million and nearly 2 million of them eligible for legal aid. But, during a three-year span, in state after state, and metropolitan area after metropolitan area, McKay's pressure resulted in mergers and consolidations until over 300 grantees had been reduced to 137.

McKay did not escape criticism for his hard-charging campaign to reduce the number of LSC grantees. In November 1998, he appeared before an assembly of grantee directors at the annual NLADA meeting in St. Louis. In the question-and-answer period, Victor Geminiani, who headed the Hawaii program and was behind one of the court challenges to the congressional restrictions, rose and shouted out: "McKay, you are destroying the legal services program and taking away the jobs of some of the best legal services lawyers. We never expected you to be a good LSC president—but at least 'please do no harm'."[115] McKay reports that in future years despite this initial hostility to his tenure as LSC president, he and Geminiani became good friends.[116]

McKay heard from another more worrisome quarter when he decided to redefine CRLA's service area to embrace two coastal counties near Los Angeles—Santa Barbara and Ventura. This would end federal funding for the tiny LSC grantees that served those two counties, both with strong roots in their communities. Those involved in the two programs had enough contacts elsewhere in the state to attract the attention of Laurie Zelon, at that time chair of the ABA's Standing Committee on Legal Aid and Indigent Defendants), one of McKay's chief allies in his dealings with Congress, and also chair of the

California Commission on Access to Justice, the sort of state-based effort he was encouraging.

After asking why he was punishing two very decent programs which were popular in their counties, Zelon said, "And aren't you putting a target on CRLA's back? The locals are likely to see this controversial program as invading their peaceful communities."

"I look at it as helpful to CRLA," McKay countered. "Remember, I'm a Republican. So I'm a Republican endorsing CRLA as worthy of taking over service in areas it hasn't reached before. If they do a decent job there, it will help build political support for them outside rural California."

Zelon replied, "I see what you're doing,"[117] although Zelon remained unconvinced of the wisdom of the LSC president's move.[118]

Consolidation of grantees was one part of McKay's vision; the other was statewide coordination among the remaining grantees. Although receiving renewed emphasis by McKay, state planning did not start with him. It had begun in 1995 while Forger was still LSC President. As McKay described the process as it evolved under him, all grantees in a state were required, as a condition of their grants, to meet and develop an annual statewide plan with several components. They were to provide comprehensive coverage insuring all geographic areas, including rural ones, had access to LSC-funded lawyers. They were to increase overall funding by cultivating nonfederal sources of support. They were to develop and institute delivery mechanisms that would enhance efficiency and allow them to serve larger numbers of needy clients. And, to the extent feasible, they were to find alternative means for handling cases the congressional restrictions prohibited LSC grantees from accepting.[119]

Unlike consolidation, this McKay initiative didn't run into resistance from LSC grantees. In fact, SCLAID and the NLADA already had moved in the same direction, partnering in a program called SPAN— Strategic Planning Assistance Network. SPAN provided resources and assistance to LSC-funded and other grantees as they worked on developing systems for coordinating legal services in their states and expanding non-LSC revenue sources, usually at the state level.[120]

The statewide plans that emerged from LSC's required process varied in quality and thoroughness and also in their implementation of the blueprints the assembled LSC grantees produced. In fact, the requirement LSC grantees produce annual statewide plans barely survived beyond McKay's term as LSC president.[121] But the statewide focus on legal services delivery, in part encouraged by the McKay's commitment to coordination as well as NLADA's SPAN program, did continue in many jurisdictions.

By the mid-1990s, LSC-funded programs in a few states had begun looking for state government funding to replace some of what they had lost from the federal government. Often with the help of state and local bar associations, they had taken their case to the state legislature or occasionally local government. Sometimes they succeeded in persuading lawmakers to allocate a portion of court fees to support civil legal aid and in a few states the legislators appropriated general revenues for that purpose.[122]

Because the state of Washington had been one of the pioneers on that front, McKay was astounded to find few others had seen that opportunity. It was one of the reasons he had pushed so hard for statewide planning. As McKay saw it, state planning had several purposes—among them more total funding for legal services, and also as a way of dealing with the congressional restrictions. With careful planning and a mix of LSC and non-LSC grantees, a state could fill the service gaps the restrictions had created.

Other reasons and other forces also were at work that moved developments in the direction of state-oriented planning and a broader focus than increasing and coordinating the supply of legal services lawyers in the state.

A NEW FRONTIER: THE RISE OF STATE ACCESS TO JUSTICE COMMISSIONS

Independent of McKay's state planning initiative, the mid-1990s saw the birth of a new concept and a new institution that over the next two decades spread to over 25 states—the "Access to Justice Commission."

The idea was born, almost accidentally, in 1989, several years before the Gingrich Congress decimated federal funding of legal services for the poor. The Washington state bar had asked William Gates Sr., a named partner in one of Seattle's preeminent corporate law firms, Preston Gates, to chair a new "long-range planning" committee.[123] (Coincidentally, William Gates's son, Microsoft founder Bill Gates, was then busy plotting his company's dominance of the computer industry.)

During the planning committee hearings, Gates gave Ada Shen-Jaffe, then in her mid-40s and the executive director of Washington's largest legal services agency, a 15-minute slot to present the needs of the poverty community. In the current day, Ms. Jaffe probably would have used a polished "PowerPoint" presentation to illustrate her message. But in 1989, she only had a placard on which she had represented the complex world of legal services needs and responses with a series of hand-written circles, a chart that soon became famous among bar members in that state as "Ada Shen-Jaffe's 'circles' chart."[124]

Three hours later the planning committee finally completed its consideration of Shen-Jaffe's 15-minute presentation and her chart. When the Gates committee issued its report the members "identified access to justice as the number one issue facing the bar," pointing out "the public and lawyers alike have a vested interest in the system working. If the legal needs of all people cannot be addressed, then the system as we know it will break down."[125]

Responding to the recommendation of the Gates committee, the Washington state bar commissioned an Access to Justice Task Force to spend the bar's 1992–93 year formulating a plan for improving access in that state. Chaired by Tom Chambers, a future state supreme court justice, and with more than 25 members, the task force did not seek to study the barriers to access or devise potential solutions. Instead the members focused on planning an institution that could undertake those tasks in the future. In a crucial decision, they chose to recommend an independent board rather than a standing committee of the bar as the best structure.[126] The task force settled on a nine-member board, including two non-lawyers from the low- and moderate-income communities. The Washington bar would recommend candidates but the Washington Supreme Court would appoint the members of the board.[127] The mission was to expand resources, coordinate the delivery system, develop new approaches, and sponsor an annual access to justice conference.[128] Recognizing the job was too big for a nine-member board, the report recommended creation of a half-dozen committees and specifically instructed that non-board members should be included on those committees.[129] Finally, emphasizing this was a joint endeavor of the state bar and the state supreme court, the access to justice board was to file annual reports with both.[130]

On May 10, 1994, all nine Washington Supreme Court Justices signed an order authorizing a Washington State Access to Justice Board for a pilot period of two years. In defining the board, its functions, structure, and other provisions, the supreme court's order tracked closely the recommendations in the state bar's report.[131] The court extended this authorization by five years in 1996 and made it permanent in 2000.

While the Washington state bar was still awaiting approval from the Washington Supreme Court of its fully developed proposal for an access to justice board, a similar approach was just entering the early planning stage two states to the south, in California. This effort, in turn, evolved from an earlier failed "access to justice" initiative at the national level which had begun in late 1990. The ABA president-elect, Talbot (Sandy) D'Alemberte had asked a small group of experienced legal services advocates to craft a plan for enhancing access to justice that could be the centerpiece of his year as president. This group included Gerry Singsen, Victor Geminiani, Esther Lardent, and myself.

The 60-page memo we prepared proposed broadening the access to justice movement in three ways. First, broadening the strategies for achieving access beyond legal services to include development of simpler forums where lawyers weren't needed, simplifying the law, and other structural reforms, while also seeking more and often different sources of funding for legal services as well. Second, broadening the population to benefit from these changes beyond the poor to include the lower-middle class. And third, broadening the base of support beyond the legal profession to embrace a full range of other interest groups—labor, business, senior citizen organizations, the League of Women Voters, and the like.

To organize and administer this national access to justice movement, our memorandum to D'Alemberte called for the creation of a broad-based "National Access to Justice Commission" charged with developing and implementing a national commitment to access to justice as a matter of right.[132]

For most ABA presidents this would have been too ambitious and far-reaching a proposal to put forward as the main goal of his term as ABA president. But D'Alemberte was not a typical ABA president. He had all the attributes to win election to that post and indeed was so popular no one was willing to oppose him the year he ran. On the outside, D'Alemberte was a charming, nonthreatening man, who had paid his dues within the ABA by chairing a variety of important committees, along the way making friends with hundreds of lawyers active in ABA affairs. Like most ABA presidents, he had been a partner in a major corporate law firm, in his case one of Miami's largest, Steele Hector, and Davis. But unlike most, earlier in his career he had been a state legislator and now was dean of the law school at Florida State University (FSU)—and later FSU's president.[133] More significantly, he was a visionary, who could see and work toward a better future, and also a risk-taker, all masked by his patient, friendly demeanor.[134]

Consequently, it was not a great surprise when "Sandy" D'Alemberte enthusiastically adopted as his own the recommendations in the document the group had prepared. He assigned the task of making that dream a reality to a committee I chaired that, unfortunately, was buried deep within the ABA structure as a part of the Consortium for Legal Services and the Public. Also unfortunately, one of the central premises of the proposal doomed it to failure, because it required more time to develop than circumstances were to allow. That central premise deemed it important that the yet-to-be assembled "commission" composed primarily of non-lawyer interest groups—labor, business, seniors, and the like—should be responsible for developing the detailed plan for achieving the project's objective—a guarantee of equal justice for all. By the time the ABA had assembled the citizen commission and it held its first meeting, the election that gave the nation the Gingrich "Contract with America" Congress was about to happen. The ABA and the entire legal services community were forced into a defensive mode and the national "Citizens Commission for Equal Justice" never met again.

**Talbot (Sandy) D'Alemberte, ABA president
1991–1992. (American Bar Association Archives)**

I had become discouraged about the process at the national level even before the commission fell apart. By happenstance, a good friend of mine, Harvey Saferstein, had been elected president of the State Bar of California in the fall of 1993. Independent of what might happen at the national level, it seemed worthwhile to foster a backup plan in California. I mentioned this idea to Saferstein at a party he was holding for the bar's board of governors in his home.

Saferstein was quick to acknowledge the need for a broader coalition to support the goal of equal justice for the poor, and also a broader concept of how that could be achieved—the same notions the national plan had embodied. But this time I suggested that people familiar with the legal system, mainly lawyers, first study the status of access to justice in California and then develop a set of findings and detailed recommendations. Only after we had that blueprint would we enlist other interest groups in a coalition in support of those recommendations. This avoided the fatal flaw in the national plan, which first formed the coalition of outside interest groups and expected that coalition to analyze the problem and produce goals and recommendations.

Saferstein asked for a memo laying out this plan, which I drafted. After further discussions, in the spring of 1994 he appointed a "California Access to Justice Working Group," including two members who were simultaneously deeply involved in defending LSC against Gingrich's efforts—Jack Londen, head of "Californians for Legal Aid," and Laurie Zelon who chaired SCLAID and the ABA's grassroots campaign during much of that same period. Another member, Gerald Caplan, had been on the OEO-LSP staff in the mid-1960s and acting LSC president during the first Reagan board's tenure, 1982. At the time of his appointment to the working group, Caplan was Dean of McGeorge Law School in Sacramento. The other members were leading legal services lawyers such as Ralph Abascal from CRLA, bar leaders, and academics, including a social scientist, Professor James Meeker, from the University of California-Irvine.

Two and a half years later the California Access to Justice Working Group issued its 88-page report, *And Justice for All*, documenting the state of access to justice in California. In comparison with many other countries and even a number of comparable states in this country, it was not a pretty picture. The report then set forth a detailed list of recommendations,[135] coupled with a proposal that the California state bar establish a permanent "Commission on Access to Justice" to implement the recommendations.[136] This commission was to be far different from the regular state bar committees, with a majority of its members selected by organizations representing other interest groups—labor, business, senior citizens, the consumers attorney organization, along with the courts, the executive and legislative branches of government and other nonlegal groups whose help was needed if access to justice was to be improved in California.[137]

In late 1996, a few months after the Gingrich Congress's LSC funding cutbacks took full effect, the State Bar of California's board of governors accepted the working group's report and authorized the creation of the permanent commission. On June 7, 1997, the members had been appointed and the *California Commission on Access to Justice* held its first meeting, with Laurie Zelon as chair. Thus was born the second "Access to Justice Commission" in the United States.

At its first meeting, the commission reached a consensus on its immediate priorities. Although the working group's report had laid out ambitious long-term goals, the commission resolved to begin with a few of the shorter-term recommendations in hope it could build the organization's credibility with some early victories. A year and a half later it scored one such victory when the state legislature adopted a proposal the commission's funding committee had lobbied hard to achieve—California's first appropriation of general revenues to support civil legal aid. Not a large sum given the huge hole in California's legal aid funding the Gingrich Congress had dug in 1996, but nonetheless a welcome $10 million in state funding.[138] This was followed shortly by a series of initiatives that enhanced access to justice in the state courts—among them, self-help centers to assist unrepresented litigants in many counties,[139] a requirement that new court rules and procedures be examined for their impact on access for low-and moderate-income individuals,[140] and a campaign that resulted in 18 large law firms pledging to devote three to five percent of their lawyers' time to pro bono representation of low-income people.[141]

About the time the California Commission was born, the ABA in conjunction with the NLADA started SPAN—the State Planning Assistance Network, mentioned earlier, to assist state-based initiatives around the country. It was not long before helping states create state Access to Justice Commissions became a high priority for SPAN. In part because of that assistance, more than a dozen more state commissions came into existence before the end of the century.[142] In many states, the chief justice or other judges in the court system assumed responsibility for forming a statewide Access to Justice Commission, and elsewhere it was the state bar association that led the effort, and in others a combination.[143]

Along with the state IOLTA committees, these access commissions gave many states a permanent structure with a commitment to equal justice and some power to advance that goal. As an important byproduct, in almost all states the Access to Justice Commission movement enlisted the judiciary as full partners in the effort to make the courts and the entire legal system accessible to poor- and moderate-income people. It has given the judges a stake and a responsibility they seldom felt in the past.

With the access commissions, LSC has partners in those states where they exist that can help fill some of the gaps Congress has created through its restrictions and the always inadequate and too often suddenly reduced funding levels. The commissions also were partners that could take other steps LSC and its grantees couldn't, for instance promoting reforms in court procedures and structures that could help lower-income litigants in other ways. Nonetheless, there were regions of the country, especially in the Southeast and the mountain states, where LSC remained virtually the only source of funding for civil legal aid and LSC-funded organizations the only institutions available to help the poor with their legal problems. The result was a patchwork pattern where no state was able to provide low-income people adequate access to the legal system, but where some jurisdictions lag much further behind than others.

WITH ONE EXCEPTION, THE FEDERAL APPELLATE COURTS OFFER NO FURTHER RELIEF FROM THE CONGRESSIONAL RESTRICTIONS

For LSC grantees hoping the courts might give some further relief from the restrictions, the Ninth Circuit opinion in the LASH appeal arrived early in 1998. But it was a disappointment, because the court affirmed the trial court decision upholding the restrictions and also adopted most of the lower court's rationale.[144]

It was almost a year later, in January 1999, before the Second Circuit issued its opinion in the *Velazquez* case.[145] That decision opened a small crevice in the wall of restrictions the Gingrich Congress had thrown around LSC grantees and their lawyers. While concluding all the other restrictions were at least "facially" constitutional, the Second Circuit panel found by a 2–1 vote the "welfare reform" provision amounted to "viewpoint" discrimination. This provision allowed legal services lawyers to argue in favor of welfare reform laws, but not against them, when representing welfare recipients. The court found this violated a well-settled principle of First Amendment jurisprudence—government cannot favor one viewpoint over another by preventing or restricting expression of the position it doesn't like.[146]

The Second Circuit also left a small opening for legal services supporters to file future "as applied" challenges against the other restrictions the court had found acceptable when subjected only to the initial "facially unconstitutional" claims Neuborne had filed.[147] In this appeal the Second Circuit had only been asked whether the language of these restrictions was unconstitutional "on its face" and thus in whatever conceivable factual circumstances it might be applied. As to all but the "welfare reform" prohibition, the answer to that question had been "no." But the court had no occasion to address and thus did not rule on whether one or more of the other restrictions might be applied in an unconstitutional manner to a certain set of facts. In that instance, the restriction would be invalid in some circumstances and valid in others.

Both sides sought review of the Second Circuit opinion in the U.S. Supreme Court. Lawyers representing the LSC wanted to overturn the ruling on the "welfare reform" issue, of course. And, despite renewed opposition from those who still feared a loss of support in Congress, Neuborne hoped the high court might strike down some other of the restrictions as "facially unconstitutional," if it had the chance. Thus, he and his team also filed a cert petition.

On April 3, 2000, the Supreme Court granted certiorari, but limited to the issue Neuborne had won in the Second Circuit—the constitutionality of the "welfare reform" restriction. As to all other restrictions, the Second Circuit's opinion upholding their constitutionality remained in effect, at least as to the "facial" validity of those provisions.[148] This was not a hopeful sign as the legal services community awaited argument and decision in the Supreme Court. The best they could do was preserve the small victory they had won, with no prospect the high court would rid them of any of the other limitations on services they could offer clients—and a good chance even that small victory would prove temporary.

THE LEGAL SERVICES CORPORATION'S TUMULTUOUS CLINTON YEARS COME TO A QUIETER CLOSE

As the 20th century drew to a close, legal services supporters had only limited and possibly temporary success resisting the restrictions, but they did receive comforting news on the funding front. By 2000, it was clear the message of reassurance had finally succeeded. When Congress took up the FY 2001 appropriation for LSC, the bill passed with a voice vote, the "no's" so minimal no one in the House asked for a roll call.[149] Although McKay and John Erlenborn did more than their share, as certainly did NLADA, McKay gave the ABA the lion's share of the credit for that. "In my view, the ABA saved the Legal Services Corporation from the Gingrich Congress's attempt to kill it. SCLAID and the ABA's legislative advocates and the lawyers they mobilized were very, very effective. I personally think it was the association's proudest moment."[150]

The bad news was that the LSC appropriation remained at the reduced level the Gingrich Congress had imposed in 1995–96. Even though LSC funding crept up a tiny bit each year and in 2000 reached $330 million,[151] the increases seldom were enough to match inflation and fell nearly $400 million below what would be required to match the "minimum access" level achieved in 1981.[152] With the Clinton administration as well as the century winding down, any hopes for filling that yawning gap in the federal appropriation or relief from any of the restrictions rested with the election of a more favorable Congress and a willing president. The legal services community held its collective breath as the 2000 elections—congressional as well as presidential—drew toward their dramatic and messy conclusion.

REPORT FROM THE FIELD: The Invention of I-CAN!—Bringing Computer Assistance to Unrepresented Litigants and Low-Income Taxpayers

Sometimes the most important contributions legal services lawyers make don't happen within the courtroom or the law office. Instead they result from the creative process—conceiving new ways of bringing justice to their clients. One of the most innovative lawyers over the past four decades has been Robert Cohen, since 1980 the executive director of the Legal Aid Society of Orange County (LASOC) in California. During the early 1980s he quarterbacked the effort to pass California's Interest on Lawyers' Trust Accounts (IOLTA) law, the second IOLTA program in the land and the first created through legislation. In the mid-1990s, when LSC funding dropped suddenly by one-third, he devised a three-tier program to combine a hotline, self-help assistance, and full legal representation, seeking to maximize the numbers his program could reach with reduced financial support.

But Bob Cohen's real "light bulb" moment came in the late 1990s after he returned from a conference where Richard Zorza described a document assembly program lawyers could use on their computers to produce court pleadings. Why couldn't that same basic technology be used by poor people to do the same. Cohen realized it would require a technological breakthrough for his idea to work. It is one thing to make it possible for lawyers to run a software program that produced legal documents and quite another to create one that was so simple and straightforward that non-lawyers, even those with little education, could operate. Nonetheless, he was determined to try.

Cohen first shared his idea with Alan Slater, the CEO of the Orange County Superior Court, because he knew many of the unrepresented people he wanted to help would first show up at the courthouse. Slater suggested Cohen should try to develop a system that used free-standing kiosks rather than computers, because at that time many people weren't computer literate if not afraid of those machines. After two unfortunate experiences with outside software developers, Cohen hired A. J. Tavares as a staff member at LASOC. Cohen credits Tavares for the computer program that exists today. Another staff member, Crystal Sims, came up with the system's name—Interactive Community Assistance Network chosen because of its perfect acronym I-CAN! In 1999, Cohen launched the system in Orange county.

Using I-CAN! is easy. Kiosks are located at courthouses and legal aid offices and some public law libraries. A user sits down at a kiosk facing a screen that asks a series of questions the user answers. When the last question is answered, the kiosk prints out the appropriate court document—a complaint for a plaintiff, or an answer for a defendant, or some other form courts require. The user then can watch videos that demonstrate how to locate courthouses, find parking, navigate to court rooms and offices, file forms, serve papers, prepare for court appearances, present cases, and more.

In Orange county, I-CAN! is now available in Spanish and Vietnamese, as well as in English. Librarians have been trained to assist those who have problems while operating the software at their facilities. And a few years after its first launch in the kiosks, LASOC introduced a version of I-CAN! for the Web, so users can access it from any computer. Since 1999, I-CAN!™ Legal has facilitated the pro se creation of over 120,000 court pleadings in Orange county. In recent years, I-CAN! Legal also has spread to a number of other areas of California and several other states, among them Georgia, North Carolina, Minnesota, Oklahoma, and Virginia.

Cohen did not stop innovating after his success with the basic I-CAN! Legal program. He and his lawyers noticed many of their clients were either not taking advantage of their eligibility for the earned income tax credit or were being ripped off by commercial tax-preparation services. These firms made extra money when preparing returns that gave taxpayers earned income tax credits by extending refund anticipation loans, commonly called RALs. These loans were very profitable for the tax-preparation services but costly for the taxpayers, because the effective interest rates on these loans ran as high as 700 percent. Cohen figured it would be possible to adapt the basic I-CAN! software to generate tax returns just as the original version spewed out court documents. So LASOC developed a program that would allow low-income taxpayers eligible for earned income tax credits to prepare and file their own returns by answering a few questions that appeared on kiosk or computer screens. This program called I-CAN! E-File became operational in 2003. Since then it has allowed clients using the system to receive over $600 million in earned income credit payments and without paying fees and onerous interest costs.

Cohen faced resistance from the Internal Revenue Service (IRS) when he asked the service to list I-CAN! E-File on the IRS Free File website. This would have alerted taxpayers they didn't have to go to a commercial tax preparer to prepare their returns applying for earned income tax credits. IRS first claimed it did not control this (their own) website and referred Cohen to a consortium of private companies that did. This consortium denied LASOC's request to be listed on grounds that it was a nonprofit organization. When LASOC filed a formal complaint with IRS about this discrimination against nonprofits, Cohen received a surprise visit from two treasury agents. They wanted a detailed exposition of LASOC's concerns about the IRS website. Fortunately, LASOC already had prepared a PowerPoint on that exact subject. After watching the PowerPoint presentation for only a few minutes, one of the agents turned to Cohen and said, "Why don't you just sue us, that's the only way you will get any change."

Eventually, faced with the prospect of an embarrassing and probably successful lawsuit against the discriminatory treatment of nonprofit tax-preparation organizations, IRS relented. In 2008 I-CAN! E-File was added to the IRS Free File website. Although legal services programs in a few other states have made I-CAN! E-File available to low-income people in their states, Cohen has been pushing hard for all legal services programs to do the same in their states. He argues that billions of dollars of earned income tax credits are not claimed each year because low-income taxpayers are unaware the program exists or that they are eligible. And he is equally concerned because hundreds of millions of dollars are siphoned from eligible taxpayers who do file by commercial tax preparers through exorbitant interest rates charged for "refund anticipation loans."

When it comes to impact on the lives of low-income people in the United States, Bob Cohen's innovations in service delivery rank right up there with the biggest victories legal services lawyers ever won in the U.S. Supreme Court. If there were a "Thomas Edison of civil legal aid" he probably would be the one deserving the title.

Chapter 28

A Time of Respite and Risk

*The Legal Services Corporation Finds a
Measure of Peace and Progress while Courts
Decide the Fate of IOLTA and the Restrictions*

We must be vigilant when Congress imposes rules and conditions which in
effect insulate its own laws from legitimate judicial challenge. Where private speech is involved, even Congress' antecedent funding decision cannot
be aimed at the suppression of ideas thought inimical to the Government's
own interest.
> —Justice Anthony Kennedy *Legal Services Corp. v. Velazquez*
> 531 U.S. 533, 549 (2001).

The George W. Bush administration took office early in 2001 with
two veterans of earlier legal services controversies in top positions—
former Office of Economic Opportunity (OEO) director Don Rumsfeld as the secretary of defense and his former special assistant, Dick
Cheney, now above Rumsfeld as vice president. This could have
been bad news for the Legal Services Corporation, its grantees, their
lawyers, and clients. And certainly many in the legal services community were apprehensive about the future under another Republican
president. During Ronald Reagan's tenure the LSC was viewed as a
target for destruction and the George H. W. Bush administration had
considered it a problem entity requiring careful scrutiny and feeble
support. So John McKay, still the LSC president, and others waited for
signals as to the direction the new administrations might take.

BETWEEN PRESIDENTIAL ADMINISTRATIONS,
IOLTA SUFFERS ANOTHER BLOW

It was the courts not the administration, however, that took center
stage as George W. Bush was about to assume office in 2001, after the
most divisive and extended election in recent U.S. history. What was
at stake was the survival of the Interest on Lawyers' Trust Accounts
(IOLTA) programs that existed in all 50 states and represented the second largest source of funding for legal services in the country. Just a

week before inauguration day, a three-judge Ninth Circuit panel reversed the Washington trial court that had dismissed the Washington
Legal Foundation's case in that state.[1] In resurrecting the WLF lawsuit that threatened IOLTA programs and the funding they supplied
around the country, the appellate court relied on the Supreme Court's
1998 opinion in the Texas IOLTA case, which had been issued a few
months after the Washington district court reached its decision.[2]

Writing for the three-judge panel, Judge Alex Kozinski, the circuit's
most renowned conservative judge, explained their view:

> The circuits had been split [on whether the interest in IOLTA accounts
> was the clients' property], and were when the district court ruled. Sub-
> sequent to that ruling, the Supreme Court definitively answered the
> question, in *Phillips v. Washington Legal Foundation:* the clients own the
> interest.[3]

Later in the opinion, Judge Kozinski conceded:

> IOLTA programs spread rapidly because they were an exceedingly intel-
> ligent idea. Money that lawyers deposited in bank trust accounts always
> produced earnings, but before IOLTA the clients who owned the money
> did not receive any of the earnings that their money produced. IOLTA
> extracted the earnings from the banks and gave it to charities, largely to
> fund legal services for the poor. That is a very worthy purpose.[4]

But that "worthy purpose" did not dissuade Kozinski or the other
two judges on the panel from holding IOLTA's feet to the constitutional fire. Judge Kozinski then addressed the two issues the Supreme
Court reserved for another day in its *Phillips* decision—whether the
IOLTA arrangement constituted a "taking" and whether it was "without just compensation."

> When the government permanently appropriates all of the interest on
> IOLTA trust funds, that is a per se taking, as when it permanently ap-
> propriates by physical invasion of real property. . . . [G]overnment ap-
> propriation of that interest for public purposes is a taking entitling [the
> depositors whose funds the law firm place with the bank] to just com-
> pensation under the Fifth Amendments. But just compensation for the
> takings may be less than the amount of the interest taken, or nothing,
> depending on the circumstances, so determining the remedy requires a
> remand [to the trial court].[5]

This was the opinion of 3 judges out of the 25 then on the Ninth
Circuit Court of Appeals. Hoping a majority of the others would have
a different view on the issues in the case, the losing IOLTA parties
petitioned for an *en banc* review. In the Ninth Circuit *en banc* means
a rehearing before 11 of the circuit's judges, randomly selected. If the
petition for review was successful, the opinion the 11-judge panel
filed would replace the original three-judge panel's decision as the

law of the circuit on the issues decided. But the full court—all 25 active judges—had to ponder the original opinion and the record, then vote whether to grant a request for an *en banc* rehearing. This review typically takes several months and while many an *en banc* hearing is requested, few are granted. So as of January 2001, Judge Kozinski's opinion remained the last word on the constitutional validity of the nation's IOLTA programs.

With both major sources of their funding now in jeopardy, one because of the courts and the other because of a suspect incoming presidential administration, as the year 2001 started LSC's grantees had reason to be worried about their future.

WHITHER THE YOUNGER BUSH'S ADMINISTRATION?

A week after that Ninth Circuit decision, George W. Bush was sworn in as president and his administration took over the federal government. Initially, John McKay had been fairly optimistic after Bush's election, because he knew George W. Bush had been quite friendly toward legal services grantees as the governor of Texas. But McKay had begun to get queasy while on Christmas vacation in Oregon. He learned the president was appointing John Ashcroft as attorney general. Ashcroft had a long record as an LSC opponent while serving in the House and later the Senate. Then McKay learned Bush's new Office of Management and Budget (OMB) had recommended zero funding for the Legal Services Corporation—signaling a return to the Reagan years.

McKay knew he had to do something about that OMB budget recommendation. He had a friend on the Bush team, Ron Walker, who had especially close ties to Vice President Dick Cheney. Earlier, Walker had offered to do anything for McKay that he could. So the LSC president decided to call in that chit.

"I have only one thing to ask," he said to Walker. "Please get a message to the vice-president-elect about the OMB 'zero-budgeting' the Legal Services Corporation. And ask him if he can intervene to change that mark."

"Sure, I can do that."

"And you might want to mention to the vice president that we have enough support in Congress to win—to get our current appropriation—even if the administration were to ask for nothing. So why should this brand new president want to embarrass himself by picking a losing fight with Congress. There are so many more important fights to fight."

"I'll get the message across," Walker promised.

A few weeks later, the OMB issued a new budget recommendation. This one proposed an appropriation for LSC—at its current level.[6]

Except for this initial misstep by OMB, the George W. Bush administration didn't evidence any animosity toward the LSC. Indeed it left the Clinton-appointed board in charge for nearly two years, rather than rushing to replace them with recess appointees.

In the long run, the LSC cause was aided by the presence of legal aid supporters holding influential positions in the White House. One of those was Harriet Meier, later to be President Bush's first choice for a seat as an associate justice on the U.S. Supreme Court.[7] A valued advisor to the new president since his days as Texas governor, Meier had a proven commitment to legal services for the poor. While a partner in a major corporate law firm, she had been active with legal aid organizations in Texas, receiving an award from Legal Services of North Texas, chairing the Texas State Bar Association's legal services committee, and also had been a member of the ABA's Consortium on Legal Services and the Public in the 1980s and the ABA Standing Committee on Legal Aid and Indigent Defendants (SCLAID) in 1998–99. She also was deeply involved in bar association activities— as president of both the Dallas and Texas bars, as chair and member of a half-dozen different ABA committees, and with the Texas delegation in the ABA House of Delegates. These activities exposed Meier to the work LSC-funded lawyers were doing for the poor around the nation and also to the political and funding problems they often faced. It also gave legal services supporters, especially those in the ABA leadership, a friend they knew and could talk with in the Bush White House.[8]

Another of the president's closest advisors was his first White House Counsel, Alberto Gonzalez, later to be attorney general during Bush's second term. He also had been Bush's counsel in the Texas state house, service that was rewarded with an appointment to the Texas Supreme Court in 1996. Gonzalez was such a strong advocate for legal services to the poor that the State Bar of Texas gave him its "Presidential Citation" in 1997 for his "dedication to addressing basic legal needs of the indigent."[9] While a member of the Texas Supreme Court, he also was one of the defendants the WLF sued in the Texas IOLTA litigation. Some indication of Gonzalez support for LSC can be gleaned from John McKay's report to the LSC board, "We continue to receive excellent cooperation and assistance from the White House, in particular [the] White House Counsel's Office, Al Gonzalez, the Counsel to the president, and Stuart Bohen."[10]

Whether deliberating a general approach to legal services policy or dealing with specific issues such as appointments to the LSC board, with Harriet Meier and Alberto Gonzalez the Bush administration had presidential advisors close by who were very sympathetic to thet corporation and its grantees.

Douglas Eakeley (LSC board chair), Alberto Gonzalez (White House Counsel and future U.S. Attorney General), and John McKay (LSC president). (Courtesy of Legal Services Corporation)

A RESTRICTION ON THE RESTRICTIONS

Yet another court decision was about to overshadow developments at the White House and at LSC in the early months of the Bush administration. Only six weeks after the three-judge opinion from the Ninth Circuit in the IOLTA litigation, the U.S. Supreme Court brought better news for LSC-funded lawyers on another issue they had been following for several years. On February 28, 2001, the high court finally ruled in *Velazquez v. Legal Services Corporation*. This will be remembered as the New York case legal services supporters filed four years earlier raising constitutional objections to nearly all the restrictions the Gingrich Congress had imposed in 1996. The Second Circuit had struck down only one of those restrictions, the one prohibiting legal services lawyers from challenging "welfare reform" rules when litigating for their welfare recipient clients.[11]

The Supreme Court reached the same result as the Second Circuit had.[12] Justice Anthony Kennedy authored the 5–4 majority opinion and pointed out the courts as well as the litigants had a stake in the outcome of this particular case, predictably drawing a dissent from Justice Antonin Scalia.

As interpreted by the LSC and by the Government, the restriction prevents an attorney from arguing to a court that a state [welfare] statute conflicts with a federal statute or either a state or federal [welfare] statute by its terms or in its application is violative of the United States Constitution. . . . Interpretation of the law and the Constitution is the primary mission of the judiciary when it acts within the sphere of its authority to resolve a case or controversy. . . . An informed, independent judiciary presumes an informed, independent bar. Under [the welfare restriction], however, cases would be presented by LSC attorneys who could not advise the courts of serious questions of statutory validity. . . . By seeking to prohibit the analysis of certain legal issues and to truncate presentation to the courts, the enactment under review prohibits speech and expression upon which courts must depend for the proper exercise of the judicial power. Congress cannot wrest the law from the Constitution which is its source.[13]

We must be vigilant when Congress imposes rules and conditions which in effect insulate its own laws from legitimate judicial challenge. Where private speech is involved, even Congress' antecedent funding decision cannot be aimed at the suppression of ideas thought inimical to the Government's own interest. . . . For the reasons we have set forth, the funding condition is invalid.[14]

Yet, joy among LSC grantees over the demise of the "welfare restriction" was muted by the fact that four years after the Gingrich Congress imposed them, more than a dozen other restrictions had survived despite vigorous constitutional challenges. True, LSC-funded lawyers representing individual clients could now argue a given welfare law was inconsistent with federal statutes or violated the U.S. Constitution. But they still could not file a class action making that same argument. Nor could they present an argument to a legislature urging that a welfare law, although legally valid, was defective or unfair or counterproductive or otherwise unwise. And, of course, outside the field of welfare law they still had no relief from the other limitations the restrictions imposed.

But, nonetheless, there was no doubt the Supreme Court's opinion in *Velasquez* was of great importance to the many clients who depended on public assistance for their very survival. The rationale of the *Velasquez* decision also placed some limits on what Congress could do in the future to immunize other areas of the law from being challenged in the courts by LSC-funded lawyers.

JOHN MCKAY'S TENURE AS LSC PRESIDENT COMES TO AN END

John McKay had never been a fan of the lawsuits some legal services lawyers and others had filed challenging the congressional restrictions. Along with many other legal services supporters, he saw the restrictions as essential to the survival of LSC and its appropriation. That was because he firmly believed the bloc of 50 to 60 moderate Republicans whom McKay counted on to vote with LSC and against their party's leadership relied on the continuance of those restrictions.[15] It gave them cover with their fellow Republicans in Congress as well as their own constituents back in their districts. It allowed them to defend their votes for LSC by saying, "We've ended the 'abuses' by LSC-funded lawyers through these restrictions. So why punish poor people by denying them the lawyers they need to get justice in this country."

As it turned out, any fears McKay or others might have entertained that the Supreme Court's opinion cancelling the "welfare reform" restriction would cause a revolt in Congress proved to be groundless. Rather than punish the corporation in any way or seeking to amend the LSC act to evade or neutralize the *Velasquez* decision, Congress quietly, without any furor in committee or on the floor, merely amended the LSC legislation to remove the offending language.[16] Whether the moderate Republicans would have been so forgiving of an opinion striking down some of the broader restrictions—against class actions, legislative advocacy, representation of undocumented aliens, and the like—is not so clear, however.

By the time the Supreme Court issued its *Velasquez* decision, John McKay was nearing the end of the fourth year of his initial two-year commitment to the job of LSC president. With his success in persuading the administration to include a decent appropriation for LSC in its budget and having completed most of the policy initiatives he had sought to accomplish, he decided it was time to make a move. McKay was ready to return to his home town, Seattle, and there was a choice job open, if he could get it—the U.S. Attorney for the Western District of Washington. His older brother, Mike McKay, had occupied that position during George H. W. Bush's administration, which only added to the attraction.[17]

So John sent his application to the White House, and soon learned he had been chosen. This was the first time in history two brothers had served as U.S. Attorneys in the same federal District.[18] (Some five years later, John McKay was one of seven U.S. Attorneys the Bush administration fired because they refused to bring politically motivated prosecutions, a scandal that made headlines around the country and led to congressional investigations. Ironically, McKay's close ally when he was LSC president, Alberto Gonzalez, was on the other side of the dispute as the attorney general instrumental in the discharge of McKay and the other U.S. Attorneys).[19]

Once McKay warned his last day as president would be June 30, the chair, Doug Eakeley, and the rest of the Clinton-appointed board members were in a difficult position. What should they do about the vacancy? It made no sense for this board—whose members could be replaced any moment—to select a new president the successor board might not like. At the same time, this remained a sensitive period for LSC, requiring a deft hand at the wheel in dealing with Congress as well as the LSC grantees.

A consensus soon developed around a perfect solution. Ask John Erlenborn, the board's vice chair and McKay's right-hand man with Congress, if he would be willing to serve as interim president for the few months before a Bush-appointed board was appointed and had time to select its own permanent president. After all, Erlenborn already lived in Washington and, after nearly a decade on the board, was familiar with the staff and the issues. The added bonus—as a former 20-year Republican congressman, his presence at the helm would be reassuring to Congress and probably to the Bush administration, as well.

Despite his advancing age, in mid-2001 Erlenborn accepted this short-term assignment as LSC president.[20] Little did he know he would still be in that job two years later.

At McKay's last meeting as LSC president, he received accolade after accolade from board members, none more meaningful than the

Douglas Eakeley, LSC board chair, John McKay, LSC president, 1997–2001, and John Erlenborn, LSC board member and LSC president, 2001–2003. (Courtesy of Legal Services Corporation)

one from Bill McCalpin, who spoke from the perspective of someone who had been deeply involved in the federal government's legal services program since 1964 and in one leadership role or the other witnessed all the ups and downs that program had suffered before and during the existence of the Legal Services Corporation.

"My recollection," McCalpin began, "is that at the very first meeting of this board we went around the table, and each of us was asked to express our view, our hope, for what might be accomplished during our tenure in office. As I recall, I said at that time that my hope was that by the time we left the Legal Services Corporation might become as accepted and noncontroversial as the Head Start Program. And I would like to say that particularly in the last four years, under the leadership of this president, we have come measurably, markedly closer to that aspiration than, not knowing then about the 1994 elections, I would have viewed possible."[21]

At that same June 30, 2001, meeting, in addition to praising the departing LSC president, the board finally responded to the furor from the field generated by one of his main management initiatives—reducing the number of grantees through mergers and consolidations. It passed a resolution establishing a committee, chaired by John Broderick, to examine the criteria, at that time unwritten, which the staff applied in redefining service areas and putting them out to bid. This Broderick committee was given a tight time deadline, expected to present an interim report for discussion at the September meeting.[22] From one perspective, it was closing the barn door a bit late, since so many important mergers and consolidations already had been completed. Although both his consolidation and state planning initiatives faded away after his departure, McKay had managed to alter the landscape of the legal services world in many ways.

THE FULL NINTH CIRCUIT DECIDES WHETHER TO GIVE IOLTA A REPRIEVE, AT LEAST TEMPORARILY

Judge Alex Kozinski's January 2001 opinion on behalf of a three-judge panel of the Ninth Circuit, a decision which threatened to end IOLTA funding throughout the country, proved to have a short shelf life. Four months later, on May 9, 2001, a majority of the 25 judges on the full court voted to grant an *en banc* hearing. This meant a randomly selected panel of 11 Ninth Circuit judges would rehear the appeal and their decision, whatever it might be, would supplant the original three-judge opinion.

So the nation's 50 IOLTA programs and all the LSC grantees and other legal aid organizations dependent on the funding those programs provided regained some hope this major source of financial support might survive after all. The vote to grant an *en banc* hearing was encouraging but hardly conclusive. All it meant was that a majority of the Ninth Circuit judges felt this issue was worthy of consideration by a broader range of the circuit's bench.

Six months later, on November 13, 2001, after another round of briefing and oral argument before the 11 judges of the *en banc* panel, Judge Kim Wardlaw wrote the majority opinion for seven of the panel members, with Kozinsky and three others dissenting.[23] A comparatively young Clinton appointee from one of Los Angeles' largest corporate law firm, O'Melveny & Meyers, Wardlaw was well equipped to deal with the complex economic issues implicated in the case. In ruling Washington's IOLTA program was constitutional, Judge Wardlaw explained:

> The Takings Clause does not prevent the Government from being able to regulate how people use their property but limits that ability to what is "just and fair." . . . Although "the government may impose regulations to adjust rights and economic interests among people for the public good," it may "not force some people alone to bear public burdens which, in all fairness and justice, should be borne by the public as a whole." Here, neither Brown nor Hayes [parties objecting to IOLTA] is being singled out to bear a burden that should be borne by the public as a whole. They, as participants in our legal system, are required to place their money in IOLTA trust accounts that generate funds at no cost to them and that expand access to the legal system from which they benefit. Given the highly regulated nature of the banking and professional industries the IOLTA rules affect, this additional unobtrusive regulation does not exceed what is "just and fair"—especially where Brown and Hayes would have earned no interest absent IOLTA. We therefore conclude that Washington State's IOLTA program does not take either Brown's or Hayes's property.[24]
>
>   There is a second reason why Washington State's IOLTA program does not work a constitutional violation with regard to Brown's and Hayes's property: Even if their property was taken, the Fifth Amendment only protects against a taking without just compensation. Because of the way the IOLTA program operates, the compensation due Brown and Hayes for any taking of their property would be nil. There was therefore no constitutional violation when they were not compensated.[25]

IOLTA programs and the legal services lawyers they supported rejoiced over the Wardlaw opinion, but with reservations. This victory could well be as short-lived as the Kozinski defeat had turned out to be, because this case almost certainly was on its way to the U.S. Supreme Court where it awaited an uncertain fate. The Ninth Circuit was the nation's most liberal federal appellate court and one that therefore was frequently reversed by the far more conservative Supreme Court.

FINALLY, A NEW BOARD OF DIRECTORS FOR THE LEGAL SERVICES CORPORATION

As 2001 came to an end and 2002 began, the Clinton-selected LSC board remained in control and John Erlenborn continued as its president. The George W. Bush administration was taking its own good time assembling a full complement of nominees for the LSC board. Obviously more favorably disposed to the LSC and its grantees than the two previous Republican presidencies—Reagan and his father's—Bush's aides evidently wanted to avoid a series of recess boards, the approach George H. W. Bush had adopted, while also avoiding the sort of contentious confirmation hearings that characterized the Reagan years.

Finally the Bush administration had a list of nominees they felt had a fair chance of passing muster before the Health, Education, Labor, and Pensions Committee (usually called HELP). In late March 2002, President Bush formally announced a slate of five nominees—all Republicans—to fill seats of some LSC board members whose terms had expired.[26] If confirmed, they would join holdovers from the Clinton-appointed board. But Senators Kennedy and Daschle immediately placed "holds" on Senate consideration of those nominees until they could see who Bush proposed for the Democratic seats. This kept the initial nominations in suspense, and left the Clinton-appointed board in full control of LSC.

Most of Bush's first five nominees had records as political moderates and a few were known supporters of legal services for the poor. Two, however, raised questions in many quarters. They were members of the Federalist Society, a national organization of conservative lawyers not known to be friendly toward legal services lawyers or many of the cases those lawyers had taken and won. The society had grown in influence with Bush's election. A large percentage of Bush's judicial appointees came from the ranks of the Federalist Society, a guarantee they would make conservative decisions on the bench. Federalist Society members also occupied many of the key legal positions in the new administration and on many congressional staffs.[27]

One of the two proposed Federalist Society members, Lillian Bevier, was a law professor at the University of Virginia—and a member of the society's national board of visitors. The other, Frank Strickland, was the long-time chair of the society's Atlanta chapter. All of this raised concern in the ranks of legal services lawyers. But they would have ample time to stew over these nominees, because the Kennedy and Daschle "hold" delayed confirmation for over a year. In the meantime, the Clinton-appointed LSC board and its interim president, John Erlenborn, remained in control of the LSC and operated largely in a "caretaker" role while awaiting their replacements.

THE U.S. SUPREME COURT FINALLY RESOLVES THE
QUESTION—ARE IOLTA PROGRAMS CONSTITUTIONAL?

When the Supreme Court granted certiorari, agreeing to hear the Ninth
Circuit opinion upholding the constitutionality of the Washington
IOLTA program, it came as no surprise, especially given the high court's
decision in the Texas IOLTA case (see chapter 27).[28] But it definitely was
a matter of concern to the nation's other IOLTA programs and the hundreds of grantees they financed, including many non-LSC-funded legal
services agencies entirely dependent on IOLTA for their existence. The
odds did not favor an affirmance of the Ninth Circuit opinion by what
was a much more conservative Supreme Court.

The oral argument in the nation's highest court was held on December 9, 2002, with many IOLTA and legal services staff members
attending—and praying. The case pitted two former solicitor gener-
als, both professors, against each other. Walter Dellinger, who served
under President Clinton and had been a Duke professor, defended
IOLTA, and Charles Fried, Reagan's solicitor general and a Harvard
professor, argued the program was unconstitutional.[29] Although they
and the justices engaged in a spirited exchange, the oral argument
yielded few clues as to the likely outcome.[30] Those counting on the
survival of IOLTA programs had to continue praying.

On the morning of March 26, 2003, the speculation ended when
Justice John Stevens announced the court's decision from the bench.
Quoting from the written opinion, he first went through the convo-
luted reasoning that led the court to the conclusion the transfer of interest from IOLTA accounts to finance legal services did constitute a
"taking" of something that belonged to the depositors.[31] In adopting
this position, the Supreme Court differed from the Ninth Circuit opinion, which was based in part on a finding no "taking" occurred. Not a
good sign for the IOLTA programs.

But then Justice Stevens turned to the third and final issue—whether
the depositors were denied "just compensation" for the "taking" of
the interest earned in IOLTA accounts. The Stevens opinion explained
IOLTA accounts could only hold accumulated funds that were incapable of producing net interest for any of the individuals whose money
was included in the account. If a lawyer erroneously placed a client's
funds in an IOLTA account that could have yielded net interest for
that client if deposited in a separate account the client would have a
legitimate claim against the lawyer, but not against the IOLTA fund
or the government. The depositor's "just compensation" for the un-
authorized taking of interest the depositor could have earned would
have to come from that lawyer. None would be owed by IOLTA or
the government.[32] To put it another way, by definition funds properly
placed in an IOLTA account could not earn any net interest for the
depositors whose funds were in that account. Thus, they lost nothing

even though IOLTA grantees gained something. The Supreme Court had long held that just compensation was measured by the claimant's loss, not by the government's gain.[33] Having lost nothing those depositors were not owed any "just compensation" for the theoretical taking they experienced.

Justice Stevens then concluded by summarizing the court's holding.

> A law that requires that the interest on those funds [in an IOLTA account] be transferred to a different owner for a legitimate public use, . . . could be a *per se* taking requiring the payment of "just compensation" to the client. Because that compensation is measured by the owner's pecuniary loss—which is zero whenever the Washington law is obeyed— there has been no violation of the Just Compensation Clause of the Fifth Amendment in this case. . . . Accordingly, the judgment of the Court of Appeals is affirmed.[34]

After five years in jeopardy of extermination, the nation's IOLTA programs finally received a welcome guarantee of their constitutionality from the final authority on that issue, the U.S. Supreme Court. Not only the IOLTA programs, but their hundreds of grantees, their thousands of lawyers, and millions of clients, breathed a collective sigh of relief. The second largest supplier of funding for civil legal aid had survived.

With confidence in its future came more willingness to explore ways of increasing IOLTA's revenues. More states began moving from voluntary to mandatory programs—requiring all lawyers in the state to maintain IOLTA accounts. Several states also began pressing banks to pay higher interest rates on those accounts. Some even began requiring "comparability," that is, interest or dividend rates on IOLTA accounts that matched the rates banks paid their favored depositors.[35] This became necessary because IOLTA earnings too often lagged behind what commercial clients received from the same bank.

THE NEW LSC BOARD FINALLY TAKES OVER

Only a few weeks after the Supreme Court's IOLTA decision, in April 2003, Senators Kennedy and Daschle lifted their hold on Bush's nominees to the LSC board. When they did, things moved speedily. Without bothering to hold hearings, the Senate's HELP Committee voted unanimously to recommend confirmation. A week later, the full Senate confirmed the nominees, also unanimously. Once confirmed, the administration advised the new nominees which of their number it wanted to chair the board—Frank Strickland. Thus, at the new board's first meeting, on April 23, 2003, Strickland was elected the chair and his fellow Federalist Society member, Professor Lillian Bevier, the vice chair of the LSC board.[36]

The LSC board of directors chosen by President George W. Bush along with Helaine Barnett, LSC president (Photo taken in 2009). (Courtesy of Legal Services Corporation)

On the surface, these choices spelled trouble ahead for LSC grantees, their lawyers, and clients. But Strickland was an unusual Federalist Society member. True, he had been very active in Republican politics, starting shortly after his graduation from law school in 1966. At that time, the Republican Party didn't even bother holding statewide primaries in the state of Georgia, because their candidates stood little or no chance in the general elections against whoever won the Democratic primary. Strickland spent years working toward turning Georgia into a two-party state and along the way became friends with many candidates and other leaders in the state Republican Party. For years, Strickland owned coastal property with Paul Coverdell, one of the few Republicans in the Georgia House of Representatives, a friend who later became the Peace Corps director under George H.W. Bush and then a U.S. senator. Although never a candidate for partisan office, Strickland served as general counsel of the Georgia Republican Party and on the board of the Republican National Lawyers Association.[37]

But Strickland also was active in causes beyond the Republican Party. His public service included 11 years as a member of the Fulton County Board of Registration and Elections and several years as a member and chair of the State Ethics Commission. But of most relevance, he had been deeply involved in legal aid for almost two decades—serving on the executive committee of the Atlanta Legal Aid

Society and the boards of both the Federal Defender Program and the Georgia Legal Services Program. In the mid-1980s, while president of the Atlanta Bar Association, Strickland led the effort to provide pro bono lawyers for Cuban detainees held at the Atlanta Federal Penitentiary, a program that earned the Atlanta bar the prestigious Harrison Tweed award from the ABA. Strickland also was an active member of the ABA, and even served in its policy-making body, the House of Delegates.[38]

Strickland's work with the Atlanta Legal Aid Society earned the admiration of that organization's long-time executive director, Steve Gottlieb, also a national leader in the legal services community. Strickland's bar association work as well as legal aid activities likewise brought him into contact with Bucky Askew, a member of Clinton's LSC board. Askew, remember, had a three-decade involvement in civil legal aid going all the way back to his service on the staff of the OEO-LSP in the 1960s and including leadership positions on both the LSC and National Legal Aid and Defender Association (NLADA) staffs. Askew was impressed enough about Strickland's commitment to legal services that, shortly after George W. Bush's election, he had called Strickland and suggested he might want to put in his name for a seat on the LSC board. Strickland thought about it for a while and then sent in his application to the White House. With his deep and long-standing Republican roots, it was no surprise he was not only nominated to the LSC board, but asked to be its chair.[39]

But few in the legal services community knew of these positive signs and even fewer trusted Strickland's commitment. Many still had memories of the "bad old days" when Reagan's boards tried to kill the LSC and even more of them were just recovering from the wounds the Republican Congress had inflicted on the program while Gingrich was in power. For most, it was hard to imagine George W. Bush would appoint a board friendly to legal services grantees and their lawyers. So Strickland and his board took over amidst an atmosphere of uncertainty and distrust.

Strickland was aware the incoming board undoubtedly would be viewed with some suspicion. At an early meeting at LSC headquarters, he called together all the corporation staff members. After the usual introductions and preliminaries, Strickland rose to speak for the first time to the nearly hundred assembled in the conference room, many of whom had never known any LSC board but the one Clinton appointed over a decade earlier. He faced a solemn group, with many crossed arms in the audience.

"How many of you know Steve Gottlieb, the director of the Atlanta Legal Aid Society?" Strickland asked. Almost half of the audience raised their hands. "Well, I want you to know something. I consider Steve my mentor in the legal services field. I was fortunate enough to serve on his board for many years. I learned a lot from him—and continue to do so."[40]

This comment was intended to convey a message to the LSC staff and perhaps through them to LSC grantees and their lawyers around the country: this new LSC board did not view legal aid lawyers as the enemy, nor consider what they did for their clients as something that should be stamped out.

On that same visit to Washington, Strickland asked for a meeting at the White House with President Bush's Domestic Policy staff. He wanted to know the White House's intentions toward the LSC. Early in the meeting Strickland made his own position clear. "If you want to eliminate the Legal Services Corporation or starve it for funds, I'm not your man. So I want to know if you expect to include a decent appropriation for the corporation in the president's budget for the next fiscal year."[41]

The response was unequivocal. The Bush administration had no problems with the LSC. The president's budget again would include a request maintaining the LSC at or near its current level. (In fact, nearly

Frank Strickland, LSC board chair, 2003–2009.
(Courtesy of Legal Services Corporation)

every budget year the Bush administration requested a flat appropriation of $310 million, even when that would represent a cut from the
higher level Congress had set the previous years.)[42] Strickland and
his board were free to operate the corporation without interference
from the administration. And indeed, this proved to be the last contact
Strickland had with the Bush White House the remainder of his term
as LSC chair—other than one informal meeting with OMB staff and
several conversations about prospective candidates when the administration was considering new appointments to the LSC board.[43]

Strickland soon learned this was to be a more demanding and
time-consuming job than he had expected. Although the new board
had inherited an effective and highly regarded interim president, John
Erlenborn, by this time the elderly former congressman was beginning
to experience serious health problems. He was seldom able to come to
the office to supervise the staff or make the hard decisions. As a result,
Strickland soon found himself wearing two hats—board chair and de
facto president of the Legal Services Corporation. This required him
to commute between Atlanta and Washington on a regular basis, jug-
gling his full-time law practice and nearly full-time job as head of the
LSC.[44] This made it all the more urgent the board pick a permanent
LSC president to replace the failing John Erlenborn.

Despite the dual burden he was already carrying, Strickland appointed himself chair of the presidential search committee. At his
suggestion, the committee hired an international executive recruiting
firm, Heidrick and Struggles, which has a large office in his home city
of Atlanta. That firm assigned Ellen Brown to lead the LSC search.
She was a lawyer who had handled pro bono cases when in private
practice, and thus had some sense of what the assignment involved.[45]

While the search for a permanent LSC president was proceeding,
Strickland turned to another critical task. Having made overtures to
the grantee community and the Bush administration, he now had to
take some soundings with another critical constituency—Congress.
He had the help of the LSC's director of government relations, now
Tom Polgar who had monitored the Reagan board for Senator Rudman in the 1980s. They set up private meetings with a dozen of the
critical senators and members of Congress—primarily the chairs and
ranking members of the appropriations and oversight committees in
both houses. In most instances, Strickland was able to sit down with
the legislator himself or herself, although in three, the meeting was
with the member's chief of staff.[46]

He received warm receptions from most, among them Democratic
senator Tom Harkin and Republican senator Pete Domenici, both
strong supporters of the corporation.[47] Harkin, in fact, was a former
legal services lawyer and an influential member of the HELP committee. Domenici had assembled the coalition that defeated Senator

Gramm's attempt to phase out LSC in the Senate during 1996. Nearly everywhere, Strickland was treated cordially. Although John Erlenborn was too ill to accompany Strickland on most of these visits, a number of the Republican lawmakers remarked the presence of their old colleague at LSC gave them comfort.[48]

Erlenborn was able to accompany Strickland to an early appropriations committee hearing, however, which proved helpful. "John obviously was greatly respected by members of Congress," Strickland said. "Those good feelings washed over the rest of us and over LSC." Nevertheless, some Republican committee members stressed they would be watching Strickland and his board closely and checking how well they kept LSC grantees in check.[49]

Although Strickland's first round of meetings in senatorial and congressional offices were cordial and often productive, later on he had a less happy experience, leading to a confrontation that tested Strickland's mettle. An aide from a congressional office that had no jurisdiction over the LSC asked Strickland to come over for a chat. When the LSC chair arrived, however, he was confronted with staff members representing a half-dozen other Republican Congress members. One of them began with a classic cross-examination question: "Isn't it true, Mr. Strickland, that . . .?"

Strickland soon realized he had been set up. Instead of responding to further questions, he objected firmly, "Number one, I was invited by one person for a private meeting to answer his questions—not anyone else's. Instead I find all of you here. Number two, I don't intend to be cross-examined by anyone."

After a moment of stunned silence, the atmosphere changed. The intimidators had been intimidated—or at least made aware they weren't facing someone whose job depended on gaining their favor. The meeting then continued under the original ground rules and in a civil manner. Strickland answered most of the questions and promised to follow-up on the rest. He left feeling he may have garnered renewed respect for the Legal Services Corporation among the staffs of some of the corporation's chief critics.[50]

Had he happened to read the right wing publication, *Human Events,* well regarded by an element within Congress and a favorite outlet for Howard Phillips, Strickland might have been especially thankful he didn't face more trouble in his meetings with lawmakers. In its March 16, 2003, issue, which came out shortly before Strickland was sworn in as LSC board chair, *Human Events* named its "Ten Most Outrageous Government Programs." At the top of the list—the Legal Services Corporation which Strickland had signed on to run. The *Human Events* list was compiled by 18 "conservative public policy experts," among them Howard Phillips, Phyllis Schafly, and Dick Armey. Other government programs marked as "outrageous" included the

McCain–Feingold Campaign Finance Reform Act, which came in second, and Amtrak, which came in seventh. To prove the panel of "conservative policy experts" was nonpartisan, the article pointed out that 6 of the 10 outrageous programs were created by Republican presidents—five (including LSC) by Nixon and one by Herbert Hoover.[51]

"CIVIL GIDEON"—A MOVEMENT ARISES SPONTANEOUSLY OUTSIDE THE LSC AND THE EXISTING STATE COORDINATING BODIES

The George W. Bush years also saw the birth of a new movement that someday may overtake the LSC as the main advance in the development of equal justice for the poor in the United States. The history of civil legal aid during the final four decades of the 20th century and the first decade of the 21st century has centered on LSC and its grantees, augmented more recently by the activities of IOLTA committees and Access to Justice Commissions at the state level. In the past few years, however, a new initiative sprung up spontaneously and has brought new energy and spun a new vision for the future of civil legal aid in the United States—the notion that poor people should have legal counsel as *a matter of right* not mere charity or legislative discretion or plain good luck.

People had been advocating for that right over the years[52] ever since the Supreme Court found a right to counsel in criminal cases in its 1963 opinion, *Gideon v. Wainwright*.[53] The principle gained additional credibility from the fact most European countries and several elsewhere in the world already had a right to counsel in civil cases going back decades and even centuries.[54] In 1979, the European Court on Human Rights went further, holding that since the language of the European Convention entitled indigent civil litigants to a "fair hearing" this meant they had a right to free counsel in civil cases because it was the only way for them to receive that fair hearing.[55] This right to counsel extended to all nations in the European Community and raised an obvious question. If most of the world's industrial democracies gave their poor people a right to free counsel in civil cases, why not here? (These foreign developments will be discussed in more detail in chapter 30.)

This growing momentum came to a screeching halt, however, when the U.S. Supreme Court issued its *Lassiter* opinion in 1981.[56] For nearly two decades there was no movement and little talk about the issue in the United States. But then in the late 1990s, independent of each other, a few lawyers in Maryland and the state of Washington began exploring the possibility a right to counsel might exist under their state constitutions—so-called "independent state grounds" not based on the U.S. Constitution or the U.S. Supreme Court's interpretation of that constitution. If a right to counsel could be found in a provision within a state constitution, the U.S. Supreme Court's decision in *Lassiter* would be irrelevant for poor people in that state. Under the "adequate and independent state grounds" doctrine, the nation's high court would refrain from using its interpretation of the federal constitution to override a state court's interpretation of its own constitution.[57]

In Maryland, the impetus came from some lawyers involved in the Public Justice Center (PJC), a private nonprofit organization focused on major public interest legal advocacy. Among the leaders on this issue were Clint Bamberger, a former PJC board member, Wilhelm Joseph, who headed Maryland's statewide legal services agency, Professor Michael Millemann from the University of Maryland's law school, and Steve Sachs, a former Maryland attorney general and for several years a pro bono volunteer at the center.[58] In Washington state, it was the so-called "Jurisprudence" Committee of the Access to Justice Board chaired by Leonard Schroeter that, starting in the late 1990s, spent several years researching the potential arguments for a civil right to counsel. Schroeter was in his 70s, a wealthy, semiretired personal injury lawyer who had begun his career a half century earlier on the staff of the NAACP Legal Defense Fund in the days that office was building toward its victory in *Brown v. Board of Education*.[59] So he was familiar with constitutional litigation as a route to justice.

Slowly, those behind the Maryland and Washington right to counsel initiatives began exposing others in their legal communities to the theories and arguments favoring the right. They wrote articles in local legal publications, sponsored panel discussions, and brought in outside speakers.[60] Soon judges and other lawyers who had never entertained the possibility of a right to counsel in civil cases had at least begun to think about the concept. The ground had been seeded and it was time to bring a case—which happened in both states early in the 21st century. In 2002, Maryland's Public Justice Center filed a brief in *Frase v. Barnhart,* appealing a denial of appointed counsel to a mother in a child custody case, among the many in which the legal aid program lacked the resources to provide representation.[61] In 2003, advocates in Washington filed an appeal in a similar child custody case, *King v. King*.[62]

Still, these two state initiatives at opposite ends of the country remained local anomalies until the November 2003 NLADA conference. Debra Gardner of Maryland's Public Justice Center and Debi Perluss, from Washington's Northwest Justice Center, led a panel discussion on this topic that had mostly lain fallow since 1981. After articulating the several constitutional bases for a right to counsel in civil cases, they urged a state-by-state strategy that completely ignored the federal courts and thus avoided *Lassiter*.[63]

At the end of the well-attended panel discussion, Gardner invited anyone who wanted to participate in a continuing conversation via conference call to sign on to a list at the back of the room. Dozens of attendees provided their names, phone numbers, and e-mail addresses. Thus was born the "National Coalition for a Civil Right to Counsel," which quickly grew to over 150 members in more than 30 states and still holds monthly conference calls. The participants included legal services lawyers, several law professors, and partners in major corporate law firms, among others. With this new loose-knit coalition carrying the banner and "civil Gideon" as its rallying call, the right to counsel movement entered the national scene.[64] In the next few years, the movement would experience successes and disappointments, form a small consortium to support and coordinate the coalition,[65] employ a full-time staff member,[66] refine its ultimate goal, expand the strategies for reaching that goal beyond constitutional litigation,[67] and face resistance from unexpected quarters.[68] But it has moved forward—in a sense, against all odds.

THE LSC FINALLY GAINS A NEW PRESIDENT

In November 2003, at about the same time the "civil Gideon" movement first surfaced at the NLADA conference, the search for a permanent LSC president neared its conclusion. LSC had posted notice of the position in June 2003. After the selection committee screened scores of applications and interviewed nearly 15 semifinalists, it finally was in a position to submit three finalists at the November meeting of the full LSC board.[69]

After the board interviewed all three finalists, they selected Helaine Barnett as LSC's new president, an unexpected choice for a Republican-appointed board given she was a veteran legal services lawyer. Barnett was the first former legal aid lawyer to be chosen as LSC president since the Carter board hired Dan Bradley a quarter century earlier. While Bradley had been in the first "Reggie" class in 1967, he only worked as a frontline legal services lawyer for two years before joining the OEO-LSP staff. As a result, most of his legal aid experience was as an administrator at the funding agency not providing legal representation to poor people. Barnett, on the other hand, had spent her entire 37-year career on the staff of the Legal Aid Society of New York. A graduate of NYU Law School, among other assignments she had served in the appellate unit and personally argued more than 100 appeals on her way to heading the society's civil division with its 8 offices and 130 lawyers. Because the Legal Aid Society had given up LSC funding after the Gingrich Congress restricted what the society could do for its clients, Barnett's civil division could report its lawyers had benefited 200,000 poor New Yorkers through class actions as well as the 30,000 individual clients it was able to represent.[70]

Not only was Barnett the first legal aid lawyer to be chosen as LSC president, she also was the first woman, although three—Alice Daniel, Emilia DiSanto, and Martha Bergmark, had each served brief stints as interim president while earlier boards searched for replacements. Barnett was all the more remarkable for being married to the long-time CEO of a large international corporation. A woman who could have spent her life in leisure, Barnett instead had chosen to labor long hours in service to New York's poor, not for a year or two but for nearly four decades. While Barnett was managing the civil division, she also had been very active in the organized bar, occupying several leadership positions, capped by a three-year term as the first legal aid lawyer to serve on the ABA board of governors, the small group that runs the 400,000 member organization.[71]

In the end, Helaine Barnett's selection as LSC president was a near unanimous choice.[72] The combination of commitment to legal aid, her

Helaine Barnett, LSC president, 2003–2009.
(Courtesy of Legal Services Corporation)

stature in the legal profession, and leadership experience proved irresistible. The Bush board's selection of a career legal aid lawyer as the LSC's president had the additional virtue of sending an unexpected but reassuring message to LSC grantees, their lawyers, and clients.

HELAINE BARNETT'S FIRST TEST AS LSC PRESIDENT

Barnett assumed office on January 20, 2004, relieving Frank Strickland of his second assignment as the *de facto* LSC president. She had barely settled into her office at LSC headquarters when she had to defend the LSC before a congressional oversight committee on two issues.[73] That committee was now chaired by Congressman Chris Cannon, one of the most conservative lawmakers in the country. He was in his fifth term from one of the nation's most conservative districts—the Utah third—and enjoyed a 96 percent rating from the Conservative Caucus.[74] Cannon had voted against LSC at every opportunity and, over the next four years, seemed bent on making life as difficult as possible for the LSC staff and board.

This was Barnett's initial exposure to Cannon or a congressional committee hearing of any sort. The first issue on the agenda revolved around whether the clients of LSC-funded programs should be required to make copayments for the services they received, representation that currently was entirely free. Barnett handled this inquiry rather easily, documenting Congress had rejected this policy change on several occasions.[75]

Congressman Cannon then called an outside witness, Jeanne Charn, who headed Harvard's large clinical office. She explained Harvard's program did charge copayments and thought this was a good policy. But during questioning, she also revealed that the Harvard office didn't ask clients with incomes under the poverty line to make copayments unless they won a substantial monetary recovery as a result of the program's representation. Harvard only expected upfront copayments from the lower-middle class clients its lawyers and students served, a population they could represent because LSC was not funding the program.[76] So the discussion with the subcommittee members dissolved into a philosophical exchange expressing regret LSC grantees were limited to providing legal services to the truly poor and couldn't reach up to others who so often couldn't afford to hire counsel.[77]

But another issue had prompted Congressman Cannon to convene the oversight hearing—some charges against California Rural Legal Assistance. As usual, agribusiness—this time in the form of the Western United Dairymen—had persuaded a California congressman to present the original complaints in September 2000. But after a thorough investigation, LSC had dismissed those charges as having no substance. In a December 18, 2000, report [during John McKay's tenure as LSC president], the investigation team sent out by LSC's Office of Compliance and Enforcement concluded, "A review of the totality of circumstances . . . has demonstrated that CRLA did not act in violation of the applicable restrictions and that CRLA maintained program integrity with the Foundation."[78] (The "Foundation" was California Rural Legal Assistance Foundation [CRLAF], the independent but affiliated non-LSC-funded entity that litigated class actions and carried out other restricted representation CRLA itself was barred from offering their clients.)

Another California congressman had been prevailed upon to request a second investigation on June 11, 2001. This time LSC's inspector general received the complaint and undertook a 30-month investigation. The IG's report stated the investigators had found CRLA guilty of several violations.[79] Under LSC's regulations, CRLA had an opportunity to respond—either agreeing with an allegation, disagreeing, or changing its policies to cure the problem. To the extent CRLA disagreed with the IG, the LSC staff was to try resolving the differences. If unsuccessful in those negotiations, the LSC president was to appoint a neutral "arbitrator" whose decision would be final.[80]

Barnett's testimony on the CRLA issue was limited to explaining the total three-stage process after the IG issues a report and pointing out that process had not yet run its course when Congressman Cannon convened his oversight subcommittee to review the IG's allegations.[81] A Democrat on the subcommittee, William Delahunt of Massachusetts, picked up this theme from Barnett's testimony and hammered the point home. "When viewed in the larger context of our responsibilities, for us to be conducting this inquiry . . . is premature, without having the administrative oversight function that we've invested in LSC concluded."[82]

This may have been Barnett's first exposure to a congressional hearing as LSC president, but not for Jose Padilla, CRLA's long-time executive director, when he took the witness chair. As he explained, "During my [20 year] tenure alone, CRLA has gone through five extensive Federal audits and a number of investigations. . . . During my tenure—and indeed since the Legal Services Corporation Act was enacted in 1974—no program review, audit nor investigation has found any instance of material noncompliance by CRLA with the Act and its implementing regulations."[83]

IG Kirt West's investigation was the longest and most extensive CRLA had undergone since the veto controversy and hearings in 1971. But at this stage of the process, little remained outstanding between West and CRLA that LSC would be required to resolve. As Padilla pointed out in his testimony, "After the extensive review by the IG of hundreds of case files, hundreds of financial transactions, numerous staff interviews, and weeks of on-site field office visits, there was good news. No financial irregularities, no violation of LSC rules were found that required any form of penalty, nor any form of formal Federal intervention."[84]

Only three issues remained for the committee to probe.

First, $514 in interest CRLA did not charge the CRLAF when it collected overdue rent payments owed on premises it rented to this affiliated corporation. The IG considered this a violation of the LSC regulation prohibiting an LSC-funded program from subsidizing an affiliated program that carried out prohibited representation. Padilla argued this $514 was a *de minimus* "subsidy." But when pressed by Congressman Cannon, the CRLA head pledged to collect interest on overdue rent payments in the future.[85]

Second, the IG charged CRLA had "shared" some staff members with CRLAF in the sense that part of the salaries of some CRLA lawyers were paid by CRLAF for work on CRLAF cases. Padilla pointed out LSC regulations permitted such sharing, if limited to 10 percent of total staff time, and that only 2 percent of CRLA's staff hours were shared with and paid by the foundation. He volunteered to place a 5-percent limit on CRLA, even though LSC's standard remained at 10 percent. But he disagreed with West's proposed requirement only junior CRLA lawyers be allowed to spend time working part-time for the foundation.[86]

The final open issue was whether CRLA had to divulge to the opposing parties in their litigation the names and the alleged complaints of everyone who sought their services, even those who chose not to participate in the cases CRLA filed. The fact one has become a lawyer's client is ordinarily considered confidential under state ethical codes and what you tell your lawyer about your problem is even more carefully protected. In California, a lawyer revealing that information is subject to discipline from the state bar. Padilla explained the reasons many of CRLA's clients wanted to keep their identities confidential.[87]

> Where clients have explicitly chosen not to be plaintiffs [and thus not have their names included on public pleadings filed in court] for fear of landlord or employer retribution, the choice must be honored. The IG's position appears to be inconsistent with the requirements of the LSC regulation, statutory language, and with our own ethical responsibilities.[88]

Understandably, the congressmen had no questions or comments about this issue.

During the hearing, the congressmen sometimes mentioned they would be asking Barnett more questions about the CRLA investigation. But they never returned to her after interrogating Padilla. If the new LSC president took anything from her first exposure to a congressional committee, it would have been that what she and LSC did was under close scrutiny. Fair warning—when making decisions in her role as LSC president, remember Congress was looking over her shoulder.

In her six years as LSC president, this was to be one of eight congressional hearings at which Helaine Barnett testified. But it was the last one focusing on the alleged misbehavior of an LSC grantee or significant substantive policy issues. Instead in the future she was to find Congress and the corporation's IG holding a magnifying glass on matters closer to home—the conduct of the LSC board and staff.

THE "CIVIL GIDEON" MOVEMENT HAS A MIXED RESULT IN ITS FIRST COURT TEST

From its beginning at the 2003 NLADA conference, a guiding tenet of the new "civil *Gideon*" movement had been that state courts and state constitutions were the best hope. By that time, the first case to test this state-by-state strategy, *Frase v. Barnhart,* was on its way to the Maryland Court of Appeals (the highest court in that state). The trial court had refused to appoint counsel for an indigent mother in a child custody case where the other side had hired a lawyer, and the mother had lost at trial. Steve Sachs, the former state attorney general, represented Ms. Frase in her appeal to the Court of Appeals. His brief raised constitutional issues based on the due process and "access to justice" clauses of the Maryland constitution. Sachs coupled these constitutional arguments with an innovative common law claim based on Maryland's status as one of the original 13 colonies that apparently adopted the civil right to counsel the English Parliament had first enacted in 1495.[89]

When the Maryland Court of Appeals' opinion came down on December 11, 2003, it was both disappointing and tantalizingly encouraging. That court has seven members. All voted to reverse the lower court's decision against the mother, Ms. Frase. But a majority—four of the seven—refused to reach the denial of counsel issue, arguing it was moot because they already had decided in the mother's favor on the merits.[90] The other three, however, including Chief Judge Robert Bell, not only would have reached the right to counsel issue but also argued the mother had a legal right to have appointed counsel.

Writing for his two colleagues, Judge David Cathell first explained why the majority opinion was wrong in refusing to reach the right to counsel issue:

> The majority declines to address an issue I believe to be properly presented that goes to the very center of the American constitutional, and extra-constitutional promises—equality under the law. I am fully aware that there may be serious concerns the reaction of the other branches of government, of the organized Bar (and other members of the profession)

and of the people, in respect to any decision this court might reach in addressing this most important question: do the poor receive equal treatment in a matter concerning the most basic of fundamental, and constitutional, rights—the matter of the custody, visitation, and control of children by their parents? Rather than answer, or attempt to answer it, the question is avoided by a majority of the Court.

It is always easiest to decline to address controversial issues. It is, perhaps, the safest thing to do, even for courts. But the avoiding of such issues is best left to the political processes of the other branches of government. It is our branch of government, the judiciary, under the express and implied doctrine of the separation of powers, to which the toughest and most difficult decisions are delegated. It is our primary role to ensure that the fundamental constitutional rights, which are reserved to the people, are protected. One of the most important roles of the judiciary is to see that the laws equally protect all people—the poor as well as the wealthy.[91]

Judge Cathell then explained why the right to counsel issue was so crucial to society as well as the woman before the court:

I think it can be agreed that the quality of justice received, even in our system, arguably the best system of justice ever conceived, is impacted by the presence or absence, and the quality of, legal representation of the respective parties. I readily understand that it may well be beyond our power to create a perfectly equal system, but, that acknowledged, there is no acceptable reason to avoid doing what we can do, even if it is perceived that what we do may not be well received by other governmental entities that will have to address the impact of our rulings.

* * * * *

While I certainly cannot speak for the individual judges of this Court, it is my belief that there is no judge on this Court that believes in his or her heart or mind, that justice is equal between the poor and the rich. . . . With the constraints of the adversarial court system, and the prohibitions it (and our cases) place upon judges not to assist either side, the poor, unrepresented parent faced with experienced counsel on the other side is at a great, system-built-in, disadvantage.

[A]s to the "due process" and "law of the land" provisions contained in the Declaration of Rights of the Maryland Constitution, we are not constrained by the limitations the United States Supreme Court has appeared to place upon the interpretation of federal constitutional provisions.

* * * * *

We should all try to imagine how it must feel to be utterly poor and to receive a summons from the hands of a sheriff informing us that we are required to appear in court because either the State or some third party is attempting to terminate our parental rights, or to interfere with them, and we don't have any money with which to hire a lawyer. The poor face fears without the security of the money that many others have. And it can be terrifying, to realize how helpless you are when others are attempting to take your children from you.[92]

Finally, Judge Cathell announced how he and his two colleagues would decide the issue they felt was properly and urgently before the whole court.

> I would reach the [right to counsel] issue. More important I would resolve it by holding that in cases involving the fundamental right of parents to parent their children, especially when the parent is a defendant and not a plaintiff, counsel should be provided for those parents who lack independent means to retain private counsel. Whether there should be a panel that weeds out frivolous cases, whether there should be permanent civil public attorneys, whether courts should have the power to appoint counsel and apportion the costs to specific entities, are for others to resolve, or, perhaps, a matter for this Court to resolve in a different context under our rule making authority and our role as the overseer of our profession.[93]

So the civil *Gideon* movement lost a court decision in Maryland by a single vote, while gaining an eloquent and persuasive opinion signed by three judges that offered some hope for the future. Meanwhile, in the nation's capital, the LSC was busy with the here and now not the future and the hope.

LIFE UNDER THE MICROSCOPE: WHEN THERE ARE NO BIG PROBLEMS, LITTLE ONES WILL HAVE TO DO

In contrast to the previous two decades and three presidents, the eight years of the George W. Bush administration brought a period of relative calm to the Legal Services Corporation, its grantees, their lawyers, and clients. The March 2004 oversight hearing on CRLA proved to be a blip not a trend. While LSC failed to gain any significant increases in its LSC budget during the Bush years, it didn't suffer any cuts either. Each year the appropriations sailed through Congress without controversy and usually with voice votes. Indeed, in most years, Congress gave LSC more money than the Bush administration requested.[94] The onerous restrictions remained, but no new ones were imposed.

Unlike some LSC boards in times past, particularly during the Reagan years, the members themselves got along exceedingly well, socializing at dinners after business meetings. Several friendships developed, the most unexpected one between Tom Fuentes, the longtime chair of the Orange County, California, Republican Party, also the board's most conservative member, and Herbert Garten, a prominent Maryland Democrat.[95] Also unlike the first Reagan board that ran into serious problems with Congress over major financial issues, such as allegedly profiteering by claiming compensation at levels nearly as generous as directors of General Motors and other major manufacturing corporations earned, this time LSC's fiercest opponents inside and outside Congress were reduced to sniping about rather trivial expenditures and housekeeping details.

Congressman Cannon was one of the members Strickland had met with during his initial round of meetings, because he occupied a key role as chair of the House Oversight Subcommittee with jurisdiction over the LSC. This, more than any others within the legislative branch, was to become an ongoing relationship for Strickland and Barnett. Unlike prior oversight committees, however, the Cannon committee fixated primarily on happenings at LSC headquarters, rather than what legal services grantees and their lawyers were doing in the field.

The first of these "little problems" produced a huge cloud of smoke but in the end not even a spark to say nothing of a fire. It began when Congressman Cannon raised a furor while Strickland was still doing double duty as board chair and de facto president. It revolved around a transaction Strickland inherited from the Clinton-appointed board—the purchase of a building to house LSC's headquarters. For the first quarter century of its existence the LSC had bounced around the District of Columbia, leasing space in a series of private office buildings. While he was LSC president, John McKay had become convinced it was important for the corporation to have its own headquarters building—for both practical and symbolic reasons. It would signal to all that the Legal Services Corporation was here to stay, a permanent part of the nation's governmental structure.[96]

McKay found a location, a virtually empty lot, perfectly situated only a few blocks from the Capitol building, the Senate and House office buildings, the Supreme Court, and the Georgetown Law School campus. But that deal fell through when LSC couldn't come up with the financing. So it was after John Erlenborn took over as the interim LSC president before the board found a new building and put together a creative financing arrangement that would allow the corporation to become the owner—eventually.

This building was traditional in appearance—four stories of dark red brick—and located far from Capitol Hill in an area of Georgetown on the Potomac River. The Bill and Melinda Gates Foundation provided $4 million for a down payment. A new separate nonprofit entity, Friends of the Legal Services Corporation, was formed to own the building, hold the mortgage, and act as landlord. LSC staff occupied roughly three-quarters of the space and other tenants rented the remainder. The LSC made its lease payments from funds it otherwise would be using to pay rent on a private office building somewhere in Washington. When the mortgage was paid off, the Friends of the Legal

William Gates Sr., chair of Bill and Melinda Gates Foundation, and Helaine Barnett, LSC president. (Courtesy of Legal Services Corporation)

Services Corporation would hand the building over and LSC would own the building outright.[97]

This appeared to be a sound arrangement to those involved in setting it up. But not to the LSC's IG, Kirt West, whom Strickland and his fellow board members had hired. He wrote a report lambasting the transaction, questioning LSC's legal authority to form a second corporation, or to sign a 10-year lease with that corporation.[98] Congressman Cannon shared West's concern and inquired about the issue during hearings before his oversight committee.[99] All this attention to the Friends of the Legal Services Corporation and the 10-year lease aroused Senator Grassley and he requested a Government Acountability Office (GAO) investigation of the entire arrangement.

Senator Grassley's request turned out to be a favor for LSC. On September 14, 2006, GAO's general counsel sent an eight-page letter responding to the issues the senator raised. In that letter, GAO completely absolved LSC, finding it had legal authority to do everything it had done. "The Legal Services Corporation Act and the D.C. Nonprofit Corporation Act," the opinion letter concluded, "confer broad investment authority and discretion, allowing LSC to establish Friends and to enter into a lease with Friends for office space."[100]

LSC headquarters building. (Courtesy of Legal Services Corporation)

With this exoneration by GAO, the issue of LSC's headquarters building and its financing simply faded away. By this time the building—which LSC will own in the future—already had increased 50 percent in value, LSC's rent was 10 percent below comparable buildings in the District of Columbia and less than LSC had been paying to rent elsewhere in the city.[101]

The complaint about the financial arrangements for LSC's building, although of questionable merit, at least involved high stakes—the validity of a multimillion dollar transaction and whether LSC would be able to have a permanent headquarters building. But LSC also was subjected to a succession of minor complaints, what some might characterize as "nit-picks," that were blown up to look like major scandals. As is usually true, the charges captured the headlines, the truth barely registered with the press.

Some examples will have to suffice.[102]

One charge—LSC officials are motoring around Washington in limousines when taxis or the Metro would do. The response—the only time taxis or the Metro was not used was on a single occasion when Strickland and Barnett hired a regular car—not a limousine—because they had a full-day of appointments and tight deadlines around the greater Washington area—visits to congressional offices in different buildings, attending John Erlenborn's funeral and then his burial in Arlington Cemetery, some of these locations taxis didn't frequent, then back for another meeting on the hill, and finally on to the airport so Strickland could catch his 6 PM return flight to Atlanta.

A second charge—the board was feasting on lavish desserts while the poor people their lawyers served were starving. The response, a hotel where an LSC board meeting was being held gave the name "death by chocolate" and charged $14 a head for the chocolate chip cookies, coffee, tea, and cokes it served for a mid-afternoon break.

A third charge—LSC officials regularly flew first class. The response—Helaine Barnett once flew first class on an exhausting trip to Ireland so she could attend an international legal aid conference with the heads of legal aid programs from more than 20 countries, thinking the airline was using her frequent flyer miles to upgrade her reservation from economy to first class, and upon learning otherwise paid the difference.

It had long been true that the board and staff of the LSC were held to a different standard than others paid with federal funds. Because its beneficiaries languished in poverty, LSC was expected to scrimp just as its clients had to. Any suggestion the board or staff leadership was living well on the LSC dime was viewed much more harshly than it would if personnel at some government agency or government-funded entity had done the same. That attitude came to the surface most dramatically in 1982, when as will be recalled, the first Reagan-appointed board was taken to task by a Republican congressman, Caldwell Butler, among others, for claiming compensation as high as $25,000 a year. But because Congress put an end to that possibility by cutting out compensation for anything other than board meetings, later boards including the one Strickland led were doing most of their work for LSC on a pro bono basis. And it also meant the complaints about supposedly excessive expenditures were miniscule compared to what happened in 1982—measured in the hundreds of dollars instead of the scores of thousands.

None of these alleged deeds broke or bent any statutes or regulations, even if they conceivably might have if done by federal officials, because by law LSC was not a federal agency but a private, nonprofit corporation. Other than the salary and benefits paid its president, and compensation limits on its board members, which were the subject of congressional legislation, LSC was free to set its own policies for transportation, hotel accommodations, meals, and the like for its board and staff. Nonetheless, in order to avoid any further criticism about these and any possible minor deviances from federal government practices, in 2006 LSC instituted rules that brought the corporation into line with the standards applicable to federal agencies.[103]

This near constant stream of minor accusations cost the LSC board and staff a disproportionate amount of time and resources. As Strickland observed later, "We would be forced to spend $5,000 preparing a response to a claim questioning a $500 expenditure. Usually it came to nothing. But in the meantime we had wasted time and resources that would have been better spent on running the legal services program."[104]

The LSC's own inspector general, Kirt West, filled his periodic reports with these and still other, often even less significant complaints about the LSC board and headquarters staff operations. Some board members became so frustrated with the time and expense LSC had to devote to responding to these allegations that they suggested maybe it was time to consider getting rid of West. Indeed the board's vice chair, Professor Bevier, who also chaired the performance review committee made the harshest comments. After a meeting of her committee considering West's performance, Bevier reported to the full board:

"So that to have that [LSC's good works] undermined by allegations that are deemed—that we regard as unwarranted, and that are at least, presented in an inflammatory way, . . . seems to be not in the corporation's best interest. . . . We plan to have outside counsel review that with an eye to the possibility, and I stress that, I *really stress that we are only sort of thinking about the possible worst-case scenario,* which would be possibly deciding that we had to let Kirt go, and we reduce that to writing, give it to counsel."[105]

Upon hearing about these statements by board members, some congressional critics charged that the board had fired the corporation's IG without notifying Congress as the law required. In fact, the board had not fired West. Instead they only had a speculative discussion about the possibility of taking that step. But Congressman Cannon looked on West as an ally, having shared in the unproductive inquiry into LSC's headquarters building arrangements. He filed a bill, H.R. 6101, to require 9 votes (out of 11) for the LSC board to discharge its inspector general and on September 26, 2006, held a hearing on that bill.[106] Not long after the hearing, Congressman Cannon's bill died in committee.[107] In the meantime, West had been looking for a better-paying job in the private sector and a year later finally landed one and left.[108] A year after that, 2008, Cannon lost his reelection bid, and a thorn was removed from the side of LSC.

RESPONDING TO RECOMMENDATIONS FROM THE GOVERNMENT ACCOUNTABILITY OFFICE

On two occasions in 2007, the Government Accountability Office conducted audits of LSC, again at the behest of Senator Charles Grassley.

These GAO audits failed to turn up any scandals or pervasive problems, but did call for some significant changes.[109] Rather than resist or minimize these recommendations, Barnett and the LSC board accepted all of them and used the reports to tighten the corporations' administrative procedures.

As Barnett summarized their efforts, "From the beginning, LSC took the recommendations . . . as helpful technical assistance to improve our own operations. . . . LSC has become a more modern agency; we have improved our internal working relationships; we now use more effective procedures and methods of operation; and our own governance and grants oversight has improved."[110]

That approach evidently paid off. Barnett was able to point out proudly that a follow-up GAO audit in 2009 found "LSC's board of directors and management have made progress on implementing our prior recommendations including fully implementing nine recommendations. . . . The improvements that LSC has made in its governance and accountability provide a good foundation for completing implementation of the elements needed for a strong program of governance and internal controls." In written testimony Susan Ragland, director of financial management and assurance at the Government Accountability Office, observed:. "LSC has made good progress on prior recommendations, implementing more than a dozen major actions to improve board governance, financial and grants oversight and management practices."[111]

Thus, from the mix of minor complaints usually coming from suspect sources and legitimate criticisms and solid recommendations from the Government Accountability Office, Barnett and the LSC board managed to extract some positive administrative changes. It would have been easy for Barnett and Strickland to have become distracted by the constant barrage of minor charges raised by the LSC's IG and some members of Congress. But somehow they managed to remain focused on the needs of the corporation and the performance of its grantees.

THE "JUSTICE GAP" REPORT

Every year the Strickland-led LSC board made its own budget request to Congress usually asking for a substantial increase in funding—even though the Bush administration stuck with its flat funding recommendations for LSC. After three years of failure, watching Congress stay with the Bush recommendation or very close to it, they decided a new strategy was required. Having heard some skepticism expressed by certain congressional critics about the claims of unmet need among poor people, Barnett suggested the LSC conduct its own study and publish the results. The board concurred and the study was underway.[112]

The LSC used three different methodologies in its study.

First, for a period of two months the corporation instructed all LSC grantees to keep track of all the people who came to their offices asking for representation with worthy cases. The grantees then recorded and reported a count of how many of those who applied they had the time and resources to help and how many they had to turn away.

Second, headquarters staff analyzed the nine state "legal needs" studies that universities and other research organizations had conducted among poor people since 2000. These state studies reported the number of legal problems the respondents experienced in a given year and the percentage of those cases in which those individuals or families had been able to obtain legal help—either from legal aid or private attorneys.

Third, the staff counted the total number of lawyers working in all legal aid programs in the country, both those that received LSC funding and those supported entirely by other sources—IOLTA, state governments, private donations, etc. They then divided the number of poor people by the number of legal aid lawyers available to serve them and divided the number of people in the rest of the U.S. population by the number of private lawyers available to help them with their personal legal problems—excluding those lawyers who represent corporations, unions, and the like.[113]

When Barnett shared the draft report with Strickland, he was especially struck by one statistic. For every person they were able to help, legal services grantees had to turn away another eligible person who otherwise merited their help, because they simply didn't have the resources. Strickland told Barnett and the others working on the study, "That's our headline. That's what we should feature with the press and with Congress."[114]

Barnett decided to call the difference between the huge number of legal needs poor people experienced and the negligible resources available to meet those needs the "justice gap." So the report was named, *Documenting the Justice Gap: The Current Unmet Civil Legal Needs of Low-Income Americans*. LSC sent the report to Congress, then distributed it to the media on October 17, 2005. All three methodologies confirmed a serious gap existed.

- From the two-month "unable to serve" survey, the report established that LSC funded grantees had managed to serve 901,067 poor people in 2004, but were forced to turn away 1,085,838 eligible poor people who came to their offices seeking legal assistance. "This shows that for every client served by an LSC-funded program, at least one eligible person seeking help will be turned down."[115]

- From the nine recent state legal needs studies the report summarized, "All nine . . . found that only a very small percentage of the legal problems experienced by low-income people (fewer than one in five) is addressed with the assistance of a private or legal aid lawyers. . . . [A]nalysis of these studies shows that even if the problems considered are limited to those considered to be 'very important' by the household experiencing them and understood by the household to call for legal help, a large majority of the problems are not addressed with the help of a lawyer."[116]

- Finally, the comparison of legal resources available to poor people contrasted with what was available to the rest of Americans helped explain the results of the other two phases of the study. "The count shows that despite the expansion of non-LSC funded programs in the past decade, a substantial majority of attorneys serving the poor still work in LSC-funded programs: there were 3,845 lawyers in LSC-funded programs . . . and an estimated 2,736 in programs that do not receive LSC funding. . . . While there is only one legal aid lawyer (including all sources of funding) per 6,861 low income people in the country, there is one lawyer providing personal civil legal services for every 525 people in the general population."[117]

As Strickland anticipated, the statistic that had the most impact with Congress was the million poor people a year who appeared at legal services offices those lawyers didn't have the time and resources to help. It is obvious that for every person a legal services grantee had to turn away from those who actually sought help at their offices, there were several others who didn't even come to the office. For many it was because they had heard the odds of being helped were not very good. For others it was because they lived too far away from an office to even make the attempt or just didn't know legal aid existed or that they might be eligible for those services. So the 50 percent "turn away" statistic vastly understated the unmet demand for legal services. But at least the fact legal services offices had to turn away half the people who came to them for legal help silenced those members of Congress who somehow believed that fewer than 4,000 LSC-funded lawyers and another couple of thousand other legal aid lawyers could handle the legal problems of some 50 million poor people. This in a country with over a million lawyers, meaning legal aid lawyers represented only six-tenths of a percent of the nation's lawyers, yet were expected to bring justice to nearly a fifth of the nation's population.[118]

In any event, the "Justice Gap" report appeared to have some effect. For the next several years Congress gave LSC modest annual budget increases—in each instance ignoring the lower figure in President Bush's budget. By the last year of George W. Bush's administration, 2008, LSC worked with an appropriation of $350 million[119]—$20 million higher than the first year of that administration[120] (but still some

$410 million short of the FY 1981 "minimum access" budget after adjusting for inflation and $600 million short when taking account of the 25-percent increase in poor people since 1981).[121]

ENCOURAGING PRO BONO SERVICES FROM THE PRIVATE BAR

The LSC regulations had long required local grantees to use 12-1/2 percent of their LSC funds to involve private practitioners in the delivery of legal services to the poverty community. In some places, the grantee agency satisfied this requirement by operating a small "Judicare" program paying private lawyers to represent clients in selected cases. But most grantees used this part of their budget to fund the administration of a pro bono program—enlisting local lawyers willing to volunteer their services, training them, and matching them to cases in a way that maximized their contribution to the overall effort.

At Barnett's urging and with Strickland's strong endorsement, LSC started two initiatives aimed at increasing the level and effectiveness of the pro bono component of their grantees' programs. The first was to encourage local grantees to adopt a "pro bono resolution" committing themselves to expand and improve pro bono efforts in their communities. During Barnett's tenure as LSC president, 107 of LSC's 137 grantee agencies voted to approve such resolutions.[122]

Barnett's second pro bono initiative was to honor the volunteer lawyers themselves, rather than the grantees who were administering those programs. Whenever the LSC board members met outside Washington, they would hold a ceremony and present plaques to local pro bono lawyers the grantee agency identified as having rendered special services to the area's poor people. Strickland did not present the awards, instead deferring to another board member, David Hall, a professor and former dean at Northeastern Law School in Boston. The reason the LSC chair chose this tall, broad-shouldered African American for this role was because, as Strickland remarked, when he spoke in his deep, resonant voice it was a "Moses moment." As Hall finished extolling the virtues of pro bono and the accomplishments of the award recipients, most in the audience had goose bumps and all rose in a standing ovation.[123]

THE ABA JOINS THE "CIVIL GIDEON" MOVEMENT

In August 2005, when Mike Greco assumed the office of ABA president, the emerging "civil Gideon" movement caught a break that would have a payoff a year later and thereafter. Greco had a long history of supporting legal services for the poor, dating back to the mid-1980s when he was Massachusetts Bar Association president and with two other state bar presidents formed "Bar Leaders for the Preservation of Legal Services for the Poor" to counter the Reagan board's efforts to abolish the Legal Services Corporation. He had decided during his year as ABA president-elect in 2004 that he would use his opportunity as ABA president to advance the cause of legal aid to the poor in the United States by making it one of his presidential priorities.

While still president-elect, Greco was scheduled to address the Alabama Bar Foundation's annual dinner in Montgomery, on January 28, 2005. Terry Brooks, who headed the ABA Division for Legal Services, learned of the event and called Greco and filled him in about the National Coalition for a Civil Right to Counsel and its mission. Greco listened with interest to what Brooks had to say about a civil right to counsel, which ended with Brooks asking whether Greco would be willing to possibly just mention the controversial subject in his Alabama remarks. Greco asked for a memorandum providing a more in-depth discussion of the issues.

After reading the memorandum, Greco called Brooks. "Not only will I mention the subject in my speech," Greco told Brooks, "it will be the heart of the speech." He asked Brooks to prepare the first draft. After reading that draft, Greco told Brooks that when he took office as ABA president he would appoint a special presidential task force, to advance the idea of a right to counsel in civil matters. He would charge the task force with preparing a report and a recommendation to the ABA House of Delegates putting the ABA on record as supporting the civil right to counsel, and predicted that the house would approve it.

Brooks was less optimistic, pointing out that having an ABA president even mention it, as Greco was going to do in Alabama, was itself unprecedented and huge progress. Brooks predicted the gestation period would last for many years before the house would support the concept. Greco responded that he did not have many years, but only one year as ABA president, and he was confident the respected task force he intended to appoint would make it happen within his year in office.

When Greco finished speaking at the Alabama Bar Foundation's Annual Dinner he sat down, expecting the usual polite applause. Instead, he looked up to see the entire audience up on their feet, with a rousing and prolonged standing ovation. If this is the reception it receives in Alabama, Greco thought, maybe this civil right to counsel idea has a chance. Not long after that, he appointed the "ABA Presidential Task Force on Access to Justice," and asked it to produce a resolution supporting the right to counsel in civil cases involving legal

Michael Greco, ABA president, 2005–2006. (American
Bar Association Archives)

needs that are basic to human existence, such as shelter, health, and
family. This resolution, in turn, Greco planned to submit to the ABA
House of Delegates at the August 2006 annual meeting in Honolulu.[124]

Greco appointed Justice Howard Dana, twice a member of the
LSC board, to chair the task force. The members included the current
SCLAID chair, Bill Whitehurst, who along with Greco, was one of the
three cofounders of Bar Leaders for the Preservation of Legal Services
for the Poor. Others included a cross-section of legal services lawyers,
bar leaders, National Coalition leaders, and ABA House of Delegates
members.[125] Greco asked me to serve as the "senior advisor" to the
Presidential Task Force, which meant I was part of a three-member
drafting committee, along with Terry Brooks and Debi Perluss, one of
the leaders of the National Coalition.

After a half-dozen full-day meetings held at different locations over
nearly a year, most of them attended by Greco, in May 2006 the Presidential Task Force had a draft resolution and supporting 15-page report that satisfied all its members. Over the next two months Howard
Dana and other task force members managed to line up more than

two dozen cosponsors from ABA sections and state bar associations. It began to appear a near certainty the ABA House of Delegates would approve this landmark resolution by a comfortable margin.

Finally, on the afternoon of August 6, 2006, the resolution reached the floor of the ABA House of Delegates.[126] There, this best laid plan almost went agley, when the ABA family law section complained it had not been consulted and threatened to oppose. This raised the real possibility other delegates would vote to table the proposal until the next ABA meeting six months hence—in order to allow negotiations between the resolution's sponsors and the family law section. Fortunately, one of the resolution's floor managers, Jon Ross, the third cofounder of Bar Leaders for Preservation of Legal Services for the Poor, was a prominent member and former chair of the family law section. He was able to negotiate a compromise acceptable to both sides— merely adding five words to the end of the original resolution—"as determined by each jurisdiction." We on the Presidential Task Force felt this qualification was implicit in the resolution and its supporting report, thus saw no reason not to add the requested language.

Justice Dana appeared before the ABA House of Delegates and moved approval of the resolution. Then, by prearrangement, he accepted the five-word addition the family law section tendered as a friendly amendment. After a few others spoke in favor of the resolution, ABA president Greco, the final speaker to address the house on the resolution, gave an impassioned speech. He told the house that a civil right to counsel would be the defining issue for the ABA and the legal profession in the 21st century; that there have been moments in the long history of the ABA that informed the public of the legal profession's commitment to the public good; and that this was one of those moments; and that the country was waiting to hear where the ABA stood on this fundamentally important issue. He urged the house to approve the resolution, and to do so by a unanimous vote.

When the chair of the House of Delegates asked for all those voting "in favor," there was a thunderous chorus of "yeses." And when he asked for those voting "opposed," there was absolute silence. The ABA House of Delegates, the policy-making body of the nation's 400,000-member association of lawyers, in an historic moment had passed the following resolution without dissent:

> The American Bar Association urges federal, state, and territorial governments to provide counsel as a matter of right at public expense to poor people in cases involving basic human needs such as housing, health, sustenance, safety, and child custody, as determined by each jurisdiction.[127]

This ABA resolution was followed two months later by a similar resolution adopted by the California Conference of Delegates of Bar Associations, an organization composed of representatives from all of that state's local bar associations.[128] In time, the New York, Pennsylvania, and several other state and metropolitan bars followed suit.[129] Several state and local bar associations also created new "right to counsel" committees committed to advancing the ultimate goal the ABA resolution had raised on the horizon.[130] The legal profession in the United States had begun to stir to a new drumbeat.

THE QUEST FOR QUALITY—DEVELOPING PERFORMANCE CRITERIA

The year 2007 marked the fruition of a landmark initiative at the Legal Services Corporation. Except for the first two years of the Clinton administration, since 1980 no LSC board had spent much time attempting to improve the *quality* of the service legal services lawyers provided their clients. When not fighting to maintain or increase LSC's appropriation, John McKay had concentrated on increasing the *quantity* of those services—the numbers of poor people LSC-funded lawyers reached in one way or the other. Before him, the Reagan boards did their best to undermine the program and later LSC leadership was forced into a survival mode. But the relative calm of the George W. Bush era allowed the board and especially its president, Helaine Barnett, to consider how LSC could enhance the performance of the lawyers its grants were financing. "Quality" soon became the new watchword for the corporation and it grantees.[131]

Improving quality was not an easy task. Congress had stripped LSC of the very resources—support centers and a national training program—some earlier boards could rely on to upgrade the representation clients received. What could be done now? Fortunately, answering that question played to Helaine Barnett's strengths. After all, she had spent a decade before her appointment as LSC president heading the civil division of one of the nation's largest legal aid providers, overseeing the work of 130 lawyers. In that role, she had emphasized quality and had some experience with how to move a group of lawyers in that direction. As she later wrote, "From my first days at LSC, it was clear that quality would be a primary emphasis and a personal priority during my presidency. Throughout my professional life, quality has been my priority. Quality legal services are mandated under the LSC statute. . . . It is not enough for a low-income person to have access to a lawyer if it does not result in high quality service."[132]

But Barnett also knew she faced a new challenge in attempting to accomplish that mission on a national scale. It is one thing to improve the performance of a force of lawyers who work directly under you and yet another to influence the behavior of attorneys who are employed by other agencies you only provide with funding—and often just a percentage of that funding.

Convinced of the vital importance of enhancing quality and confident LSC could take steps that would advance that goal, in her first year as LSC president Barnett launched a high-visibility "quality initiative." As she explained, "we approached quality as a multifaceted concept, including a program's capacities and processes and outcomes, both for individual clients and for the population served by the LSC program. Quality involves asking whether the program is taking on the cases reflecting the most critical needs of their client population, is also integrated into the community so that it is aware of the needs of the clients and clients are aware of its services. Quality also requires that the programs are well functioning with strong leadership and motivated staff with a commitment to diversity, adequate training, self-evaluation, and effective use of technology."[133]

For the first year and more, LSC talked quality, had meetings with grantees and their lawyers about quality, and discussed quality with SCLAID and the NLADA. SCLAID was in the midst of a project to rewrite and update the "ABA Standards for the Provision of Civil Legal Aid," a document which itself was designed to improve quality among all providers whether funded by LSC or other sources. Sarah Singleton, later to join the LSC board, chaired the SCLAID task force charged with preparing those standards.[134] This was a useful complement to Barnett's own emphasis on quality.

Despite the impending publication of the revised ABA Standards, anticipated to be released in 2006, Barnett and her staff decided LSC needed to develop its own quality measures tailored to the corporation's statutory goals and limitations. Some of the ABA Standards might well call for legal aid lawyers to do for their clients things the congressional restrictions prevented LSC grantees from doing. After all, as far back as 1903 the original legal aid society's charter called upon its lawyers to "promote protective measures," often new statutes, helpful to their client community. This was something LSC-funded lawyers could no longer legally offer their clients. And indeed, when the ABA Standards were approved and published in August 2006, they included a substantial section instructing legal aid lawyers they "should advocate before legislative bodies or [for those prohibited from doing so] actively participate in a delivery system which includes such advocacy."[135] This standard recognizes that in many states, LSC-funded grantees can make use of one or more legal services agencies not receiving any funding from LSC which employ legislative representatives to advocate for lower-income people before state legislatures and executive departments.

By publishing its own performance measures LSC could both set some goals LSC-funded lawyers could aspire to attain within the bounds of the restrictions and also provide evaluators with guidance in rating and counseling grantees. These criteria could even be used in the design of the refunding application forms grantees were expected to submit and also in picking the successful applicants when a service area was open to a competitive selection process.

Thus, early in 2006, LSC set out to draft what it termed "the LSC performance criteria." Although starting with criteria first promulgated in 1993 and 1994 by the Clinton-appointed board while Alex Forger was LSC president, what Barnett contemplated was a complete overhaul and production of a more comprehensive and sophisticated document than had existed before. To ensure these revised criteria would have credibility with LSC grantees and their lawyers, LSC engaged the field as well as respected outside lawyers and academics in the process. The LSC staff was assisted by a seven-member "advisory committee" including experienced executive directors from LSC-funded grantees along with Alan Houseman and others with a broad perspective on legal services history and philosophy. As they were produced, draft sections also were sent to nine other "draft reviewers," mainly from LSC grantees. A next-to-final draft of the entire document was broadly circulated in the legal services community for comments and suggestions, some of which were embodied in the final publication.[136]

The ABA House of Delegates approved the revised ABA Standards at the association's August 2006 meeting,[137] thus making them official association policy and LSC published its "performance criteria" document in March 2007.[138] The LSC publication also cross-referenced to relevant sections of the ABA Standards. Although there were some important differences between the two documents because they had different purposes, for the most part they reinforced each other. One told LSC-funded legal services lawyers what their profession expected and the other what their funder desired.

The LSC performance criteria set forth a total of 20 criteria divided into 4 "performance areas"—(1) identifying the most pressing needs and targeting resources on those needs,[139] (2) engaging and serving low-income people throughout the service area,[140] (3) effective legal representation and other program activities benefiting the low-income population,[141] and (4) effective governance, leadership, and administration.[142]

In a sense, the "quality initiative" in general and the "LSC performance criteria" in particular constitute the flip side of LSC's compliance function. The latter tells grantees what they *can't* do because of the restrictions and punishes them if they stray beyond those boundaries. The "performance criteria," on the other hand, tell them what they *could and should* do and rewards them for doing more of that for their clients. After publication of the criteria, LSC evaluations began to look closely at both sides of the coin—quality as well as compliance—a strong signal to LSC grantees that high quality and effective lawyering within the confines of the congressional restrictions is what counts.[143]

The LSC performance criteria document was the centerpiece of Barnett's "quality initiative," but not the only important component. She and her staff also expanded the technology program inherited from earlier LSC administrations. In the fall of 2008, LSC convened a conference bringing together IT experts from academia and private law firms, as well as LSC and IOLTA-funded legal services agencies. Based on input from that conference, LSC published a report, *Technology Capacities that Should Be in Place in a Legal Aid Office Today* that was distributed to every LSC grantee, among others. LSC also began requiring each grant application to include a technology plan.[144]

Barnett and her staff also realized LSC was approaching a leadership crisis among its grantees. Fully 40 percent of local grantees were headed by executive directors who had held those jobs for a quarter century or longer.[145] They were from the "Reggie" generation. Not that all of these veteran executive directors were "Reggies," by any means, but those that weren't had joined legal services during the same time period and for the same reasons as those who were. That meant they had arrived from the late 1960s to the early 1980s, and by 2007 had been lawyers anywhere from 25 to more than 40 years. On the whole, they were superb directors of their programs—smart, knowledgeable, capable, often inspirational leaders who had learned how to survive and succeed despite an ever-changing and too often hostile political environment. Preparing the next generation of legal services leaders capable of succeeding them presented a real challenge, one Barnett recognized as critical since she herself was from the "Reggie" generation now approaching retirement. She also saw the need to further diversify the pool of prospective executive directors in the legal services community—giving more women and minorities the kind of training that would prepare them for these positions.[146]

As a start, Barnett and her staff established a pilot program to "mentor" promising younger legal services lawyers. LSC matched each lawyer selected for the pilot program with a well-regarded executive director willing to guide the prospective future director in developing the skills essential to leadership in the complex and difficult world legal services has become.[147] This pilot program provided a template for developing a diverse pool of leaders to run LSC's grantee programs in the future.

Barnett and her staff faced another challenge to quality—helping local grantees attract and retain regular staff members who too often faced educational debts of $100,000 or more by the time they left law school. How could those young lawyers hope to pay off debts of that magnitude with the salaries LSC grantees could afford to pay? The answer was to provide some form of loan forgiveness for lawyers who choose to serve the poor (or engage in other forms of public service) rather than pursuing the much higher pay offered to those who entered private practice. Called a "Loan Repayment Assistance Program" or LRAP, this approach is now offered at over 100 law schools around the country.[148] Typically, during the time a lawyer works in a legal services office or some other designated public service position, the school reduces or delays the repayment obligation on loans extended to those former students. LRAP also is available to public service lawyers through statewide programs in 24 states, some funded by state governments and others financed and administered by bar associations or foundations finance.[149]

Realizing the law school and state programs were only filling part of the need among legal services lawyers, the LSC started its own LRAP on a pilot basis in 2005, after persuading Congress to include a line item in the LSC budget for that purpose. In 2008, the program named for one of LSC's board members, the Herbert Garten Loan Assistance Program, made three-year forgivable loans of $5,600 a year on a competitive basis to some 42 legal services lawyers in 22 different grantee agencies.[150]

THE ELECTION OF PRESIDENT OBAMA RAISES EXPECTATIONS FOR LSC'S FUTURE—ONCE AGAIN

As the 2008 elections brought a new administration to power, this time a Democratic president, Frank Strickland knew his term as LSC board chair would be drawing to a close. Helaine Barnett, already the longest-serving president in LSC history, already had announced she would be stepping down on December 31, 2009, no matter which administration was in power. Both could take some considerable satisfaction in the positive contributions they had made. Rather than coasting, they had taken advantage of what was the quietest eight-year period the corporation had experienced since its birth to institute some measures that promised to enhance the quality and effectiveness of LSC's grantees. No mean accomplishment, especially given what had gone before.

But with a Democratic president on his way to the White House, and that party also in control of both houses of Congress, legal services supporters had even higher expectations for the future—hoping for far more generous LSC appropriations, an end to some of the more onerous restrictions, and an LSC board as fully supportive of their mission as the Clinton board had been. Perhaps, but not certainly, it would work out better this time with a Democrat in the White House than it had during Clinton's time in that office.

On this hopeful but guarded note, I arbitrarily conclude this history of civil legal aid. As with any ongoing institution or movement, events do not come to a halt so an author can put a convenient period at the end of a narrative and claim he has provided a complete history. In the nearly six years I spent researching and writing the foregoing chapters covering 132 years of legal aid history, the legal aid movement marched on. During those six years, its lawyers served millions of clients, opponents kept sniping, supporters continued defending, budgets went up and down, and the future remained hopeful but uncertain. As for the centerpiece of civil legal aid in the United States— the Legal Services Corporation—until a president has left office and the LSC board he appointed is replaced, what happened to legal services during that time is not yet history but remains a current event, always subject to dramatic shifts in course, as the Clinton board found to its dismay.

So the Obama chapter of legal aid history and what may follow it is for another time and another book. The remaining three chapters concern the future, only glancing at the Obama board for a moment while setting the scene for what may come as civil legal aid and justice for the poor move ahead toward what one can hope will be better days.

REPORT FROM THE FIELD: The Satisfaction of Being a Class Action Client

Nearly every class action carries the first "named plaintiff" in the title of the case. Thus it was with Evonne McCain in 1983 when the Legal Aid Society of New York filed a class action on behalf of McCain and thousands of others evicted from their apartments who then unsuccessfully sought decent emergency housing from the city of New York. In 2008, some 25 years and 50 court orders later, New York finally agreed to a settlement in the case then known as *Evonne McCain, et al. v. Michael R. Bloomberg* [New York's Mayor]. The agreement guaranteed suitable emergency shelter for 10,000 families including 17,000 children every night. In an affidavit McCain filed asking the court to approve the settlement, she explained why she had been part of that class action and why it meant so much to her years after she no longer needed the relief it provided others.

> More than 25 years ago, I went to the City for help after my children and I were evicted from our apartment. At first, the City turned us away and said there was no shelter available. Eventually, the City sent my family to the Martinique Hotel, where we stayed for several years.
>
> The mattresses we were given at the Martinique were ripped, burnt, bug-infested, and stained with urine on both sides. The sheets were greasy and stained. The rooms were infested with rats and bugs. We had little heat and often had no hot water. . . . I spent hours sponging

off the mattresses with disinfectant and trying to clean up our rooms. Because the windows in our 11th-floor rooms were jammed open and had no guardrails, I stayed up all night crying, terrified that if I didn't watch them, one of my children might fall out the window.

The Legal Aid Society helped me convince the City to give my family shelter after we had been turned away. I wanted to be part of a lawsuit that Legal Aid would bring on behalf of families like mine to make things better for other families who needed shelter and who ended up at the Martinique. I wanted the lawsuit to help homeless families like mine retain some of their dignity; just because you don't have any place to live doesn't mean you shouldn't have dignity. I didn't want other families to go through what we were going through. But I never thought the lawsuit I brought would be so important and help as many people as it has.

A lot has happened in my life in the past 25 years. In 1996, after moving from one place to another to get away from my abusive husband, my children and I were finally able to settle down in an apartment in Staten Island, which we got through a Section 8 program. I went back to school to become a counselor. My children have grown up and I am a grandmother. I am also a cancer survivor.

Recently, I found out that my cancer has come back. When my lawyer called me in September to discuss the fact that the City had agreed to settle the case, I wasn't feeling very well. But when he told me that, under the settlement, there would be a permanent right to safe, adequate shelter for families like mine, I was so happy and relieved. This is what we went to court for so many years ago, and I am so glad that I lived to see it happen.

I respectfully request that the Court approve the settlement . . ., so that other families do not have to go through what my children and I did.[1]

The Legal Aid Society of New York had given up its Legal Services Corporation (LSC) funding when Congress passed restrictions prohibiting its grantees from litigating class actions, and thus it was able to continue this class action to its successful conclusion. Had the society remained an LSC grantee, it would have had to surrender this case and it probably would have died.

---

1. The above excerpts are from Evonne McCain's 2008 affidavit reprinted in the *New York Times Magazine,* December 25, 2011, 42.

PART VI

The Future of Civil Legal Aid in the United States

Chapter 29

How Far We Have Come, How Far Yet to Go

Justice, justice shall you pursue.

—*Old Testament*, Deuteronomy 16:20

The future of civil legal aid in the United States—our country's major effort to "establish justice" for its low-income population—is being made as you read this book. Whether viewed as the future of the Legal Services Corporation, the centerpiece of the effort that has occupied so much of this book, or the future of the entire enterprise, the only certainty is uncertainty, the range of possibilities almost limitless, and tied closely, as it has been the past half century at least, to the direction the larger society takes. Based on its history so far, it seems justice for lower-income people in the United States may remain forever in jeopardy—its fortunes rising if the political tide flows in its favor as it did during the War on Poverty and sporadically for brief periods since, but then falling and sometimes flirting with the abyss when the political tide reverses.

This seems a precarious platform for something so critical to citizenship in a democracy as justice for all. Stable one year and teetering on the brink the next. Yet it appears it may be ever thus. Unless, that is, "justice for all" assumes its rightful place not as an assertion we make when pledging allegiance to our flag, but as one of the small constellation of fundamental rights given constitutional protection. Is that even possible—a constitutional right to counsel in civil cases? We will address this question later. Before looking to the future, it is necessary to examine the present.

WHERE THE UNITED STATES STANDS NOW— THE LEGAL SERVICES CORPORATION

As of the completion of the manuscript for this book, the 21st century has been a relatively peaceful period for the Legal Services

Corporation—certainly compared to the final three decades of the 20th century. As Mauricio Vivero, who staffed the American Bar Association's grassroots campaign to save LSC in the mid-1990s and headed governmental affairs for LSC later that decade, wrote, "LSC has dispelled old myths about the work of local legal aid offices and has solidified support for the core mission of the national legal services program."[1]

The explanation for this changed view of LSC and the lawyers it funds? Part reality and part perception.

For a combination of reasons, LSC-funded legal services aren't doing as many things that can stir up controversy as they were in the 1960s and 1970s. To begin with, through its restrictions Congress has taken many of the hot button issues off the table—defending drug dealers in evictions, abortion cases, class actions, legislative advocacy, and the like. An unintended consequence—those same restrictions encouraged an upsurge in non-LSC-funded organizations capable of taking on those prohibited cases and clients. At least in many areas of the country, this provided a safety valve for LSC grantees that otherwise would have to see many poor people coming to their offices go without the relief they need. And yet neither LSC nor the lawyers it finances can be blamed or disciplined for what these other organizations do.

LSC 35th anniversary banner. (Courtesy of Legal Services Corporation)

Another factor diminishing the volume of potentially controversial litigation is that there is less incentive now to take issues to the appellate courts. The conservative drift of these forums the past few decades has made them less and less hospitable to legal arguments poor people bring. The commitment to equality and to due process does not enjoy the same priority in our courts the way it did in the mid-20th century. The prospects of success are not what they used to be and so affirmative litigation is less frequent and the eye-catching newspaper headlines fewer.

At the same time, legal services lawyers have found quieter, sometimes nearly as effective ways of helping their clients. The earlier appellate victories and class actions have left the substantive law less slanted against the poor, so litigation merely enforcing the new norms has become a more viable alternative for helping their clients. Seasoned legal services lawyers also found some welfare departments and other administrative agencies didn't have to be pounded into submission through litigation, but could be persuaded to follow a reasonable interpretation of the relevant statutes and regulations. Thus, policy advocacy often takes place in the quiet of a bureaucrat's office or over the telephone rather in the glare of a public courtroom. Add to that the fact most sizeable LSC-funded grantees are led by well-seasoned executive directors who lived through and survived the political wars of the 1980s and 1990s. They know how to maximize effectiveness and minimize controversy—and almost always succeed.

So the realty has changed from LSC's adventuresome youth. Yet much of Congress's impression of LSC in the 1990s was founded not on truth but on misconceptions about what legal services lawyers were actually doing at that time—the nature of the services they were spending most of their time supplying. Nothing said more about the depth of the gulf between perception and reality than the conversion of Congressman Norman Shumway in the early 1990s. While in Congress, as recounted in chapter 25, he railed against the "abuses" committed by legal services lawyers and pushed an amendment seeking to end LSC's funding. But when Shumway became LSC's vice chair and learned firsthand what those lawyers were actually doing he began praising those same lawyers and their good deeds in testimony to the Congress on which he had served.

Even before the mid-1990s when Congress imposed the final round of major restrictions on LSC-funded lawyers, most of their time was spent on work nobody could quarrel with. As Vivero summarized, "LSC's annual statistics on grantee caseloads show that the work seen as objectionable by some in Congress never represented a significant percentage of the work performed by legal services lawyers. Prior to enactment of the new congressional restrictions, for example, litigated cases involving prisoners' rights totaled 680 and represented less than

0.05 percent of all LSC cases for 1995. In June 1996, LSC reported 630 active class action lawsuits and 2,993 cases involving representation of aliens not eligible for assistance under the new restrictions. Together, these cases represented less than one percent of all LSC cases for 1996."[2]

For a long time, senators and members of congress, especially the more conservative members, were bombarded with horror stories fed them by ideologues such as Howard Phillips and unhappy losing litigants such as some growers and their lobbyists. Perhaps the most important contribution John McKay and John Erlenborn made to the legal services cause as LSC presidents was correcting those misconceptions. Enjoying credibility with their fellow Republicans, they spent hour upon hour on the Hill refuting erroneous charges and exposing members of the Senate and House to the reality of what legal services lawyers were doing. Not that they succeeded every time, but they often did, thus over time lowering the temperature of the discussion of LSC in both chambers.

As a result of both—a sharp reduction in cases that might generate controversy and a more accurate understanding of what legal services lawyers do—the Bush administration years saw the LSC appropriation grow slowly, but never backtrack, and no longer the subject of prolonged debate. Then during Obama's first year in office as in the early Clinton years, LSC's budget rose significantly—but far short of what its supporters hoped for or expected. Although the ABA asked for $550 million and the Obama administration requested $490 million—an increase of $100 million from the last Bush budget—Congress only appropriated $440 million for FY 2010. Then the full impact of the financial meltdown hit, and the LSC budget paid a price along with most other domestic programs, receding to $348 million by FY 2012.

Either through first year naiveté or as a deliberate gamble, President Obama's administration chose to depart from the usual practice in his nominations to the board of the LSC. Prior Democratic presidents usually had nominated the most liberal Republicans they could find for the five minority seats just as prior Republicans presidents had nominated the most conservative Democrats they could. Although names of dozens of Republicans supportive of legal services were submitted to the White House, the Obama administration didn't name any of them, instead handing over the selection of the five Republican seats to Senate minority leader Mitch McConnell.

Obama's picks for the six Democratic seats included *Robert Grey*, a partner in the Richmond corporate firm that Lewis Powell once headed and himself a former ABA president, *Martha Minow,* the dean of Harvard Law School who earlier in her career was a law clerk to Justice Thurgood Marshall, *Gloria Valencia-Weber,* a Harvard law graduate and professor at the University of New Mexico Law School who specialized in Native American law and served as a judge on the

Intertribal Court of Appeals, *Laurie Mikva*, now a commissioner on the Illinois Court of Claims and the only former legal services lawyer on the board, and *Julie Reiskin*, a client representative and the only non-lawyer on the board, who is the executive director of the Colorado Cross-Disability Coalition, a disability rights advocacy organization.

As board chair the president favored John Levi, the Sidley Austin partner who more than two decades earlier had been an accidental matchmaker. It was Levi who recruited a first year Harvard law student, Barack Obama, as a summer associate and asked a young lawyer in the firm, Michelle Robinson, to orient him to the job. By the end of the summer Barack and Michelle were dating on their way to getting married—and the rest is history. The fact the new president chose as head of LSC's board the man responsible for him finding his life partner seemed a very positive sign for the future of that organization.

As a group, Obama's selections for the Democratic majority on the board were a mix of political liberals and moderates. Senator McConnell, however, chose five solid conservatives, four of them active members of the Federalist Society. Those four included *Victor Maddox*, a named partner in a Louisville law firm and formerly McConnell's recruit as counsel for the Senate Judiciary Committee, *Charles Keckler*, a professor at Penn State's law school who served in the George W. Bush administration as deputy assistant secretary for policy at the

John Levi, 2010 LSC board president. (Courtesy of Legal Services Corporation)

Department of Health and Human Services, *Harry Korrell III*, partner in a large Seattle corporate law firm who received a major award from the Federalist Society for winning a Supreme Court decision ending the Seattle school's affirmative action program, and *Sharon Browne*, who was a senior attorney at the Pacific Legal Foundation, a public interest law firm that represented business and antiregulatory positions in major litigation. The only McConnell pick not a Federalist Society member was his selection for the Republican "client" seat. For that role he named a young Dominican friar, *Father Pius*—poor enough to qualify as a client representative only because he had taken the vow of poverty required by his occupation. But before joining the priesthood, Father Pius was a University of Chicago law graduate and corporate lawyer in the same national law firm, Sidley Austin, as John Levi.[3]

It was as if the Democratic leadership in the Senate had tendered four members of the National Lawyers Guild to a Republican president. What chances would there have been that they would have been nominated to sit on the LSC board? Yet the Obama administration accepted McConnell's entire slate. If the two Federalist Society members on the George W. Bush LSC board, Frank Strickland and Professor Lillian Bevier, had not proved to be so supportive of the corporation and its grantees, the presence of four members of the Federalist Society on the Obama board may have been more alarming to the legal services community than it was. No one could quarrel with the legal credentials of the Republican nominees. All had graduated well up in their classes from good, often elite, law schools. Two had clerked for federal judges and two others had written extensively in law reviews and other publications, and several were experienced litigators. Nonetheless, many of those who had followed the travails of the LSC over the years, including this author, were concerned about the views of these nominees on legal services for the poor in general and LSC in particular—and what their presence on the board might mean for the future of the corporation. Several of us expressed opposition and urged the Senate to reject at least one of McConnell's choices. But the Senate unanimously confirmed all of Obama's 11 nominees, without holding hearings. Democrats in the Senate were simply unwilling to oppose a candidate their new president had nominated even if the Obama administration had not chosen that person.

As of the delivery of the manuscript for this book, most of the fears LSC supporters entertained about the Republican members of the LSC board have not been realized. Those five members, unlike the Donald Bogards, Clark Durants, LeaAnne Bernsteins, and Michael Wallaces before them, have not tried to defund or sabotage LSC and the lawyers it supports. Nor has the LSC board experienced the acrimony and dysfunction that divided LSC boards exhibited in the 1980s. The chair, John Levi, has gone out of his way to maintain generally good

LSC Board of Directors

LSC is headed by an 11-member Board of Directors appointed by the President and confirmed by the Senate.

John G. Levi, *Chairman*
Partner in the Chicago office of Sidley Austin, LLP.

Martha Minow, *Vice Chair*
Dean of Harvard Law School and the Jeremiah Smith Jr. Professor of Law.

Sharon L. Browne
Principal attorney in the Pacific Legal Foundation's Individual Rights Practice group and a member of the Foundation's senior management.

Robert J. Grey Jr.
Partner in the Richmond and Washington offices of Hunton & Williams LLP.

Charles N.W. Keckler
Professor at Pennsylvania State University's Dickinson School of Law.

Harry J.F. Korrell III
Partner in the Seattle office of Davis Wright Tremaine LLP.

Victor B. Maddox
Partner in the Louisville, Ky., firm of Fultz Maddox Hovious & Dickens PLC.

Laurie Mikva
Staff attorney in the Office of Legal Counsel at the Illinois Department of Employment Security.

The Rev. Pius Pietrzyk, O.P.
Priest in the parish of St. Thomas Aquinas in Zanesville, Ohio.

Julie A. Reiskin
Executive Director of the Colorado Cross-Disability Coalition.

Gloria Valencia-Weber
Professor at the University of New Mexico School of Law.

The LSC board of directors nominated by President Barack Obama, and confirmed 2010. (Courtesy of Legal Services Corporation)

relations with those in the five-vote Republican minority. Nearly all board committees are balanced with two members from each faction. Victor Maddox chairs the audit committee, and Charles Keckler chairs the operations and regulations committee, two of the most important board assignments. When it comes to significant issues, the five minority members generally have not voted as a bloc, nor has the six-vote Democratic majority.[4]

The Obama board chose LSC's longtime general counsel, Victor Fortuno, as interim president. He was in that office for almost a year

Victor Fortuno, LSC president, 2010. (Courtesy of
Legal Services Corporation)

before the board completed a wide-ranging search for a permanent
LSC president. At the end of that process, the board selected a proven
leader from a prestigious law firm, James Sandman, as its new president. Sandman had spent 30 years with a large national law firm,
Arnold and Porter, 10 of those years as the firm's managing partner.
During most of those years he also was active in pro bono programs,
which among other honors earned him the Howard Lesnick Pro Bono
Award from the University of Pennsylvania—an award named for the
first director of the Reginald Heber Smith Fellowship Program, which
began its life at that law school. Sandman also served on the board
of the Neighborhood Legal Services Program, where I had started in
legal services in 1964, and was involved with bar association work,
serving as District of Columbia bar president in 2006. The District of
Columbia legal newspaper named him one of the "90 most outstanding lawyers of the last 30 years." Unusually articulate and with a near
perfect background for the position, Sandman gives LSC a steady,

James Sandman, LSC president 2011–present. (Courtesy of Legal Services Corporation)

impressive staff leader as it moves forward into an uncertain but possibly bright future.[5]

The board has repeatedly voted to request significant increases in the LSC budget, but has only had middling success so far because of the economic crisis and resulting cutbacks in discretionary spending. In a 2012 hearing I attended in Sacramento, one of the Republican board members, Sharon Browne, delivered an eloquent plea for additional funding of legal services to the poor. So far, LSC and its allies also have succeeded in beating back repeated attempts to eliminate funding for the corporation.[6]

The LSC board has appointed task forces including board members and outside experts, which devised plans for improved monitoring of grantees' financial operations and expansion of pro bono resources.[7] It also adopted an ambitious "strategic plan" for 2012–2016.[8] Over the next few years LSC will be attempting to implement that strategic plan as well as the task force recommendations. If the unlikely marriage that is the LSC board as of 2012 stays on that course and has luck with Congress the corporation could have a solid if not spectacular future as the essential core of civil legal aid in the United States.

WHERE THE UNITED STATES STANDS—
NON-LSC-FUNDED RESOURCES

The 21st century has been a time of broadening support and considerable growth in non-LSC funding—at least until the onset of the Great Recession—and in some parts of the country those other sources have become a full partner of LSC in financing civil legal aid. As a result, a few states have been able to restore "minimum access" for their low-income residents. But is "minimum access," even where it is achieved enough to "establish justice" for that population?

The 21st century also has been a time of continuing growth in the quantity of pro bono resources donated by members of the private bar, and especially the large corporate law firms. The upswing, especially among larger law firms, began in the 1990s because of three major developments: First, the ABA's Standing Committee on Pro Bono and Public Service (Pro Bono Committee). Second, the Pro Bono Institute (PBI) founded by pro bono pioneer Esther Lardent in 1996, who had staffed one of the ABA's initial pilot pro bono projects in the early 1980s and started PBI to focus on the larger corporate firms (50 to 1000+lawyers). And third, the *American Lawyer,* a national legal newspaper that began including a firm's level of pro bono commitment in its annual rankings of law firms.

The ABA Pro Bono Committee has encouraged increased pro bono efforts among the association's members since 1980 when then ABA president Reese Smith persuaded the board of governors to fund a few pilot programs to demonstrate the value of organized and staffed pro bono programs. Among other efforts, the committee performs studies, provides publications and other resources, and honors outstanding pro bono work at the ABA annual meeting. In 2008, it published the results of a survey reflecting that a high percentage of private lawyers report they supplied some services to people of limited income on a pro bono basis during the previous year.[9] Of those reporting they provided those services, 40 percent of the clients came via referrals from legal aid programs,[10] many of them presumably from LSC grantees coordinating pro bono services as part of their obligation to use 12½ percent of their budgets for private attorney involvement (PAI).

The Pro Bono Institute promotes pro bono work among large law firms and offers resources and expertise to those who choose to participate. Probably its most successful recruitment tool is the "pro bono challenge," which asks firms to sign up as willing to devote three to five percent of the firm's total billable hours (60 to 100 hours per attorney) to pro bono work. First, a few, than dozens, and eventually more than a hundred law firms took the pledge. As Lardent observed, "In 2000, 'corporate pro bono' was an oxymoron. In 2002, it was an interesting idea. In 2005, there's an aura of inevitability about it."

By 2012, PBI could report that in 2011 corporate law firms donated 2,578,958 hours to provide legal help to low-income people or to organizations that serve that population.[11] This would be the equivalent of approximately 1500 full-time legal services lawyers, although a considerable percentage of those pro bono resources were devoted to representation in criminal rather than civil cases—death penalty appeals and post-conviction advocacy–there being no constitutional right to the latter and little public funding available for it in most states. Thus, it is not the same as if 1,500 lawyers were added to civil legal aid's resources through the pro bono contributions of major corporate law firms. Nonetheless, it is also true these pro bono contributions by large firm lawyers represent additional resources that have been very helpful where they are available, primarily in the larger cities.

The American Lawyer publishes an annual ranking of the nation's 200 largest firms reflecting their pro bono work as measured by the average number of hours the firm's individual members devote to these activities and also the percentage of firm members who spend more than 20 hours a year doing so. The top firm in the 2012 report committed an average of 54 hours per firm member to pro bono activities and 44 percent of firm members spent more than 20 percent of their time to this work.[12] These rankings influence many of the nation's top law graduates when choosing which firm they want to join because they are attracted to firms that encourage pro bono work. Not only does this work satisfy their charitable instincts but it often gives them the chance to deal with real clients and handle trials or similar hands-on tasks not offered them in the early years at the typical large corporate firm.

THE UNITED STATES HAS COME SO FAR, BUT HAS YET SO FAR TO GO

The United States started from so far behind that the progress made during the past nearly five decades can appear remarkable. Yet it is but a tiny step forward toward truly establishing justice for this nation's lower-income population. In just 15 years, from 1965, when civil legal aid depended entirely on $5.4 million in private donations, to 1981 when LSC alone supplied $321 million, expenditures for legal services to low-income people in this country exploded 60-fold—in current dollars that is. Even correcting for the high rate of inflation during those 15 years, civil legal aid funding grew more than 20-fold— from $38 million in 2011 dollars in 1965 to nearly $800 million in 2011 dollars in 1981. After reaching what turned out to be its peak in 1981, however, for the next 30 years the LSC budget has trended downward.

The funding level has not been in free fall, but instead experienced precipitous drops in the early 1980s and mid-1990s, each time followed by slow recoveries and multiyear plateaus, so that as of 2012 LSC's budget of $348 million was only eight times higher than the entirely private-funded legal aid of 1965, after correcting for inflation. This unhappy downward trajectory is illustrated in the chart below. (See Table 29.1.)

Indeed, after correcting for inflation LSC's current budget is only marginally higher than the one the new corporation inherited from the Office of Economic Opportunity in 1975. That is, $71 million in

Table 29.1
Selected LSC Budgets in Current Year's Dollars and in 1981 Dollars
(1981–2011)

Budget Years	Amount in Current Year Dollars	Value in 1981 Dollars	Percentage Decrease from "Minimum Access" Budget
1981 "Minimum access" reached	321,000,000		
1982 First Reagan era budget	241,000,000	227,000,000	–31.4%
1990 First G.H.W. Bush era budget	316,525,000	219,000,000	–33.5%
1995 First Clinton era budget	400,000,000	238,000,000	–27.9%
1996 First Gingrich Congress budget	278,000,000	161,000,000	–51.3%
2002 First G.W. Bush era budget	329,300,000	166,000,000	–47.2%
2005	330,804,705	153,000,000	–53.0%
2007	348,500,000	152,000,000	–52.5%
2008 Last G.W. Bush era budget	350,490,000	147,000,000	–52.6%
2009 First Obama era budget	390,000,000	165,000,000	–48.2%
2010	420,000,000	167,000,000	–47.9%
2011	404,000,000	164,000,000	–48.9%
2012	348,000,000	141,000,000	–56.0%

1975 dollars is the equivalent of $296 million in 2011 dollars, just $52 million short of what the present Congress is willing to appropriate for the Legal Services Corporation. Expressed another way, because of the rapid inflation from 1975 to 1981, the final OEO-LSP budget of $71 million was the equivalent of $120 million in 1981 dollars while the FY 2012 budget was $141 million in 1981 dollars. Viewed either way, the 2012 LSC budget was slightly more than 17 percent higher than the final OEO-LSP budget in 1975. (See Table 29.2.)

As another measure of the federal government's commitment to establishing justice for its lower-income population, consider the size of that budget on a per capita basis in this country. At its height, in 1981, the LSC budget was only $1.40 per person. A tiny, tiny piece of the government's budget directed toward achieving one of a democratic society's fundamental goals—equality before the law for all its citizens, irrespective of their financial means. Obviously, $1.40 per capita was not enough to provide that basic equality to all low-income people in this country, but it was enough so a meaningful percentage of that population could receive the legal help they need for effective access to the legal system. The minute size of that price also suggests how cheap it would be to make good on the Constitution's aspiration and our nation's pledge to establish justice for all, compared to the cost of several less critical services and social goals to which our government devotes far more money per capita—to say nothing of the price of any number of frivolous things on which we as individuals choose to spend our money.

And what has happened to this miniscule per capita investment in the LSC budget over the past three decades? Because our total population grew faster than the LSC budget, the nation's per capita investment in the LSC dropped from $1.40 per capita to $1.12 per capita from 1981 to 2012 as measured in current dollars. And meantime it plunged to 43 cents per capita in 1981 dollars. Another way of saying the same thing is to state both the 1981 and 2012 per capita figures in 2011 dollars, in which case the 1981 LSC budget was the equivalent of

Table 29.2
The Final OEO-LSP Budget in 1975, 1981, and 2011 Dollars

Final OEO-LSP Budget in 1975 vs. FY 2012 LSC Budget in 1975 Dollars	Final OEO-LSP Budget in 1981 Dollars vs. FY 2012 LSC Budget in 1981 Dollars	Final OEO-LSP Budget in 2011 Dollars vs. FY 2012 LSC Budget in 2011 Dollars
$71 million–$83 million	$120 million–$141 million	$296 million–$348 million

$3.46 in 2011 dollars per person in 1981 but by 2012 had plummeted to its current $1.12. (See Table 29.3.)

It also is revealing to note where the LSC budget would be if it had the same share of the federal budget today as it did in 1981 or if it still had the same share of the nation's total spending on the services of lawyers as it did that year. The answers: $1.78 billion or $3.27 billion. That is, in 1981 LSC received 0.047 percent of the federal budget of $678 billion. The federal budget for FY 2012 was $3.79 trillion and 0.047 percent of that figure comes to $1.78 billion. (See Table 29.4.) If the LSC budget had only kept pace with the rest of the federal government, it would have expanded to five times what it is today.

In 1981, the LSC budget represented 1.4 percent of the $23 billion the nation spent on lawyers at that time. By 2009 spending on the services of lawyers had exploded by 10-fold to $234 billion. If the LSC budget were still the same 1.4-percent share of the legal profession's income as it had been in 1981, the LSC budget in 2009 and subsequent years would have been in the neighborhood of $3.3 billion. (See Table 29.5.)

Table 29.3
The Decrease in Per Capita Expenditures on the Legal Services Corporation (1981–2012)

	Per Capita Expenditure on LSC in Current Dollars	Per Capita Expenditure on LSC in 1981 Dollars	Per Capita Expenditure on LSC in 2011 Dollars
1981	$1.40	$1.40	$3.46
2011	$1.12	$0.43	$1.12

Table 29.4
LSC 2012 Budget if LSC Still Had Same Share of that Budget as It Did of the 1981 Budget

	LSC Budget	Federal Budget	LSC Budget as Percentage of Federal Budget	LSC Budget if the Same Percent of Federal Budget as it Was in 1981
1981	$321 million	$678 billion	0.047%	
2012	$348 million	$3.79 trillion	0.009%	$1.78 billion

Table 29.5
LSC 2012 Budget if LSC Still Had the Same Share of the Nation's
Expenditures on Lawyers as It Did in 1981

	LSC Budget	Total Expenditures on Lawyers in 1981 and 2009 (Most Recent in 2012 Statistical Abstract)	LSC Budget as Percent of Total Expenditures on Lawyers	LSC Budget if the Same Percent of Total Expenditures on Lawyers as it Was in 1981
1981	$321 million	$23 billion	1.4 percent	
2012	$348 million	$234 billion	0.14 percent	$3.28 billion

The $1.13 per capita the federal government currently devotes to the LSC was a pimple on a pimple of the federal government's $3.79 trillion budget in 2012, which reached $12,225 per person. The LSC budget could be 5 or 10 times higher and not make a measurable difference in the nation's total outlays. At $5 or $10 per capita a meaningful LSC budget would still be dwarfed by the $1,100 per capita the government already spends on Medicaid to furnish health care to low-income U.S. citizens and far below the $80 per capita spent on food stamps for that same population.

Although the LSC obviously has not fared well financially over the past three decades, it remains the vital core of a somewhat larger enterprise—one that at the national level has accumulated combined resources including LSC's grants that approach the "minimum access" level of 1981. The OEO-LSP and the early expansion years of the LSC not only generated an explosion, albeit temporary, of new funding for civil legal aid. Of equal importance those programs attracted an infusion of extraordinary talent–lawyers and leaders–many of whom have remained through the leaner times since. Scores of the executive directors who started in those positions during the heydays of the 1970s and early 1980s are still running their programs, while others are headed by those who joined the programs as frontline lawyers in those years and later moved up the ladder to the executive director level.

No summertime patriots these. When LSC grants suddenly shrunk, they began looking for creative ways of filling the gap with other funding. Often aided by former legal services lawyers who had moved on to leadership positions in state government, the judiciary, major law firms, or the organized bar, in many states they made significant progress in augmenting the federal resources.

Chapter 28 surveyed most of these nonfederal revenue sources that have been developed since the mid-1980s. IOLTA, a slice of court fees, a tiny piece of general state tax revenues, special purpose government grants, donations from private law firms, and foundation grants—all or some of these funding sources augment LSC grants in many but by no means every state. Because state legislatures vary so greatly in their commitment to equal justice for their low-income residents, and also because large law firms and big foundations are clustered in major urban areas, the differences in available non-LSC funding are enormous from state to state—ranging from relatively generous to virtually none, and many levels in between. They also vary dramatically within states with most of the additional non-LSC funding concentrated in the state's largest city or cities, with smaller communities and rural areas starved for additional legal aid funding to augment anything they receive from LSC.

Although IOLTA now exists in every state, there are several, especially in the South, where none of the other supplemental sources are provided, except perhaps a negligible amount from private donations. In those states, LSC funding still supplies over 90 percent of the financial support for civil legal aid. Thus, the national estimates can be misleading, because they are not representative of what is happening in so many states.

In any event, combining LSC funding and all other sources of funding, there have been years recently when the national total of civil legal aid financing was at roughly the same level per eligible person as the LSC budget alone provided in FY 1981. That is, after correcting for inflation and also for the increased size of the eligible population, the $321 million in 1981 was equivalent to $1.026 billion in 2008. In that year, combined funding actually exceeded the $1.026 billion by a hundred or two hundred million. The extra hundred million or two probably was eaten up, however, serving clients whose incomes were between the federal maximum of 125 percent of poverty and the higher 200 percent of poverty level several states have established as the eligibility cap for their non-LSC funds.[13] Thus, looking at it from a national perspective, considering all sources of funding for civil legal aid, in 2008 total funding for those below 125 of poverty essentially matched the "minimum access" target LSC alone reached in FY 1981. A tribute to the perseverance, energy, and creativity shown by legal services lawyers, most of them in LSC-funded programs, and their allies in the legal profession and elsewhere in society.

What was true in 2008 was no longer true in 2012, however. Because of historically low interest rates IOLTA revenues plunged in that four-year span, several state governments were so strapped for cash they reduced or eliminated funding of legal services, and Congress cut LSC funding from $420 million in FY 2010 down to $348 million for FY 2012. As a result, LSC could not make up for the losses of other revenues, even in part. While revenues were falling, the eligible client community was surging—from 50 million in 2008 to 64 million in 2012[14]—nearly a 30-percent increase in just four years. Because of that dramatic expansion of the population to be served and some minor further inflation, it would require at least $1.4 billion in combined federal–state–private resources to match what LSC's $321 million budget could do in 1981— provide "minimum access" to those under 125 percent of the official poverty level. Coincidentally, adding in the cost of helping those between 125 percent and 200 percent of poverty in those states which target that income strata, too, minimum access would require combined resources approaching the $1.78 billion the LSC budget alone would already be if only the corporation received the same share of the federal budget in FY 2012 as it did in FY 1981.

What does this underfunding mean in human terms, not just statistical and financial ones? To serve those 64 million or more than 100 million people, depending on whether the 125 percent or 200 percent of the poverty line is used as the eligibility cap, it is estimated there are approximately 6,500 civil legal aid lawyers funded by all sources in the entire country—around 4,000 of them in LSC-funded programs. That is only one lawyer for every 10,000 eligible people, or one for every 15,000, depending on where the line is drawn, contrasted with approximately one lawyer for every 525 people in the rest of the population.

Those 6,500 civil legal aid lawyers represent about six-tenths of a percent of the nation's 1.1 million lawyers. Yet they are expected to serve at least 20 percent and as much as one-third of the nation's population. Moreover, the combined budgets of all the programs employing these lawyers is less than one-half of a percent of what the country spends on lawyers. To add yet another perspective, two corporate law firms—Skadden, Arps, Slate, Meagher, & Flom LLP and Latham & Watkins LLP—each received over $2 billion annually in legal fees during recent years to serve a comparative handful of wealthy clients.[15] This means each of those law firms earned twice as much as all the legal aid programs in the country presently receive from all sources to purportedly meet the legal needs of 64 million, or as many as 100 million, people. Several other corporate firms are in the billion-dollar range—each of them again only representing not millions but a comparatively few clients.

To say the nation's legal resources are distributed unequally clearly is an understatement. The poor are even poorer when it comes to access to justice than they are in the dollars they receive. The bottom 20 percent of the population gets 3.4 percent of the nation's income,[16] but only a half percent of its legal resources. The combined federal–IOLTA–state–private revenue figure yields a per capita expenditure of less than \$4 per person on civil legal aid, an embarrassingly low investment in something so basic to our nation's democracy as equal justice for all.

But is this underfunding of civil legal aid just inevitable? Are poor people simply never destined to receive a decent share of any nation's legal resources? Perhaps the rest of the population and its elected representatives will never devote significant public funds to supply lawyers for those unable to afford their own.

If the underinvestment in civil legal aid is inevitable, the unwillingness to pay the price for equal justice indeed inherent, one would assume it would hold true in other industrial democracies, as well. So what is the experience elsewhere? And does that experience point toward a way forward in the United States? And beyond that, what is a possible future course for civil legal aid in the United States that would ensure its survival and perhaps truly establish justice for all? Those are the subjects of the next two chapters.

Chapter 30

Removing the Blinders, Viewing Some Possibilities from Elsewhere in the World

Legal aid shall be made available to those who lack sufficient resources in so far as such aid is necessary to ensure effective access to justice.
—Article 47, Charter of Fundamental Rights of the European Union, ratified December 1, 2009

In order to glimpse what could be the future of civil legal aid in the United States, it may prove helpful to remove our "American exceptionalism" blinders for the moment. That way it is possible to examine how legal aid developed and what it has become in the rest of the world, especially among our closer cousins, the other Western democracies.

For our nation's closest relatives, those in the common law world, the history of legal representation of the poor starts six centuries ago in the mother country, England, during the 15th century. To resolve uncertainty whether the King's common law judges would appoint lawyers to represent paupers in civil trials, in 1495, only three years after Columbus discovered America, the English Parliament intervened. The lawmakers passed a statute giving paupers a right to free legal assistance in civil cases and requiring lawyers to provide the help without receiving any compensation for their services. Often referred to in this context as simply the Statute of Henry VII, the law reads in the language of the age.

> [T]he Justices . . . shall assign to the same poor person or persons, Counsel learned by their discretions which shall give their Counsels nothing taking for the same, and in likewise the same Justices attorney and attorneys for the same poor person and persons and all other officers requisite and necessary to be had for the speed of the said suits to shall appoint be had and made which shall do their duties without any rewards for their Counsels, help and business in the same.[1]

This statute used the word "shall," clearly telling the judges they had a mandatory duty to appoint counsel and instructing lawyers they had a mandatory duty to supply their services, if appointed, and to do so without receiving any compensation for that work—the combination of a right to counsel for the pauper and mandatory pro bono for the legal profession. The Statute of Henry VII remained the authority for granting a right to counsel to low-income litigants in England's common law courts for nearly four centuries, until replaced in 1883 by a revised version establishing a new system for delivering legal assistance to poor people.[2] In the meantime, the judges of the Courts of Equity created a broader right to free counsel for the poor when they appeared in those courts, again appointing lawyers who were expected to provide their services without any payment.[3]

Governments on the European continent lagged behind England in guaranteeing free counsel to their low-income citizens just as they lagged behind in developing other democratic institutions. Although English barons had wrested a Magna Carta from the English crown as early as the 13th century and parliament already had accumulated considerable political power by the 15th century, most European nations were still ruled by absolute monarchs. Many of those kings and emperors claimed the source of their power descended from God, and consequently they possessed a divine right to govern the lesser mortals who populated their countries.

Then a group of brilliant political philosophers began espousing one version or another of a brand new vision—the social contract—providing a rationale and sometimes the inspiration for reform or even revolution. As men such as Jean-Jacques Rousseau, Thomas Hobbes, and John Locke explained, a government's right to govern did not descend from God in his heavens, but from the consent of the governed right here on earth. These philosophers argued individual citizens surrendered their rights, including their right to settle disputes through the use of force, only in exchange for a sovereign's promise to provide all of those citizens justice, peace, and the possibility of a better life. This fundamental notion came to be called the "social contract"—an agreement among a nation's individual citizens and between those citizens and that nation's government. As John Locke, perhaps the social contract thinker most influential with the founding fathers of our own nation, explained:

> Political power is that power which every man having in the state of nature has given up into the hands of the society . . . with this express or tacit trust that it shall be employed for their good . . . *and to punish the breach of the law of nature in others.* . . . And this power has its origins only from *compact and agreement, and the mutual consent of those who make up the community.*[4]

One of the essential terms of that social contract is the guarantee of "equality before the law"—the principle or "precept" that citizens from different economic classes will stand equal in the courts or other forums the government provides for resolving disputes. It is based on the notion individuals would not give up their natural right to settle disputes through force unless the sovereign offered a peaceful alternative in which they have a fair chance to prevail if in the right, no matter whether they are rich, poor, or something in between. Thomas Hobbes, another influential social contract theorist spoke to this right.

> The safety of the People, requireth further, from him or them that have the Sovereign Power, that *Justice be equally administered to all degree of People;* that is, that as well the rich and mighty, as *poor and obscure persons, may be righted of the injuries done them;* so as the great may have no greater hope of impunity, when they do violence, dishonour, or any Injury to the meaner sort, than when one of these, does the like to one of them; For in this consisteth Equity; to which, as *being a Precept of the Law of Nature, a Sovereign is . . . subject.*[5]

Society, in turn, breaches this term of the social contract if its forums favor one class of citizens over those of another class—the rich over the poor, for example. Members of the disfavored class cannot be presumed to have agreed to submit to an unjust sovereign. Thus, the equal administration of justice among different economic classes is an essential underpinning of any society purportedly resting on the consent of the governed.

"Equality before the law" would have remained as only a theoretical right in Europe, as it still is in the United States, except that during the 19th century, nation after nation replaced their absolute rulers with constitutional monarchs, essentially figureheads, or with republics that functioned without a king, queen, or emperor as the head of state. As they implemented the social contract these European countries recognized there was only one way to guarantee the parity among economic classes that contract mandated and thus adopted statutory rights to counsel in civil as well as criminal cases. Shortly after its 1848 revolution that deposed one monarch before replacing him with another, France enacted a statutory civil right to counsel in 1851.[6] Italy embodied that right in its procedural laws at the moment of its birth as a nation in 1865,[7] and Germany also enacted a right to civil counsel in its "basic law" in 1877 when all the German-speaking principalities, dukedoms, and the rest, combined into a nation.[8] The rest of Europe was not far behind. By the end of the 19th century or early in the 20th century most European nations had created statutory rights to counsel in civil cases.[9]

At the time they were first enacted, these statutory rights to counsel were virtually costless to the governments creating them. That was because they conscripted private lawyers to represent indigent litigants, like England had for centuries, requiring them to serve without compensation in return for the privilege of practicing law and earning fees from those clients who could afford to pay. In most European countries, it was well into the 20th century before governments began paying for the right they had created, and some still do not.[10] (This was the system commonly used in the United States, too, but only in criminal cases. During the early years, in most states where criminal defendants enjoyed statutory or constitutional rights to counsel, the lawyers appointed to represent those defendants were expected to serve without compensation. This was true even in the federal courts until 1964.[11])

CONSTITUTIONAL ENFORCEMENT OF EQUALITY BEFORE THE LAW

The Swiss Supreme Court was the first of the European courts to confront the issue whether the constitutional guarantees derived from the social contract require the government to provide free lawyers to civil litigants who cannot afford their own. The year was 1937, a full quarter-century before the U.S. Supreme Court decided *Gideon v. Wainwright* granting indigent criminal defendants in this country a right to free counsel. The Swiss federal constitution is one of those containing an express guarantee of equality before the law but with no mention of counsel, simply providing that "All Swiss are equal before the law."[12]

In a case simply captioned, *Judgment of Oct. 8, 1937*, the Swiss Supreme Court concluded poor people could not be equal before the law in the regular civil courts, unless they had lawyers just like the rest of the citizenry. The court reasoned the constitutional "principle of equality before the law" requires the cantons to provide a free lawyer "in a civil matter where the handling of the trial demands knowledge of the law."[13] In subsequent decisions the Swiss Supreme Court has explained and expanded the circumstances when the governments of the cantons (the rough equivalent of our state governments) must supply free lawyers to poor litigants appearing in their civil courts.[14] Meanwhile, it took the Swiss Supreme Court another 35 years before, in a case decided in 1972, it finally mandated free counsel in *criminal* cases.[15]

The Swiss right to counsel decision proved to be an early precursor of a ruling with implications across the entire European continent. After World War II, most of the European nations decided it was finally time to cease the never-ending cycle of conflict that had repeatedly torn the continent apart and build a unified European community. As part of that community, in 1950 the national governments signed a Convention on Human Rights and Fundamental Freedoms—a rough equivalent of our nation's Bill of Rights—guaranteeing individuals living within their borders would enjoy certain basic minimum rights those countries could not deny.[16] To enforce the provisions of this convention, the founding nations established a Court on Human Rights drawn from the member states and empowered to consider cases brought by individuals who believed their countries were failing to live up to the convention's promises.

Among the guarantees the Convention on Human Rights and Fundamental Freedoms includes is clause 6(1), which says: "In the determination of his civil rights and obligations or of any criminal charge against him, everyone is entitled to a fair and public hearing within a reasonable time."[17] Pretty simple and straightforward—all litigants involved in civil proceedings—as well as defendants in criminal prosecutions—are to have a "fair hearing." Except, what does it take to enjoy a "fair hearing" within the meaning of the European Convention?

In 1978, nearly 30 years after the major European powers signed the Treaty of Rome creating the European Convention on Human Rights and Fundamental Freedoms, a young Irish barrister and law professor, Mary Robinson, received a message from the European Court on Human Rights. The judges wanted her to represent an indigent Irish woman, a Mrs. Airey, who had no lawyer to argue for her before the European Court. The issue in the case was whether Ireland violated the European Convention when its courts denied her request to appoint a lawyer the indigent woman couldn't afford to hire.

As Robinson knew, Ireland unlike most nations in Europe had no statutory right to counsel in civil cases, or even a legal aid program. At that time, Ireland also didn't allow divorces. It did permit a wife like Mrs. Airey to sue for "separate maintenance," however. This would allow her to live apart from her husband and impose a court order forcing him to provide financial support to Airey and her children. But as Mary Robinson learned, when the destitute Mrs. Airey went to court seeking that relief, she was overwhelmed by the complex laws and legal technicalities facing her if she wanted to prove her case. When she pleaded with the trial judge to appoint a lawyer to represent her, Mrs. Airey was told there was no right to counsel for poor people in the Irish civil courts. When she appealed that denial to the Supreme Court of Ireland, that court told her the same thing—as would a U.S. court even today. She then had sent a written request to the European Court on Human Rights claiming Ireland was denying her a "fair hearing" by forcing her to try her own case in the nation's courts without the assistance of a lawyer.

Mary Robinson later said she felt encouraged about Mrs. Airey's chances in the European Court by the fact the judges themselves had recruited a lawyer to argue for her in that court. Consistent with a fundamental precept of the social contract, Article 6 does guarantee *all* civil litigants a "fair hearing." Yet, if and when a "fair hearing" required governments to supply lawyers to litigants unable to afford their own remained a matter of interpretation and thus an open question to be decided by the European Court.

Significantly, this was not a case where an individual citizen was opposed by her government in a civil case, as it might have been if officials were trying to take something from her, such as her children, or had denied her welfare or health care or some other substantive benefit to which she thought she was entitled. No, the issue here was the essence of "equality before the law," a dispute between private citizens possessing different levels of economic resources, one of whom could not afford to employ a lawyer and the other who could and did. Moreover, Mrs. Airey was the plaintiff who had brought the case, not a defendant who had been involuntarily dragged into court. Finally, the main relief she was seeking was monetary. Because Ireland did not allow divorce at that time, Mrs. Airey could not gain freedom to marry someone else, but only the right to legally live separately from her husband and to receive "separate maintenance" out of his earnings.[18]

As a result, Mrs. Airey was presenting the European Court with what might be seen as the ultimate issue, one that an advocacy organization bent on establishing a right to counsel under the European Convention probably would have raised only after a succession of favorable decisions in intermediate situations. But Mrs. Airey wasn't an advocacy organization with a strategy for developing a right to counsel in civil cases, but just an individual too poor to hire a lawyer asking the court to establish a right to counsel for her, who happened to be a plaintiff seeking essentially monetary relief in a case against another private person.

In considering the case, however, the European Court on Human Rights did not focus on these factors, but only whether any litigant could receive a fair hearing in the regular courts in such a case without the assistance of a lawyer. After examining that question from several angles, the judges concluded the answer was no, and held the fair hearing guarantee of the European Convention required the member governments to provide free counsel to those unable to afford their own.[19] In the course of its opinion in *Airey v. Ireland,* the European Court first emphasized a party's opportunity to be physically present in court was *not* access to justice in any real sense and certainly not enough to satisfy the requirements of a democratic society:

> The Convention was intended to guarantee rights that were *practical and effective,* particularly in respect of the right of access to the courts, in view of its prominent place in a democratic society . . . The possibility of appearing in person before the [trial court] did not provide an *effective* right of access.[20]

The European Court went on to emphasize governments have an affirmative duty to provide their private citizens a level playing field when they are opposing each other in the courts—even if that requires providing a free lawyer to the side that is unable to afford her own.

> The [Irish] Government maintain that . . . in the present case there is no positive obstacle emanating from the State and no deliberate attempt by the State to impede access: the alleged lack of access to the court stems not from any act on the part of authorities but solely from Mrs. Airey's personal circumstances, a matter for which Ireland cannot be held responsible under the Convention.
>
> The Court does not agree. . . . In the first place, hindrance in fact can contravene the Convention just like a legal impediment. Furthermore, fulfillment of a duty under the Convention on occasion necessitates some positive action on the part of the State; in such circumstances the State cannot simply remain passive, and "there is . . . no room to distinguish between acts and omissions." The obligation to secure an effective right of access to the courts falls into this category of duty.[21]

The European Court on Human Rights' decision was good news for Mrs. Airey. She got her lawyer and subsequently her judicial separation and separate maintenance order. It also was good news for the poor people of Ireland. In 2005, I had the pleasure of attending a banquet in Killarney, Ireland, celebrating the 25th anniversary of that nation's legal aid program established in 1980 to comply with the mandate of *Airey v. Ireland.* It also marked the first big victory in Mary Robinson's path-breaking career. A decade after that, in 1990, she was elected the first female president of Ireland, and in 1997 left that position to become the United Nations Human Rights Commissioner.[22] But the opinion's influence extended far beyond Mrs. Airey and Ireland. *Airey v. Ireland* now controls litigation for some 45 nations and over 400 million people across the continent of Europe, comprising the majority of the world's Western industrial democracies.

Although this case was decided over 30 years ago, the European Court on Human Rights recently made it clear the principle announced in *Airey v Ireland* remains the governing law for member nations when it issued its opinion in *Steel and Morris v. United Kingdom.*[23]

England may have the most comprehensive and generously funded civil legal aid system in the world, but it still denies counsel in a few types of cases, including the prosecution or defense of libel and defamation lawsuits. This exclusion was put to test when some Greenpeace members distributed pamphlets accusing McDonald's corporation of hurting the environment. McDonald's retaliated by suing two of the Greenpeace members for libel. Lacking any income, the defendants asked English legal aid authorities and subsequently the court to appoint legal counsel to help them with their defense against these charges. The request was denied and the two Greenpeace defendants found themselves going up alone against a battery of high-priced barristers and solicitors in a legal proceeding that lasted for over a decade.

The result, as might be expected, was a judgment against the two defendants, awarding McDonald's 60,000 pounds in damages.

Ultimately, that judgment and, in particular, the English government's denial of counsel to the demonstrators found its way to the European Court on Human Rights. In *Steel and Morris v. The United Kingdom* (2005), the European Court found the failure to provide counsel to the indigent demonstrators denied them the "fair hearing" guaranteed by the European Convention on Human Right and Fundamental Freedoms. Under the precedent established in *Airey v. Ireland,* the court reversed the judgment, not only reinforcing the "fair hearing" and "effective access to justice" dimensions of the Airey opinion, but also introducing "equality of arms" between competing litigants as a governing principle.

> The Court recalls that the Convention is intended to guarantee effective rights. This is particularly so of the right of access to court in view of the prominent place held in a democratic society by the right to a fair trial (see the *Airey v. Ireland* judgment of 9 October 1979, Series A no. 32, § 24). It is central to the concept of a fair trial, *in civil as in criminal proceedings,* that a litigant is not denied the opportunity to present his or her case *effectively* before the court (ibid.) and that *he or she is able to enjoy equality of arms with the opposing side.*[24]

The European court then proceeded to explain how and why the appellants lacked effective access and did not enjoy equality of arms against McDonald's team of lawyers, even though they had some limited legal assistance from pro bono counsel and the trial judge was helpful to them.

> They received some help on the legal and procedural aspects of the case from barristers and solicitors acting *pro bono* . . . The Government have laid emphasis on the considerable latitude afforded to the applicants by the judges of the domestic courts, both at first instance and on appeal, in recognition of the handicaps under which the applicants laboured. However, the Court considers that, in an action of this complexity, neither the sporadic help given by the volunteer lawyers nor the extensive judicial assistance and latitude granted to the applicants as litigants in person, was any substitute for competent and sustained representation by an experienced lawyer familiar with the case and with the law of libel.
>
> In conclusion, therefore, the Court finds that the denial of legal aid to the applicants deprived them of the opportunity to present their case effectively before the court and *contributed to an unacceptable inequality of arms* with McDonald's. There has, therefore, been a violation of Article 6 § 1.[25]

In this case, the European Court made an interesting and quite revealing choice of language—"equality of arms"—to describe what governments must provide in the judicial context. It underscores the social contract origins of the duty. In order to honor the promise of "equality before the law" that induced individual citizens to surrender the natural right to use "arms" in the sense of using weapons to forcibly resolve disputes with their neighbors, governments must guarantee those citizens they will enter the courtroom with the modern equivalent of the "arms" necessary to give them a fair chance in that arena, that is, lawyers. Elsewhere in the opinion, the court makes it clear governments are not required to provide a poor person an *absolute* equality of arms with his or her opponent, but rather *rough* equality.[26] For instance, if the affluent party has the highest-priced, most qualified lawyer in town, the government need not furnish the legal aid client with one possessing the same level of skill. On the other hand, according to the opinion any lawyer appointed would have to be to be fully familiar with the specialized body of law involved in the case.

The European Court in *Steel and Morris* also demonstrated how it could encourage European governments to abide by the duty to provide counsel in the civil context. The judges knew they didn't have the leverage they wield in criminal cases. There governments face the reversal of criminal convictions their prosecutors have won, unless they supply the defendants with counsel. But a government suffers no particular loss if a civil judgment gained by a represented private party is reversed because it failed to provide counsel to the indigent party. So what did the court do in *Steel and Morris v. United Kingdom?* It not only reversed the judgment against the two Greenpeace members in *Steel v Morris,* but also awarded the successful defendants over 80,000 Euros in damages and costs—to be paid, not by the McDonald's Corporation, but by the English government for its violation of the defendant's right to counsel under the European Convention.[27]

For some in the United States it may be an embarrassment and for others a mark of pride, but if our nation was a signatory to the European Convention on Human Rights and Fundamental Freedoms, our legal system would be in violation of that convention. Indeed our courts would be witness to thousands of individual violations of that charter every day of the work week because on every one of those days throngs of poor people appear needing a lawyer and are denied that assistance. A sobering thought for anyone who thinks this nation's legal system is the best in the world.

NOT A RIGHT TO COUNSEL IN EVERY CASE, BUT A "RIGHT TO EQUAL JUSTICE" IN ALL CASES

Whether it were to be established through a constitutional decision or through legislation in the United States, the right in civil cases is likely to be quite different and also more complex than the right to counsel the U.S. Supreme Court declared in criminal prosecutions. As interpreted by the U.S. Supreme Court, the Constitution guarantees an absolute right to counsel in criminal cases; that is, to representation by a full-fledged lawyer in all cases.[28] This is a simple and straightforward, although quite expensive, right to enforce. In criminal cases, this right is easily justified, not only by the seriousness of criminal penalties, but also by the complexity of the criminal process. The Constitution not only guarantees counsel, but also dictates the essential elements of criminal procedure that make the assistance of counsel essential to equal justice for criminal defendants. It is distinctly adversarial and features such elements as jury trials; complex rules of evidence; constitutional rights against self-incrimination and illegally obtained evidence that must be raised or waived in the heat of the courtroom battle; ever more intricate and onerous sentencing schemes; and a dozen other guaranteed, or at least universal elements that make self-representation, or representation by anything less than a skilled lawyer, a foolish alternative.

In contrast, the civil—or, more accurately, the noncriminal—arena is far more diverse. There is no single model—but rather an array of models (and potential models) for resolving disputes. The regular civil courts—the forums in which traditional contract, tort, and property litigation occurs—often are every bit as complex as the criminal courts, indeed sometimes more so. Hence, lawyers are as essential for civil litigants in these forums as they are for criminal defendants in criminal trials. As the European Court emphasized in both the *Airey* and *Steel and Morris* decisions, in these proceedings the assistance of a lawyer is essential to a fair hearing and to effective access to justice. Any parties who face represented opponents without a lawyer of their own in such proceedings lack the "equality of arms" the European Court found essential in *Steel and Morris.* Consequently, there can be no equal justice without a right to counsel when low-income litigants appear in the traditional civil courts or any other forums where the procedures and/or substantive law approaches the complexity found in the criminal process.

But in its *Airey* decision, the European Court on Human Rights also recognized the possibility some civil disputes might be decided in forums and through processes in which the parties would have effective access to justice and enjoy fair hearings without being represented by lawyers.

> Whilst Article 6 para.1 guarantees to litigants an effective right of access to the courts for the determination of their "civil rights and obligations," it leaves to the State a free choice of the means to be used towards this end. The institution of a legal aid scheme—which Ireland now envisages in family law matters—constitutes one of those means but there are *others such as, for example, a simplification of procedure.* In any event, it

is not the Court's function to indicate, let alone dictate, which measures should be taken; all that the Convention requires is that an individual should enjoy his *effective right of access* to the courts in conditions not at variance with Article 6 (1).[29]

With those words, the European Court on Human Rights qualified its holding in *Airey*, requiring member governments to provide free counsel to indigent litigants in civil cases. The court mandated counsel only in cases where the procedures or the substantive law is sufficiently complex that the expertise of lawyers makes a substantial difference to the litigant's chances of success. The holding left open the option for governments to offer forums where low-income litigants could enjoy effective access to justice without legal counsel. Thus, what the European Court of Human Rights has announced for the signatory nations to the European Convention in *Airey* and *Steel and Morris* is not a right to counsel as such, but more accurately a right to equal justice. That is, the guarantee of a fair hearing in which indigent parties enjoy "effective access to justice" and when opposed by better-heeled adversaries, "equality of arms" with those adversaries.

On December 1, 2009, the European Community embraced something approaching the above formula when the Treaty of Lisbon finally came into force, enacting a series of major revisions to the community's basic structure.[30] Included was a Charter of Fundamental Rights. This charter includes a provision that guarantees legal aid in civil cases while still allowing alternative strategies for delivering effective access to justice. Found in the charter's section on "justice," Article 47 reads as follows, with the legal aid guarantee appearing in the final sentence:

Article 47

Right to an Effective Remedy and to a Fair Trial

Everyone whose rights and freedoms guaranteed by the law of the Union are violated has the right to an effective remedy before a tribunal in compliance with the conditions laid down in this Article.

Everyone is entitled to a fair and public hearing within a reasonable time by an independent and impartial tribunal previously established by law. Everyone shall have the possibility of being advised, defended and represented.

Legal aid *shall be made available* to those who lack sufficient resources in so far as such aid is necessary to ensure effective access to justice.[31]

One could imagine what it would mean if the United States adopted similar language as a guarantee of what lower-income litigants would enjoy when they appeared in tribunals deciding their disputes and enforcing their rights. It could come from a court, no longer fearing it was imposing an obligation that would mandate the expense of providing lawyers in every case in every forum, even where lower-income people could enjoy truly effective access to justice through less costly approaches. After setting the standard governments had to satisfy, the court could leave it to the other branches to work out the details. Or alternatively, the guarantee could result from a legislative effort that not only articulated the standard of "effective access to justice," but designed, tested, and installed the full range of institutions and services required to achieve truly *effective* access to justice—but with lawyers guaranteed in forums and cases where they are needed to ensure equality before the law.

WHAT THE UNITED STATES MIGHT LEARN FROM COUNTRIES WITH "RIGHTS-BASED" LEGAL AID

Because so many European nations have had statutory rights to counsel in their regular civil courts for so many years, they have accumulated a vast amount of experience in implementing such a right. Should the United States contemplate moving in that direction, it stands to gain some valuable information and insights from the design and often redesign of those foreign programs.

In no country does the existence of a right to counsel in civil cases mean a low-income person can simply march in and demand a lawyer sue somebody. All impose some sort of "merits" test. That is, before the legal aid program will provide legal representation to a financially eligible applicant, the applicant's prospects for a successful prosecution or defense of the claim must pass some threshold. That threshold varies and is expressed in different language in different countries—as a "reasonable probability of success,"[32] in others as a "reasonable grounds for bringing or defending" the case[33] and yet others will grant legal aid unless the applicant's case is "manifestly inadmissible or devoid of foundation."[34] Most nations also impose a "significance" test, again framed in different ways in different statutes. Some nations do so by merely excluding "trivial" cases.[35] Others require the applicant's pursuit of the case to pass a "reasonableness" test in addition to means and merits tests[36] or that the litigation costs are not "unreasonable in relation to the possible gain or loss."[37] In most nations, the right to counsel doesn't apply to all types of cases, but usually covers all but a few categories such as defamation, election disputes, and alienation of affections.[38] Some countries also limit the statutory right to cases heard in the regular courts, and leave citizens to their own devices when appearing in administrative proceedings before "tribunals," "administrative courts," and the like,[39] although the government may provide advice and assistance short of representation in those forums.[40]

All countries, of course, impose a financial means test. But in many of the European and common law countries, government-funded legal services are not confined to those near the bottom of the income ladder. In the Netherlands, for instance, nearly half the population is eligible for some level of government-subsidized legal aid in civil cases.[41] Instead these programs provide free services to the poor and partially subsidized services to those whose incomes put them above that level.[42] (Another way of characterizing these subsidies is to refer to the clients' share of the total cost as a copayment, with the level of the required copayment rising along with the clients' income.)

Most countries, no matter where they started, have settled on independent national bodies, public or quasi-public and not unlike our nation's Legal Services Corporation, as the best approach to administering their legal aid programs.[43] In some, however, the national entity doesn't just fund independent local organizations that deliver the services, as we do in the United States. Instead they employ the local administrative staffs, and also any salaried lawyers used to deliver legal services to the client community.[44] This is not that much different from what Arthur von Briesen proposed Congress should create for our country over a century ago, a single "national legal aid society."

Programs also differ as to who determines an applicant's eligibility to receive legal aid services—in Germany, the judges,[45] in France, local committees of lawyers and representatives from government agencies,[46] and in England and most other nations, salaried lawyers or administrators.[47] In most nations that have a rights-based legal aid system, applicants who are turned down have a right to appeal.[48] In some, it is only an internal administrative appeal.[49] But in others, an unsuccessful applicant also can appeal to or at least receive review by the judiciary,[50] thus allowing court decisions to occasionally refine the criteria applied in future eligibility determinations.

The United States has followed such a different path than most of the rest of the world with respect to civil legal aid, it has little exposure to the variety of delivery systems that have developed elsewhere in the world. Lacking a right to counsel, the United States has relied principally on a "fixed resource" approach in which we employ a limited number of salaried lawyers and ask them to serve as many poor people as they can, supplemented by pro bono services contributed by private attorneys. The many poor people salaried lawyers and the available pro bono lawyers are unable to serve simply go without counsel.

Should the United States, or a state, move to a "rights-based" system, it can no longer count entirely on a "fixed resource" to implement the right. Because they would have a legally enforceable right to counsel, financially eligible people with "meritorious" and "significant" claims or defenses could no longer be turned away as they are now, even if the salaried lawyer force was at full capacity.[51] If too many clients showed up, it would be physically and mentally impossible for those lawyers to handle the volume—to be in three courts at the same time, to have time to properly research a huge pile of legal problems the clients presented, or to draft the host of legal documents those clients need. So the legal aid system needs a flexible resource, one that can expand when the number of applicants increases and contract when the demand eases, for one reason or the other. The need for a flexible resource appears to inevitably require involvement of the private legal profession, at a minimum as a "safety valve" for the overflow from salaried offices. This is what Ireland does. When the salaried staff lawyers cannot handle all the applicants arriving at their offices in a timely fashion, the staff begins assigning cases to private lawyers from one of three subject-matter panels.[52]

In addition to the need for a flexible resource, there are other reasons for including private lawyers in a "rights-based" system that plans to cover most kinds of cases. Some clients are likely to arrive presenting unusual legal problems with which salaried lawyers are unfamiliar yet within the specialty of some private lawyers. It would seem to be less expensive and more effective to send such cases to the specialist in private practice. The foreign experience suggests there also may be some potential political advantages in having the entire legal profession invested in the government-funded legal aid program—not just as a matter of professional principle or pride, but as a matter of self-interest.

Several other nations with "rights-based" civil legal aid systems make greater use of private lawyers than Ireland does. Germany[53] and France[54] rely entirely on compensated private lawyers—similar to our country's "Judicare" programs. Private solicitors and barristers remain the dominant but not exclusive source of legal aid in England.[55] Finland[56] and Quebec Province,[57] on the other hand, give clients the option between having their litigation handled by a staff lawyer or a private practitioner—once the staff finds they are eligible for legal aid. And, Ontario Province assigns two large categories—family law and criminal defense cases—to private lawyers,[58] and the rest to salaried lawyers in legal clinics scattered across the province.[59] The Netherlands legal aid system divides the work by function. "Law counters" staffed with salaried lawyers and paraprofessionals[60] furnish all the legal advice and brief service,[61] with compensated private counsel handling all the litigation.[62]

As can be seen, foreign countries provide a wide range of alternative models for every dimension of operating a "rights-based" civil legal aid system. The main lesson may be that a civil right to counsel can be made to work, because it has been in comparable democracies, more than once and in different ways. By proper screening of cases, lower-income people can be guaranteed access to justice without inflicting injustice on others. It is possible to contemplate, at least, extending services to those in the lower-middle class and even the middle class, on a partially subsided basis. And, there are several ways to mix salaried lawyers and compensated private counsel to provide a resource flexible enough to satisfy the variable demand from year to year.

After removing the blinders, and glimpsing how other countries have gone about seeking to "establish justice" for their lower-income people, it is time to consider how the United States might combine those experiences with our own history and envision a better future for civil legal aid and equal justice in our country. That is the subject of the next chapter.

Chapter 31

Establishing Justice for All: Possibilities and Prospects[1]

> It was the boast of Augustus . . . that he found Rome of brick and left it of marble . . . but how much nobler will be the Sovereign's boast when he shall have it to say that he found law dear, and left it cheap; . . . found it the patrimony of the rich, left it the inheritance of the poor; found it the two-edged sword of craft and oppression, left it the staff of honesty and the shield of innocence.
> —Lord Brougham, speech on Law Reform, House of Commons, 1828

If the United States is ever to truly "establish justice," as promised, for those without the financial resources to employ lawyers, it will have to guarantee them *effective* access to the legal system and equality of arms with their opponent, in other words, a *right* to equal justice not merely a hope. In many situations that means a right to be provided a lawyer because without one effective access and equality of arms are impossible. For far too long, when it comes to equal justice for all, this nation has promised the reality but only delivered a myth. It is time to become serious about repairing this deep rupture in the very foundation of our democracy. In this chapter, we discuss the possible ingredients and general shape of a rights-based system guaranteeing equal justice for all in the United States.

POSSIBLE MODEL FOR A CIVIL RIGHT TO COUNSEL IN THE UNITED STATES

In 2010, a working group within the American Bar Association (ABA) completed drafting a "model statute" designed to offer a head start for any jurisdiction that wanted to implement a right to counsel in civil cases. With representatives from a dozen ABA sections, this Civil Right to Counsel Working Group spent more than a year researching, writing, and circulating tentative drafts to a wide range of individuals and organizations for their input. Finally, in August 2010, the working group was ready with its final draft, which was the fifth or sixth version, and submitted it for approval by the ABA House of Delegates. It passed with an overwhelming voice vote, along with a companion document, "Basic Principles for Implementing a Civil Right to Counsel."[2]

In some sections, the ABA's "Model Civil Right to Counsel Act" resembles one or the other of the foreign statutes mentioned above—containing merits and significance tests, for instance. But there is one obvious difference. Instead of extending the right to virtually every types of case, as most nations do, this model act proposes as a first step creating a right for poor people only in cases where basic human needs are at stake. These basic human needs are listed as including "sustenance, safety, health, housing, and child custody."

The model act also focuses almost exclusively on the right to a full-fledged lawyer and did not purport to cover lower cost alternatives that might provide *effective* access to justice in selected situations. Yet this may be an important element of any plan for comprehensive, cost-effective right to equal justice in the United States.

WHEN, IF EVER, CAN SOMETHING LESS THAN A LAWYER GUARANTEE A RIGHT TO EQUAL JUSTICE?

There appears to be little doubt that the United States has much to learn from other countries about the willingness to invest enough to guarantee their citizens equality before the law and some alternative approaches to making that guarantee a reality. Yet if there is an upside to our failure to adopt a rights-based system thus far, it is that it has compelled the legal aid organizations and, in some jurisdictions, the courts, to innovate. The scarcity of resources has forced these elements of the justice system to develop tools that will allow them to deliver some level of justice to as many low-income people as they can with what they have available. Whether that level is sufficient to provide low-income litigants equality before the law is a threshold question. Yet properly mixed with a much larger quantity of lawyer resources, these innovations offer the possibility of building a cost-effective system for implementing a right to equal justice for lower-income people in this country. The next few pages explore the four most promising developments—(1) self-help assistance to unrepresented litigants, (2) lay (non-lawyer) advocates in administrative cases and perhaps simple court proceedings, (3) technological advances applied to the delivery of justice, and (4) aggregate remedies for common claims.

(1) Self-Help Assistance to Unrepresented Litigants

The first of these developments involves fundamental changes taking place in the adjudication of disputes in family law courts. These courts often have larger caseloads than the regular civil courts and touch more lives. Of significance to the future of justice for the poor, nationwide these forums not only hear millions of cases a year involving lower-income people, but family courts are one of the few venues where both sides are generally from the same economic strata and thus less often pit an unrepresented party against a lawyer in the courtroom. Instead, more often than not, neither side has a lawyer.

The fundamental changes that have been introduced represent no less than a shift from the adversary model of deciding cases in the direction of the inquisitorial model. This means replacing a model that places the primary responsibility for finding the facts and the governing legal principles on the private parties who are opposing each other before the court in favor of a model which asks the judge to do most of that work. An approach that expects the judge to take an active role in asking most of the questions not just evaluating the answers witnesses give to questions the parties or their lawyers ask. And also, one that leaves it to the judge to figure out the law that controls the outcome, without lawyers bringing the applicable statutes and cases to the judge's attention.

My home state of California was not the first to start down this road. But in recent years it probably has gone further than most other jurisdictions. Beginning at least a decade ago, judges began to realize poor people and those somewhat above that line were flooding California's family law courts, appearing without lawyers, and asking the courts to give them justice as "pro pers." ("Pro per" in legal jargon refers to a person representing oneself without legal counsel.) In something like 70 to 80 percent of the hundreds of thousands of cases the family courts in California are expected to decide each year, either one or both parties are unrepresented by counsel.[3] It is possible this dramatic statistic means the courts just began quantifying a phenomenon that had long been true. But whatever the reason, there is no doubt the majority of litigants appearing in California's family law courts—and, truth be told, in family law courts around the country—lack lawyers and are proceeding on a pro per basis. And, despite the Nolo Press, the paralegal forms–preparation services, and the Internet, as of the late 1990s the vast majority of that vast majority were appearing with defective pleadings, with no notion of what evidence they had to find and present, and no idea of how to conduct themselves in the courtroom.

This left the judges and the judicial system with only two choices. One alternative—allow unrepresented parties to stumble along, ask the judge to try guessing what each side was trying to present, and make a call that carried a great risk of being the wrong one—in other words, in far too many cases to deliver injustice rather than justice. The other course, and the one the California court system elected to follow, was to provide assistance to self-represented litigants. Through a combination of group classes and one-on-one assistance the court's self-help centers seek to allow unrepresented litigants to produce decent written pleadings, to give them an idea of what evidence they have to collect and present to the judge, and some preview of how the judge will expect them to behave when they enter the courtroom.[4]

This kind of quickie legal education can only go so far, however. It rarely can turn even a college-educated litigant—to say nothing of the typical lower-income individual—into someone capable of constructing and presenting a persuasive case consistent with the rules of evidence and directed to the issues critical to making the correct decision. Those determinative factual issues, in turn, are defined by the law— the legal principles governing this particular dispute, which lawyers not pro pers are trained to know or identify through research. Yet this is what the adversarial system counts on the opposing litigants packaging and presenting to the judge.

Those fostering self-help assistance programs within the judicial system were quick to recognize the essential need for "active judges" if their approach was to work. The Administrative Office of the Courts in California has developed a benchbook for judges when presiding over family law cases in which unrepresented litigants appear.[5] This manual expressly justifies this inquisitorial role for judges when the parties are unrepresented by counsel.

> To decide cases fairly, judges need facts, and in self-represented litigant cases, to get facts, judges often have to ask questions, modify procedure, and apply their common sense in the courtroom to create an environment in which all the relevant facts are brought out. In short, judges have found as a practical matter that a formalized, noncommunicative role in dealing with cases involving self-represented litigants can lead to serious decision-making problems. Without the additional facts that active judicial involvement brings to light, judges are at risk of making wrong decisions.[6]

On the opposite coast, the New York County Bar Association drafted a set of "protocols" addressed to judges sitting in New York's housing courts where 90 percent of tenants are unrepresented and 90 percent of landlords have lawyers. Like the California benchbook, the New York protocols define what is essentially an active, what some would define as an inquisitorial, role for the judge in the hearing and resolution of cases in those courts.[7]

For those cases and when the competing parties and other circumstances are right, there is good reason to expect these proceedings to produce just results. And, to the extent these courts and these processes can succeed in doing so they reduce the need for government to provide lawyers to the litigants and thus could contribute to the cost-effectiveness of the entire justice system.

Nonetheless, it is important to recognize some limitations to this approach. Once one of the parties has a lawyer and the other doesn't, it is difficult to the point of impossible for a judge to make the sides equal. To expect the lawyer on one side to question and cross-examine witnesses and otherwise present the client's case, while the judge is doing the same for the unrepresented party is unlikely to produce the appearance of impartiality. Yet if the judge fails to assume that responsibility, the contest will be so unequal it will lack either the reality or appearance of equal justice.[8] Even when both sides are unrepresented, often there will be situations when one or both parties are incapable of even the modest levels of participation the inquisitorial approach requires—because of a lack of English language facility, mental capacity, or otherwise. There also will be many cases where the law to be ascertained and/or the facts to be uncovered are simply too complex for the judge to unearth without the assistance of counsel on both sides—in other words, without a true adversary proceeding.

A few words of caution are in order when viewing self-help assistance as an alternative to the traditional lawyer-intensive adversary system. Some skeptics, concerned self-help assistance may be nothing more than a cheap excuse for avoiding the cost of providing lawyers to the millions of litigants needing them, raise questions.

To begin with, they ask, is it absolutely certain an inquisitorial court coupled with self-help assistance will necessarily cost the public less than an adversarial forum with two lawyers, even if one or both of them is paid by the government? A trial judge might have to spend considerably more time teasing out the relevant facts from the unrepresented parties in an inquisitorial hearing than that same judge would listening to lawyers who honed in on the decisive law and facts in an adversarial proceeding. Lawyers also are more likely to settle cases than unrepresented parties, especially in cases as contentious as those heard in family courts. To the extent they do, the judge need devote little if any time to those cases. Some argue research that has yet to happen may reveal taking account of all the expenses government incurs—judicial time, the cost of self-help assistance, and attorney compensation—that it would cost the government less to handle a court's caseload by paying lawyers for one or both sides than paying the judge and self-help assistance office to decide each case in an inquisitorial hearing.

Other questions raised about the inquisitorial model revolve around the judges.

First, can U.S. judges who are socialized in the adversarial approach and its superiority truly accept the inquisitorial role and transform themselves into effective practitioners of that fundamentally different way of conducting a hearing? If they don't, and merely sit back asking the unskilled parties to give it their best shot at making a case for their position, what are the chances of a fair process and a just result? This is the reason for the California handbook and the New York protocols and apparently the re-socialization has worked with some judges in those jurisdictions, at least. But how about the rest?

Second, does the judge presiding over a given hearing have sufficient mastery of the relevant law himself or herself to arrive at a legally correct decision without input from lawyers representing the competing parties? This may not be a problem when the case arises in a narrow, self-contained area of the law, but it could be a major concern if the inquisitorial model were to expand to subject areas interlaced with complex rules—statutes, regulations, appellate court interpretations, etc. No judge has or, as a practical matter can, have that command of the law. Much of what lawyers do when litigating is present competing interpretations of legal issues to the judge who, after profiting from this education can determine the proper legal rules controlling the case.

Finally, will the judge's inquiry into the facts be distorted by prejudices he or she harbors or will the judge be able to maintain complete objectivity in asking questions and evaluating credibility? One of the presumed virtues of the adversary system is that it forces judges to at least hear about facts and law that may not fit their worldview and personal prejudices.

The answers to these and other questions should be answered as U.S. jurisdictions continue expanding their use of the inquisitorial model combined with self-help assistance and learn from experience whether and when this model works. Properly done research also might speed the process of finding those answers. But until then, it will be difficult to gauge the proper reach of this alternative to the traditional adversarial model.

(2) Lay Advocates in Administrative Proceedings and Perhaps Simple Court Cases

At a midpoint in cost between full representation by a lawyer and some self-help assistance lies another alternative that holds promise for contributing to a cost-effective justice system—using lay advocates instead of lawyers in administrative hearings. This alternative developed relatively early in the history of the federally funded legal service program when it became apparent lay persons could be trained to properly represent recipients in welfare fair hearings. The procedures in these administrative forums are quite informal and the substantive law, although relatively complex, is self-contained. Once lay advocates became educated about that body of law and had access to advice from a supervising lawyer, they could provide quality representation to welfare recipients. A study confirms this is true in some other administrative proceedings as well.[9] This is especially significant because so many cases involving lower-income people are decided in administrative forums rather than the courts, because this is where nearly all disputes over government benefits—social security, public assistance, public housing, and the like—are decided.

As was true of self-help assistance, however, substituting lay advocates for lawyers in the representation of the poor also requires that the forum hearing the case adhere to some principles. If poor persons have lay advocates at their side, the agency defending the adverse action likewise should be represented by a lay advocate not a lawyer. This balanced advocacy is essential to fairness and more likely to produce a correct result. (It also is less expensive for the government than paying a lawyer's salary for the agency's side of the case.)

Whether this lay advocate model could be transferred beyond the administrative arena to the courts is an open question and a problematical proposition, especially given the monopoly the legal profession enjoys over representation in the judicial system. To give that monopoly to non-lawyer advocates so lawyers couldn't appear in certain cases in the regular courts may not be either feasible or wise. Nor does the option of guaranteeing lower-income litigants only lay advocates to face full-fledged lawyers in judicial proceedings offer the "equality of arms" that is essential to equal justice. Nonetheless, with so many disputes involving poor people being decided in nonjudicial forums an increased role for lay advocates in those forums offers the prospect of an effective but overall less costly system for giving lower-income people a right to equal justice in this nation.

(3) Technological Advances Applied to the Delivery of Justice

A third development holds promise for reducing the cost while maintaining the quality of justice lower-income people enjoy—ever more sophisticated applications of technology to the delivery of justice to government-funded clients. The past few years have seen the growth of telephone "hot lines" offering legal advice and referrals at far lower cost than those services could be delivered in person and to populations often far removed from the legal services offices.[10] By comparison, this is an obvious utilization of long-existing technology on a wide scale.

Newer technologies have tended to be deployed on a pilot or experimental basis with varying degrees of success. Among them are computerized kiosks that coach unrepresented litigants through a series of questions and spill out court pleadings—a complaint, or an answer, or an order. In a court with e-filing, it is technologically feasible to file this pleading by pressing a button and feeding it to the clerk's office over the Internet. Otherwise the pleading can be printed out and filed in person.[11] The kiosk also can show a video to litigants, explaining what evidence they should bring to court and how they should present their cases to the judge. These same types of computer programs can be set up to operate over the Internet rather than at a kiosk, thus offering even easier access, at least for more sophisticated pro pers who have access to a computer either at home or at a library or other convenient location. In effect, however, this is only a computerized system for providing self-help assistance to pro per litigants. It helps in those situations where this level of assistance is enough to give litigants truly effective access to justice, but once those litigants arrive in court they are subject to all the potential limitations and conditions described in the discussion of other forms of self-help assistance

The Internet also has facilitated wide distribution of legal information, court forms, process recommendations, and sources of legal help. Several years ago, for instance, the California judicial system opened a huge website with hundreds of pages of information—now in Spanish as well as English—that receives scores of thousands of "hits" every month.[12] This may be the largest but not the first nor the only example of these state-wide legal information websites. In fact, the majority of states now have a legal information website, the outgrowth of a program LSC started in 2000—Technology Initiative Grants (TIG).[13] Once again, however, these websites are helpful primarily to pro pers, and not the many lower-income litigants who require assistance or representation that goes beyond self-help guidance whether that guidance comes in person or over the Internet.

Technology can offer opportunities to lower the cost of delivering full-fledged legal representation, as well. When time and distance are involved, teleconferencing allows lawyers to meet with clients or witnesses located far from the legal aid center without losing hours of travel time. Computerized "banks" of briefs, pleadings, and the like combined with "document assembly" programs can avoid the cost of reinventing the wheel, especially in handling repetitive issues or routine cases.

Technological advances in the future, both predictable and unpredictable, could well dwarf these and other present applications in their effect on the judicial process and its cost. Merely as an example, the convergence of ever-improving voice recognition and language translation software might someday soon allow the simultaneous translation of testimony from non-English speaking witnesses while allowing non-English speaking clients to comprehend what was being said in English by others, all without the expense of interpreters. Or artificial intelligence might finally reach the stage where it shortens dramatically the time required to research the law and produce legal documents and arguments tailor-made to the precise issues of the particular case. Analyzing the issues, researching the law, and coming up with an answer or a position—the most time consuming and thus expensive tasks lawyers typically perform—could become a matter of minutes not hours or days.

On the other hand, the *possibility* technology may one day dramatically reduce the government's cost for providing full-fledged legal representation to lower-income people in the United States should not be allowed to delay their realization of a right to equal justice in this country. Even were that future cost reduction a certainty, it would not justify denying justice to millions of the nation's citizens for years to say nothing of decades or conceivably generations while waiting for those technological breakthroughs to occur. The fact it is far less than a certainty these cost savings will materialize or be as significant as optimistic techies might hope for adds a further reason to move ahead vigorously in the present to guarantee justice as a matter of right. At the same time, legal services providers should be encouraged to continue experimenting with applications of existing and emerging technologies and adopting those that prove successful to increase efficiencies and improve results in their delivery of justice to lower-income clients.

(4) Aggregate Remedies for Common Claims

Ironically, because of restrictions Congress imposed in the mid-1990s, legal aid organizations—at least those funded by the federal government—are barred from using some of the legal system's most cost-effective tools. No longer can they bring class actions or engage in legislative advocacy to magnify the number of poor people they can help with their limited resources. Restoration of the ability to deploy these important legal tools would certainly enhance the cost-effectiveness of the legal services delivery system.

It is wasteful bordering on foolish to require every customer of a business victimized by that firm's illegal practice to sue or defend in an individual lawsuit. It is wasteful of court resources, wasteful of the legal aid program's budget, and of any government funds invested in that legal aid program. If the ban on class actions is good for anyone, it is the businesses, because cash-strapped legal aid programs will only be able to afford representing a few customers. Settle with those few and the business can continue the practice, even if it is illegal.

It is not only the business–customer relationship for which this is true. Among the many others, consider employer–employee, government agency–benefit recipient, bank–depositor, credit agency–debtor, insurer–insured, and several others where the dispute is between an institution and an individual. The institutional litigant holds most of the cards versus an individual and is a "repeat player" able to average gains and losses, litigating strategically. Only by "ganging up" in a class action can the individual parties even the scales and not only recover their losses but end the institutional party's practices that hurt them in the first place—whether it is the sale of a dangerous or defective product, an illegal denial of government benefits to a certain class of claimants, illegal underpayment of some group of employees, or the like.

Some lawmakers seemed to view class actions as class warfare, instead of what they are, a cost-effective tool for litigating cases involving a large number of people with claims they were adversely affected by the same conduct. Restoring the ability of those lawyers receiving government funds to bring class actions, when appropriate, would help make a "rights-based" legal aid system more cost effective, as it would one that was not rights-based.

The same is true of legislative advocacy. In appropriate circumstances, it can be the most efficient way—and sometimes the only way—to deal with a client's problem. With a single successful change in the law, it can put an end to practices or potentially change questionable legal rules that harm thousands of people or sometimes more, thus also reducing the number of people coming to legal aid offices seeking relief from the effects of those practices or legal rules. But legislative advocacy, although both efficient and effective, when successful, raises some unique issues in the context of a rights-based legal aid system. These issues will be explored later in this chapter.

ANOTHER ESSENTIAL ELEMENT—AN ACCURATE "TRIAGE" SYSTEM FOR MATCHING PROBLEM WITH SOLUTION

In the medical context, the term "triage" can easily conjure the image of a mass-accident scene, with a few harried doctors choosing who they will spend time trying to save, among scores or hundreds of injured people. The barely injured and the already dead and certain-to-die go to the end of the queue while the doctors focus their energies on those seriously hurt but deemed salvageable. In the justice system context, for decades legal service providers in the United States have been employing "triage," consciously or unconsciously, systematically or haphazardly, to choose which applicants are to be served and which left to fend for themselves—in other words, who gets justice and who suffers injustice.

The easiest triage principle for legal services lawyers to apply is "first come, first served," which also means "next come, not served." But few legal services providers use that technique. Most have identified a set of high priority subject areas, from among housing, income maintenance, domestic violence, consumer problems, child custody, and the like. In the main, these providers accept as many people as possible who appear with problems falling within the chosen subject areas and turn away virtually all who come with other problems.[14]

None of these is the type of "triage" referred to in this section. It is not the choice between those to be served and those to be left out in the cold, those to live and those to die in the medical context, or those to get justice and those destined to suffer injustice in the legal context. Rather what is meant by "triage" here is the process of deciding what level of service is to be provided. It is the matching of an applicant and his or her problem to the type of service—self-help assistance, a lay advocate, limited representation, or full representation by a lawyer—required to give that person a fair and equal opportunity for a just result.

Designing an effective "triage" system to accomplish this critical task will not be an easy proposition. It cannot be done by relying on gross or rigid categories. For instance, thousands of people would suffer injustice if a triage system diverted all family law cases to the "self-help assistance" track. True, one could expect a rough parity rather than an "inequality of arms" in most family law cases involving low income contestants, because both sides—husbands and wives, fathers and mothers—ordinarily are from the same economic strata. Still, depending on who was the primary "breadwinner," one side might have a lawyer and the other not, creating an inequality of arms in the courtroom. Even if the triage criteria only assigned family cases to "self-help assistance" when both parties were unrepresented, there would be a substantial subset in which legal counsel was needed for a truly fair hearing. If a case turned on complex facts or legal rules, for instance, both sides might flail around, leaving the judge to guess at what happened and hope the resulting decision was correct. Legal counsel might also be necessary if, for instance, one or both of the litigants were unsophisticated or lacked sufficient English language skills, or there was a serious knowledge or power imbalance between the spouses.

Thus, the selection criteria must be fairly detailed and precise, but presumably also allow some flexibility and some measure of subjective judgment, if they are to properly match the problem with the solution. Although it may be possible to devise an initial set of criteria based on common sense assumptions and the experience of lawyers and self-help providers, that initial set should be subject to modification based on evaluations of the various tracks and how accurately the triage system in place is accurately picking the correct tracks for the clients' problems. These assessments would have to take account not only of the criteria established, but how well the professionals making the choices were implementing those criteria.

WHAT ABOUT "PROMOTING MEASURES FOR THEIR PROTECTION"; DOES IT HAVE A PLACE IN A "RIGHTS-BASED" LEGAL AID SYSTEM?

As chapter 1 of this book revealed, from the beginning civil legal aid in the United States, in concept if not always reality, has been about more than access to the courts and the availability of legal advice. Access to justice in this country means access to the entire legal system, to the government, the right and ability to "petition" those who hold the power to make laws and to redress grievances, whether they sit in court rooms or prowl the halls of congress or labor in some government department or administrative agency. Although some "protective measures" for the poor will arrive as the natural and inevitable consequence of giving them effective access to the courts, especially the appellate courts, others can only happen thorough advocacy in the legislative arena, in the administrative rule making process, or elsewhere in government.

Yet even in concept, advocacy for legislative change or reform of administrative regulations and rules entails a wide grant of discretion about whether and when to proceed. It fits in as an adjunct not an integral part of a rights-based regime. Lawyers in the original Legal Aid Society became involved in legislative advocacy during the 19th century as a by-product of their representation of individual poor people—a pattern that continued with legal services lawyers in the 20th and 21st centuries. In all three centuries, through these frontline experiences, the lawyers identified laws that harmed their clients and needed to be changed as well as harmful practices that screamed for a new law to end them.

Once identified, the lawyers could consider the political feasibility of a legislative fix for the problem, knowing full well any new law that passed would not come in time to benefit the individual clients whose cases revealed the need for change—except perhaps if they were to face the same problem in the future. As a result, almost by definition and of necessity, legislative advocacy was and is for the collective benefit of a community not the individual benefit of a specific individual client. (Since 1996, LSC-funded lawyers cannot themselves advocate for changes in legislation or administrative rules, but once they have identified the need for a change they can seek out an organization not tainted by receiving LSC money to carry out the campaign.)

Yet legislative advocacy—the possibility of making a case for change in statutory or regulatory law—is an essential element of any system that claims to truly offer access to justice for the persons it serves. This means that the legal aid system serving a given community should have the right to engage in legislative advocacy, when appropriate under all the circumstances, but that individual clients should not have the *right* to this form of advocacy in their particular case. This would be true even in a jurisdiction that otherwise operated as a "rights-based" system.

The reason for the distinction? There may be merit in seeking the legislative or regulatory change the client wants to happen, and that change might be significant. But that claim is not going to a court that has a duty to make a reasoned and rational decision. Instead, the request for change must enter the political maelstrom, where merit and significance are of only secondary importance and where decisions about timing and strategies and tactics must be made without regard to the individual client's best interests. For instance, the client may want to see the legislative proposal introduced right now, but the political situation might dictate it wait a year or two or until a new legislature is elected, long after there is any chance it would help that particular client. Or the political situation might make it impossible to pursue the change in a way that would help the client, but a less drastic change, unhelpful to that individual, might be feasible. Or the client's desired change, if pursued, might detract from other legal changes the lawyers were already pursuing. Only if and when the client becomes an organization or other body representative of the interests of all those likely to benefit in the future from the proposed change in the law should the lawyer's ordinary deference to client desires apply, and even then with some qualifications. Thus, conceptually, in a jurisdiction offering true access to justice, legislative advocacy would be a discretionary service attached to a "rights-based" legal aid system. Not discretionary in the sense its existence is discretionary, but rather discretionary in its execution. That is, clients would not have a right to its deployment nor to control its timing and strategy—at least individual clients shouldn't.

HOW CAN A "RIGHT TO EQUAL JUSTICE" AND TO A LAWYER WHEN NEEDED COME TO THE UNITED STATES?

Based on the experience in other countries, a "rights based" rather than merely discretionary legal aid system such as we currently have in the United States, can be achieved in one of two ways—either by statute or through a constitutional decision from the highest court in the jurisdiction. Even if a court interprets the constitution to require such a right, however, the full implementation of the mandate will entail legislative action. For instance, when the U.S. Supreme Court declared a right to counsel in criminal cases, it only meant that state governments somehow had to ensure indigent defendants had lawyers. Whether those lawyers would be paid or impressed into service, or if compensated whether representation would be through salaried public defenders or private counsel, these and a host of other issues had to be worked out by state lawmakers. As might be expected, different states came up with different solutions—some more effective and fairer to defendants than others. The same would be true if the U.S. Supreme Court or the highest court in a state were to find a civil right to counsel in the federal or or a state's constitution.

In any event, based on how these rights developed elsewhere in the world and as to criminal cases in the United States, one might anticipate the right in civil cases would begin with some state or states enacting legislation establishing such a right in all or at least some categories of cases—perhaps those involving the basic human needs identified in the ABA Model Access statute. As covered in chapter 30, the right in civil case began in England with parliament's passage of the Statute of Henry VII in 1495. On the continent it began in 1851 when France legislated a right that over the next few decades was followed by similar laws in most European nations.

This trend did not make it across the Atlantic as far as civil cases, but many U.S. states did on their own create statutory rights to counsel in criminal cases. California, for instance, less than a quarter century after joining the Union, enacted a right to counsel for criminal defendants in 1872. By 1963, when the U.S. Supreme Court finally found a right to counsel in the Constitution, at least 35 states already had created such a right usually by statute.[15]

On both sides of the Atlantic, these statutory rights began as "unfunded" mandates, in civil cases in Europe and criminal cases in the United States. Lawyers were drafted to provide the required representation without any payment for their services—although as mentioned in earlier chapters in many nations and some U.S. states the legislatures years or decades later passed bills providing the appointed counsel some level of compensation. This often was done as much for the benefit of the represented parties as for the lawyers—the extent and quality of the work influenced by the reality that you tend to "get what you pay for."

At the present time, for many reasons, it would be unrealistic to expect a U.S. jurisdiction to enact a right to equal justice that failed to provide some compensation for the lawyers who supplied representation when needed to deliver that justice. As a result, the days of a cost-free right are long over and it is not as easy as it was in 19th-century Europe or the United States for a legislative body, state or federal, to create a right that will necessitate frequent deployment of lawyers as well as other forms of paid services, such as lay advocates, self-help assistance, etc. This helps explain why U.S. states have been slow to create rights to counsel in civil cases, and in those states which have extended those rights confined them to only limited categories. In a recent article, John Pollock summarized those targeted rights to counsel:

> As a consequence of both court decisions and legislative enactments, indigent litigants in a majority of states enjoy a right to appointed counsel in some types of cases, such as termination of parental rights, abuse/neglect, guardianship, civil contempt . . ., involuntary mental health commitment, quarantine, and proceedings to grant minors a judicial waiver of an abortion statute's parental consent requirement. Moreover, in many (but not a majority) of states, indigent litigants are provided counsel in proceedings involving adult protection, paternity, nonconsensual adoption, sexually dangerous/violent person, and parole revocation. Finally, a few states provide a right to counsel in proceedings involving custody, domestic violence, special immigrant juvenile status, or certain types of benefits.[16]

There also have been exceptions, a precious few, to the general pattern that legislative rights have preceded a court's reinforcing and sometimes expanding those statutory rights with a broad constitutional decision. Switzerland is the clearest example of a supreme court stepping forward and filling a complete vacuum. The European Court on Human Rights did that for Ireland, but at a time nearly all the remaining European countries already had statutory rights to counsel in civil cases. But in Switzerland, no canton had a statutory right before the high court reminded them the national constitution guaranteed all their citizens, including the poor, equality before the law and thus free counsel for those who couldn't afford to pay for their own.

What are the prospects for the U.S. Supreme Court or a state supreme court taking the bold step the Swiss Supreme Court took over 75 years ago or the somewhat less bold action the European Court on Human Rights took over 40 years ago? Although those prospects dimmed considerably in 1981 with the U.S. *Lassiter* opinion discussed earlier it did not necessarily foreclose the possibility forever. Remember four of the nine justices hearing that appeal adopted the position that constitutional due process mandated appointment of free counsel for the mother whose parental rights were in jeopardy, even though she was a convicted murderer serving a lengthy prison sentence who had evidenced little concern for her child before or after her imprisonment. Had there been a right to counsel with any sort of merits test, she almost certainly would have been one of those who failed that test and thus been denied counsel, even in a rights-based system.

Indeed one of the encouraging signs in the long run is found in the close calls in cases at the state level where a court fell just short of deciding in favor of a right to counsel and the number of justices and judges who, in the aggregate, have agreed it is a constitutional right. In a decision of New York's highest court in 1975,[17] three of the seven justices found a constitutional right to counsel in divorce cases, which would have extended that right to a broad class of litigation and set the legal groundwork for a full-scale right to counsel in nearly all civil cases in the future. Similarly, in 2003, three of seven judges on Maryland's highest court, the Court of Appeal, found there was a constitutional right to counsel in private child custody cases, that is, cases between a mother and father and not involving the government. The remaining four judges in that case did not decide against that view on the right-to-counsel issue, but just chose not to reach it.[18] When in 1984 an unrepresented indigent civil litigant petitioned the California Supreme Court to consider a trial counsel's refusal to appoint counsel for him, three of the seven members of that court voted to hear that appeal,[19] a strong indication they were ready to overrule the trial judge. Close calls don't create precedent, but they can build momentum.

One thing that has impeded progress is what could be called the myth of *Lassiter*. Too many judges and even lower appellate courts have misread its message. They have tended to read only the case's headline—"The U.S. Supreme Court denies right to counsel in a civil case"—and interpreted that to mean there is no right to counsel in *any* civil case. In fact, an entirely proper headline for Lassiter could have been "The U.S. Supreme Court denies a right to counsel in the civil case before it, but declares there is a right to counsel in civil cases if a three-part test is satisfied." True, the majority did hold there was a "presumption against" appointing counsel for poor people in civil cases. But too many courts have treated that presumption as if it were a conclusive presumption which ends any further inquiry before the judges inform the poor clients appearing in their courtrooms that they have no constitutional right to counsel in civil cases.

But in fact, it is not a conclusive presumption but under the *Lassiter* opinion very much a rebuttable one. The *Lassiter* opinion lays out precisely what is required to rebut the presumption—three factors, two of which the majority conceded were satisfied in that case—the significance of the indigent party's interests at stake in the litigation's outcome versus, on the other side, the government's interest in not providing counsel, although the cost of that counsel to the government could not alone justify its denial. Only the third factor needed to overcome the presumption—the "risk of error" if counsel was not provided to the mother—was not present in that particular case. That "risk of error if counsel does not represent the indigent party "is another way of asking "would a lawyer have been able to make a difference?" if appointed to represent the client it that proceeding. If there ever was a case where it is clear a lawyer—even the very best one—could not have prevented a mother from losing her parental rights it was the *Lassiter* case.

The majority in the Lassiter case expected the state courts to apply its three-factor test to future indigent parents who asked for appointment of counsel. In his concurring opinion explaining why he had supplied the fifth vote to create the majority ruling against giving Ms. Lassiter the lawyer she sought, Chief Justice Warren Burger said he was willing to leave the right-to-counsel issue to "case-by-case" determination by state courts.[20] But for the most part, that is not what has happened. Instead most state trial and appellate courts simply hold there is no right to counsel, citing *Lassiter,* and don't bother engaging in the three-factor analysis the *Lassiter* opinion enunciated clearly and in some detail.

One federal trial judge, Charles Sweet, formerly a partner in a leading Wall Street law firm, did apply the *Lassiter* test, not in a decision, but in an article. In doing so, he reached the conclusion that a fair application of that test would result in the appointment of counsel in the average civil case.

> I think the most rewarding focus is on the Mathews three-factor procedural due process calculus applied by the Court which balances (1) the private interests at stake, (2) the government's interest, and (3) the risk that the procedures used will lead to erroneous decisions.
>
> To place the last first, then, analysis of the risk of erroneous decision dictates appointed counsel whenever in forma pauperis status exists. As every trial judge knows, the task of determining the correct legal outcome is rendered almost impossible without effective counsel. Courts have neither the time nor the capacity to be both litigants and impartial judges on any issue of genuine complexity.
>
> As far as the second factor is concerned, society's paramount interest must be in a just determination of a person's fundamental rights and privileges. While there will undoubtedly be a cost to providing counsel to impoverished litigants, erosion of faith in the judicial system would exact an even higher price. To put it simply, denial of representation constitutes denial of access to real justice.
>
> Finally, Mathews mandates as a third factor consideration of the private interest at stake. . . . A right to property or economic justice, to custody, or to housing, for example, is as significant in real terms as a right to a constitutional guaranty. Without representation, a litigant does not truly have access to our legal system, and it is the system, even more than the litigant, that will be the worse for the lack.[21]

A recent U.S. Supreme Court opinion in the context of a type of case that has both civil and criminal aspects has left a mixed message on the right-to-counsel issue. It arose when a father fell far behind in his child support obligations and was threatened with imprisonment for failure to pay those obligations. This is one of the rare situations where it remains legal to send someone to jail for nonpayment of a debt—but even then only if that person has the financial means to pay. These cases are like criminal cases in which there is an absolute right to counsel for indigent defendants because of the loss of physical liberty if one loses. But they resemble civil cases in that the only "crime" involved is the defendants failure to pay what is otherwise a civil debt. The other factor that is almost unique—the defendant, if imprisoned has the "keys to the jail in his pocket." All he has to do is pay what he owes in support payments and he can immediately walk out through the cell door.

In this particular case, *Turner v. Rogers*,[22] the mother was suing the father for a significant sum in unpaid support payments. Neither had counsel and the father asked the court to appoint one for him, because he faced imprisonment if he lost. In that, he was like a criminal defendant and believed he should have the same right to counsel as a bank robber or embezzler or any other person subject to losing his physical liberty in a court proceeding. After Turner was denied relief by the state trial and appellate courts his case arrived in the U.S. Supreme Court. The high court affirmed the denial of counsel, but only after finding in total the proceedings had denied Rogers due process, thus returning it to the trial court with instructions to rehear the case but with a number of changes in the process the judge used, which are calculated to offer the defendant due process without a lawyer.[23]

The outcome was surprising and discouraging to some, because it was the first time the Supreme Court had approved the denial of counsel when physical liberty is at stake. The opinion seemed to undercut the positive side of the *Lassiter* presumption that the right to counsel is automatic in cases involving the party's physical liberty, but not others. Here physical liberty was on the line and yet it was held the Constitution did not mandate counsel for the defendant.

From a right-to-counsel perspective, the opinion had relevance for two reasons.

First, the court expressly reserved the question whether the procedural protections it required would be sufficient to satisfy due process if the wife had been represented or the government had been a party, implying that due process may have required the father to have counsel in either of those situations.[24] In fact, the court expressly limited its holding to the situation where the other side was unrepresented. "We conclude that where as here the custodial parent (entitled to receive the support) is unrepresented by counsel, the State need not provide counsel to the noncustodial parent (required to provide the support)."[25] The court also made the point that if it indeed had ordered counsel for the father here it would have created an imbalance, what the court called "asymmetry" with respect to the unrepresented mother—in essence an "inequality of arms," in the words of the European Court on Human Rights.[26]

The court then explained the evils of that asymmetry when one side is represented and the other is not. This inequality of arms could introduce "a degree of formality" and "could make the proceedings *less fair* overall, increasing *the risk of a decision that would erroneously deprive a family of the support* it is entitled to receive."[27] It will be interesting to see whether the Supreme Court will be as concerned about overall unfairness and the risk of erroneously depriving an unrepresented party of financial support—or housing, or health, or child custody, or some other basic human need—when the other side already has counsel and these evils of asymmetry will exist unless the court provides a lawyer to the party asking for counsel.

Second, the Supreme Court made it abundantly clear trial courts have an affirmative obligation to ensure the process they provide parties is fair taking account of the characteristics of those parties and what they can be expected to understand. Here the court had not informed the defendant that the key issue was whether he had the means to pay the accumulated support obligations, had not provided a form on which the defendant could list his income and assets, nor had the judge even ruled whether he found the defendant had ample means to comply with an order to pay. This behavior the Supreme Court found failed to satisfy due process.[28] Trial judges cannot use a complex process only a lawyer can properly negotiate when the party is unrepresented and then deny that party a lawyer. Nor can the court simply deny counsel and then make the unrepresented party try to figure out what he is required to prove and what evidence he needs to produce, and like issues involved in making an effective case to the judge.

There is language in the *Turner v. Rogers* opinion that could lead toward a right to counsel in civil cases down the road. Whether called asymmetry or inequality of arms, that condition is equally bad whether created by appointment of counsel or through its denial. In the most optimistic reading, this could be the first tiny baby step toward the Supreme Court recognizing a constitutional right to equal justice—and to a lawyer when needed to afford equality of arms. Or it could lead in the opposite direction. Or it could prove to be a dead end, a ruling and a rationale limited to the unique situation of a civil contempt proceeding. Time and future Supreme Court decisions and possibly future Supreme Courts will have to work that out. In the meantime, the state courts and their interpretations of their own state constitutions remain the main hope for a judicially determined right to equal justice in civil cases for the foreseeable future.

One of the more encouraging developments for the long run is the emergence of trial judges as outspoken advocates for a right to counsel in their courts. When right-to-counsel cases were before both the Alaska and Washington Supreme Courts they were accompanied by briefs filed by several trial judges in those states testifying how unfair it was to unrepresented parties appearing in their courts. In the brief filed by a dozen Washington judges, they said:

> Without assistance from attorneys, pro se litigants frequently fail to present critical facts and legal authorities that judges need to make correct and just rulings. Pro se litigants also frequently fail to object to inadmissible testimony or documents and to correct erroneous legal arguments. This makes it difficult for judges to fulfill the purpose of our judicial system—to make correct and just rulings.[29]

Then in 2011, I heard a number of trial judges from another state deliver powerful oral testimony urging the importance of providing lawyers for indigent civil litigants. This occurred while attending an all-day hearing conducted by the Wisconsin Supreme Court. The full court was considering a petition asking them to issue a rule, not to create a full-scale right to counsel in civil cases but to impose a set of criteria to guide trial judges in their exercise of an existing discretionary power to appoint counsel in such cases. Under a prior decision of the Wisconsin Supreme Court, if a trial judge indeed used that discretionary power to appoint a lawyer, the local county government had to pay that lawyer.

The hearing led off with a succession of trial judges from around Wisconsin, each one telling horror stories of what happened when unrepresented litigants struggled to represent themselves in their courts. One of their number served on a specialized court that recently had received Supreme Court approval to appoint counsel on a regular basis. He spoke of the difference between the days when most litigants appeared without lawyers and the current day when most had lawyers. Not only was the process fairer and the judge more confident he was dispensing justice not injustice, but the proceedings now move much faster and with far more out of court settlements the judge need only review and approve. This witness testified that he as a judge and the court on which he sat were far more efficient as a result.

If this ripple of unrest among trial judges becomes a torrent from below, it may well affect the appellate courts and supreme courts above. For one thing, some trial judges become appellate judges and some of those appellate judges become Supreme Court justices. If they have felt or expressed frustration over what it meant to them that counsel is denied to so many litigants before them while on the trial bench, that concern will remain when they are in the position of writing appellate opinions. Secondly, appellate and trial judges interact regularly in court administration matters, training conferences, and social occasions. Appellate judges are more likely to listen to what trial judges have to say about issues like how the absence of counsel affects the fairness and quality of justice the trial courts are able to dispense than they are the usual advocates for a right to equal justice such as legal services lawyers, bar leaders, and the like.

In the absence of a statutory or constitutional right to equal justice and counsel when needed, the future of civil legal aid will be more of the same—a struggle for enough money to at least maintain "minimum access" to counsel. While waiting for courts or legislatures to finally recognize a right to equal justice and counsel in the large percentage of cases where they are needed for justice to be equal and real, those in the field can continue further refining and expanding the use of lay advocates, self-help assistance, more sophisticated technological tools, and other ways to make the system still more cost effective. Key to all of this will be keeping the Legal Services Corporation alive and at a reasonable level of funding and to harness ever more pro bono services from this nation's large private legal profession.

WILL THE U.S. PUBLIC AND ITS POLITICIANS EVER ESTABLISH JUSTICE FOR THE COUNTRY'S LOWER-INCOME POPULATION?

We have now reached the big question, the most difficult one by far. Will a United States seemly obsessed with cutting government spending and gutting so-called "entitlement" programs consider expanding several fold its investment in civil legal aid? And if not now, will it ever? By civil legal aid, in this context, I mean to include not just lawyers but lay advocates, self-help assistance, and technology that deliver legal services to those unable to afford counsel. In other words, the entire system that might implement a right to equal justice.

Consider first where civil legal aid in the United States stands now compared to other comparable nations and to its own domestic social programs serving the poor. Almost always, the first and often only objection raised when someone mentions the possibility of the United States implementing a right to equality before the law is: "It will cost too much, American taxpayers will never support that amount of funding." Often this is followed by: "Why, we don't even adequately fund health care yet." This last comment carries the clear implication—or sometimes is stated expressly: "We shouldn't invest more public funds in making the justice system fair for lower-income Americans until we have taken care of their needs for health care."

What this specie of objection raises are really only questions of political will (or willingness), comparative cost, and societal priorities.

35th Anniversary of the Legal Services Corporation, 2009

By the President of the United States of America

A Proclamation

Every day the Legal Services Corporation (LSC) breathes life into the timeless ideal, "equal justice under law." It reaches those who cannot afford the assistance they need and those who would otherwise go without vital representation. Today we recognize the 35 years during which the LSC has moved our Nation and our legal system towards greater equality.

The LSC brings legal counsel to every corner of the Nation. As the largest provider of civil legal aid to the poor, it supports programs that touch families in every State. Persons of all ethnic and racial backgrounds know its great work, and women, who represent 75 percent of LSC-supported clients, especially benefit from its expertise.

The Legal Services Corporation's work helps improve lives. It allows more people to access the public benefits they deserve, more domestic violence victims to secure the protections they desperately need, and more workers to receive the compensation they have been promised and earned.

During an economic crisis, the work of the LSC is especially important. When families face foreclosure, eviction, or bankruptcy, or when communities are targeted by predatory lenders, they need the help of legal professionals. These scenarios are far too common today. Fortunately, the LSC stands ready to meet these demands.

Because economically vulnerable communities continue to face an unmet need for legal services, my Administration has supported increased funding for the LSC. I have also recommended lifting several unnecessary restrictions on funding so that more people can receive assistance. These changes are critical to the organization's mission and work.

We have made great progress in protecting the legal rights of our citizens, and the Legal Services Corporation has played a vital role in this story for more than 3 decades. With continued support, it will serve those in need and help our Nation live out its highest ideals.

NOW, THEREFORE, I, BARACK OBAMA, President of the United States of America, by virtue of the authority vested in me by the Constitution and the laws of the United States, do hereby proclaim July 25, 2009, as the 35th Anniversary of the Legal Services Corporation. I call upon legal professionals and the people of the United States to honor the contributions of this vital organization.

IN WITNESS WHEREOF, I have hereunto set my hand this twenty-third day of July, in the year of our Lord two thousand nine, and of the Independence of the United States of America the two hundred and thirty-fourth.

President Barack Obama's Proclamation on the occasion of the Legal Services Corporation's 35th anniversary in 2009. (Courtesy of Legal Services Corporation)

We will first explore them in the light of what some other comparable industrial democracies have been willing to spend on civil legal aid. Then we will turn to what the United States spends on civil legal aid compared to what we already spend on health care for that population.

Comparing U.S. Expenditures on Civil Legal Aid with Other Western Democracies

As mentioned earlier, several comparable industrial democracies, most but not all in Europe, invest anywhere from 3 to 10 times as much of their nation's income on civil legal aid as does the United States. These comparisons are reflected in Table 31.1.

The expenditure statistics were compiled from "national reports" prepared by legal aid administrators or in some cases academics from the nations included on the chart and submitted for the 2013 conference of the International Legal Aid Group.[30] The expenditure figures include only *public* funding and *not private* sources of funding, whether those private funds were derived from client contributions, court-awarded fees, foundation grants, or private donations. Most of the data are from calendar or fiscal year 2011 or 2012. When a nation's data are from an earlier year, that is indicated on the chat. Even for the many nations which have a unified civil and criminal legal aid system, the expenditure data is limited to the civil component.

As Table 31.1 makes quite apparent, in no country, even the most generous, is the investment in civil legal aid anything but a thin slice of the nation's GDP. At one end, the United States' investment in civil legal aid was less than seven-*thousandths* of a percentage of our GDP in 2012. At the high end, England's was still only seven-hundreths of a percent of that nation's GDP that same year. To put it another way, the United States was at *seven*-thousandths and England at *seventy*-thousandths of a percent of their respective national GDPs—making England better than 10 times more generous than the United States in its commitment to providing equality before the law for its lower-income people. Yet even England's investment seems negligible compared to the nation's ability to pay and also compared to the fundamental nature of the national promise of "justice for all" that expenditure fulfills.

Another revealing comparison is presented in Table 31.2. It is based on the $15.9 trillion GDP the World Factbook reported the United States earned in 2012 and shows what the U.S. *public* expenditure on civil legal aid would be if this country invested as much of its GDP for that purpose as eight of these other nations did in 2012.

Table 31.1

Comparative Public Expenditures on Civil Legal Aid (2012)

Nation	Total Public Civil Legal Aid Investment[1]	Population[2]	Public Civil Legal Aid Investment Per Capita	Gross Domestic Product (Per Purchasing Power) Per Capita[3]	Public Civil Legal Aid Investment as Percentage of GDP (in Thousandths of a Percent)
United States	$1.050 billion[4]	314 million	$3.31	$50,700	Less than 7-thousandths of a percent
Germany	$520 million (2010)	82.4 million	$6.44	$38,200 (2010)	16-thousandths of a percent
Ireland	$38.2 million	4.58 million	$8.36	$42,600	19-thousandths of a percent
Hong Kong	$77.3 million	7 million	$11.20	$52,300	21-thousandths of a percent
Ontario, Province, Canada	$136.8 million	13.50 million	$10.13	$46,500	29-thousandths of a percent
Scotland	$78.5 million	5.25 million	$15.00	$37,500 (for United Kingdom)	40-thousandths of a percent
Norway	$107.6 million	4.7 million	$22.9	$55,900	41-thousandths of a percent
Netherlands	$355 million	16.65 million	$21.32	$42,900	50-thousandths of a percent
New Zealand (2009–2010)	$80 million	4.4 million	$18.20	$29,500 (2010)	62-thousandths of a percent
England and Wales	$1.49 billion	56.6 million	$26.30	$37,500 (for United Kingdom)	70-thousandths of a percent

[1] With the exception of New Zealand, the civil legal aid expenditure figures are from the "national reports" prepared by national legal aid administrators or academics from those countries and submitted to the 2013 conference of the International Legal Aid Group held in The Hague, Netherlands, during June, 2013. Unless otherwise noted, those expenditure figures are for calendar year or fiscal year 2012, converted from local currency to U.S. dollars based on the average conversion rates for the year 2012 (for instance, Euros = $1.28 and British pounds = $1.58). The New Zealand data are from the 2009–2010 annual report of the New Zealand Legal Services Agency, the final year before that nation's Ministry of Justice assumed responsibility for administering the legal aid system.

[2] The population figures are from the World Factbook (2012), published by the U.S. government.

[3] Ibid. The per capita GDP figures reflect "purchasing power parity" GDP, not "official exchange rate" GDP.

[4] As is true for other nations in this table, the U.S. civil legal aid expenditure figure only includes public sources of funding, for example, from the Legal Services Corporation, IOLTA, and state, local and non-LSC federal government grants, but not private foundation grants, donations from law firms and other private sources, client contributions, court-awarded fees, among others.

Table 31.2
U.S. Expenditures on Civil Legal Aid If It Invested the Same Percentage of Its GDP in Civil Legal Aid as These Nations (2012)

Ireland	Germany	Hong Kong	Ontario	Norway	Scotland	Netherlands	England* and Wales
$3.0 billion	$2.5 billion	$3.3 billion	$4.6 billion	$6.5 billion	$6.4 billion	$7.95 billion	$11.1 billion*

*Changes the English government implemented in 2013 may reduce civil legal aid expenditures by 20 to 30 percent in future years.

In addition to comparative per capita and per-GDP statistics, other revealing comparisons focus on the justice system itself. Unfortunately, the statistics are difficult to obtain and thus only a single two-nation snapshot was available at this point. But that snapshot was rather dramatic. A decade ago in England, the government's investment in civil legal aid represented 12 percent of that nation's total spending on lawyers by all individuals, businesses, governments, and other possible clients,[31] whereas in the United States civil legal aid received less than a half a percent of our nation's total expenditures on lawyers.[32]

Another revealing measure compares nations in how they allocate the publicly funded resources they commit to the dispute resolution function. Table 31.3 portrays a nation's willingness to expend resources on civil legal aid compared to its willingness to expend resources on the courts. The data used to calculate the percentages for the European countries reflected on the chart come from a recently published report "European Judicial Systems" prepared by the European Commission for the Efficiency of Justice and published by the Council of Europe.[33] Because the "European Judicial Systems" report only supplied a combined figure for civil and criminal legal aid, it was not sufficient by itself as a source for comparisons of investments on the judicial and civil legal aid components of the justice system. Thus, the only nations included on the chart were ones for which data was available from other sources regarding the level of civil legal aid funding (independent of funding on defense of the criminal accused).[34]

An adversarial system such as the United States uses depends on the private parties rather than the judges discovering the relevant facts and the operative legal principles then presenting them to a neutral fact finder (judge or jury). In contrast, an inquisitorial system expects the judges to play a major role, independently and actively discovering the facts and applicable law as well as deciding the case. Thus, one would expect a nation using an adversarial system to devote more funds proportionately to subsidizing private parties who could not afford to perform these vital functions on their own than does a nation

Table 31.3
Comparison between Civil Legal Aid Expenditures as Percentage of Judicial Expenditures in Selected Nations

Nation	Civil Legal Aid Budget as Percentage of Judicial Budget	U.S. Civil Legal Aid Expenditures Out of Public Funds if They Were the Same Percentage of U.S. Judicial Expenditures as This Nation's Civil Legal Aid Expenditures Are of its Judicial Expenditures
Finland	13.6%	$2 billion
Netherlands	27.0%	$4 billion
Ireland	35%	$5.25 billion
Northern Ireland	37%	$5.5 billion
Scotland	63%	$9.4 billion
England/Wales	79%	$15.8 billion
United States	5%	$1 billion

using an inquisitorial approach where the publicly funded judiciary is doing more of this difficult and expensive work.

With the exception of the United States (which uses an adversary system), this expectation is confirmed by the limited number of nations included on the above chart (Table 31.3). In Finland, which uses a system that is fairly close to a pure inquisitorial approach, the civil legal aid budget is only 13.6 percent as large as the judicial budget. The Netherlands uses a system that has elements of both the inquisitorial and adversarial systems and its civil legal aid budget is 27 percent as large as its judicial budget. But in those countries using a classic adversarial system the civil legal aid budget ranges from 35 percent to 79 percent the size of the judicial budget. The United States is the outlier—indeed on the outer fringes—only spending an estimated five percent as much on civil legal aid as it does on the judicial system.[35]

Thus, ignoring competition from other societal priorities, it is apparent that by comparison to other jurisdictions from which we have data, the U.S. justice system is out of balance—failing to allocate nearly as much of its total justice system resources to subsidizing counsel for those who cannot afford their own in civil cases as our fellow common law countries do.

U.S. Expenditures on Civil Legal Aid Compared with Other
Public Expenditures Benefiting the Poor

In order to make some relevant comparisons, the starting point is the share of total legal resources civil legal aid organizations presently have to serve the population eligible for their services. Recall, at the present time that share is less than one-half of one percent. This miniscule percent of legal resources is expected to serve 64 million people—more than a fifth of the nation's total population. That 64 million figure, in fact, represents the *minimum* number who need civil legal aid—those who are under 125 percent of the federal poverty line and thus eligible for LSC-funded legal services. But many states have decided another strata of people are unable to afford counsel and drawn the line at 200 percent of the poverty line.[36] Applying this standard, by 2011 over 120 million people—two out five U.S. citizens—would be eligible for civil legal aid.[37]

This means that at the current time civil legal aid is funded from all sources an average of $19 a year per eligible poor person assuming the 64 million figure represents the total population needing their services and less than $10 per poor person if we adopt the more realistic estimate of 120 million needing free counsel for most legal problems they face. Think about it for a moment, how much of a lawyer's time could you expect to buy with $10 or even $19? One typical prepaid-legal insurance company charges premiums of as much $300 a year—and that doesn't even cover litigation expenses if the insured needs to go to court.[38]

Another relevant statistic contrasts the roughly $1 billion in public funding (LSC, IOLTA, state and local and other federal funding, but not foundations or private donors) for civil legal aid with the $351 billion annual nationwide government expenditure on medical care for the poor. Medicaid, the major component of that health care expenditure on the poor, unlike civil legal aid, is presently a "rights-based" program. That is, if an applicant is financially eligible and has a health problem covered by the program that patient is legally entitled to government-paid health services to address that problem. Medicaid serves essentially the same low-income population as are eligible for LSC-funded civil legal aid in the United States. This means that at this point, the United States spends on justice for the poor less than a third of a percent of what it spends on health care for the poor. Another way of expressing the stark difference, and one that makes it easier to comprehend, is that the Medicaid budget provides over $7,000 per eligible patient while civil legal aid only has $19 per eligible client.

On another and more relevant scale of comparison, the combined federal–state Medicaid program expenditure of $323 billion[39] in 2010 represented fully 15 percent of the nation's total public and private spending on health care that year, which amounted to slightly over $2.1 trillion.[40] (The total spending statistic includes all the private health insurance premiums individuals or their employers pay, their personal copayments and noninsured payments to providers, as well as Medicare, Medicaid, and other government health programs.) Thus, poor people are receiving *fifteen* percent of the nation's health care expenditures, but only a *half of a percent* of its expenditures on "legal care."

The lesson of these statistics is not that civil legal aid should be funded at or near the level of Medicaid. It rather is to highlight two points. First, poor people receive a far larger share of the nation's health care resources than they do of its legal resources. And second, the nation's investment in civil legal aid could be increased rather dramatically without making a dent in the funds devoted to medical care. A 500-percent increase in funding for civil legal aid, for instance, would only represent a little over 1 percent of the Medicare budget. So it makes little sense to say the United States is unable to afford to give its low-income population the resources needed to afford them equality before the law until it fully funds their health care. Foregoing adequate funding for civil legal aid adds nothing meaningful to the resources available for health care—and similarly, adds little to the public resources available for education or public financial assistance to the poor.[41]

THE ROAD TO EQUAL JUSTICE FOR THE POOR

In 1919, Elihu Root, one of the most venerated lawyers and public servants in U.S. history, a man who served as secretary of state and won the Nobel Peace Prize among other notable achievements, also wrote the foreword to Reginald Heber Smith's landmark book, *Justice and the Poor.* In that foreword, Root observed:

> New projects are continually suggested for improving the condition of the poor by the aid of government, and as to many of them there is a debatable question whether they come within the proper province of government. . . . No one, however, doubts that it is the proper function of government to secure justice. In a broad sense that is the chief thing for which government is organized. Nor can any one question that the highest obligation of government is to secure justice for those who, because they are poor and weak and friendless, find it hard to maintain their own rights.[42]

Root wrote this passage long before our federal government created social security, Medicare, Medicaid, welfare, and like programs for improving the condition of the poor and sometimes other people in this country. Given his own record during the Progressive era, it seems doubtful Root would now object to those initiatives. But he most certainly would be disappointed if not befuddled by the comparatively low priority accorded what he saw as the "highest obligation of government," that is, to secure justice for the poor.

As Root recognized, the rationale for government investing in civil legal aid is different and reposes at a more fundamental level than is true for social programs such as Medicare, Medicaid, and welfare. Equality before the law is at the core of the social contract just as peacefully resolving disputes between citizens, including between citizens of different economic and social classes is as Root wrote, the "chief reason," but obviously not the only purpose for government itself.

The primacy of the dispute resolution function and the necessity it be performed justly was recognized by the U.S. Supreme Court in *Boddie v. Connecticut.*

> Perhaps no characteristic of an organized cohesive society is more fundamental than its erection and enforcement of a system of rules defining the various rights and duties of its members, enabling them to govern their affairs and definitively settle their differences in an orderly, predictable manner. . . . Without [the] guarantee that one may not be deprived of his rights, neither liberty nor property, without due process of law, the State's monopoly over techniques for binding conflict resolution could hardly be said to be acceptable under our scheme of things. Only by providing that the social enforcement mechanism must function strictly within those bounds can we hope to maintain an orderly society that is also just.[43]

In a very real sense, a citizen's right to equality before the law in civil cases is as important as his or her right to vote in a democratic society—and as critical to full participation as a citizen in that democracy. Without the ability to effectively litigate in court, citizens are in no position to enforce the substantive rights and benefits their votes may have allowed them to gain. Unenforceable rights are no rights at all. For those lacking counsel, the law does not exist as a practical matter—at least as a benefit and not just a threat—and their right to vote gains them little. Low-income people can be sued and lose as defendants despite laws favoring their position that they have no way of knowing about or being capable of asserting. Conversely, they have no way of affirmatively enforcing legal protections they possess under the law because if they try to sue to compel obedience to the law they have virtually no prospect of winning.

For all these reasons, equality before the law and the right to counsel when needed for that equality is an inherent if as yet unrecognized element of citizenship. As a consequence, civil legal aid is more than a social program but rather an inherent and essential term of the social contract. Indeed, without that equality before the law, poor people are far less than full citizens in our democracy.

California Chief Justice Ron George recognized this fundamental truth when he warned that state's legislature in 2001 that, "If justice for all becomes justice only for those who can afford it, we threaten the very underpinnings of our social contract."[44] Unfortunately, of course, we are already violating the social contract because we are not providing justice for all, but justice only for those who can afford it or who are lucky enough to find a legal aid lawyer or a pro bono lawyer with enough time to take on their cases. That, as we know, is a distinct minority of the nation's lower-income people.

And so, one might ask, as Elihu Root certainly would, why has civil legal aid lagged behind so many social programs in the government's funding priorities? Part of the reason is probably historical and a product of our distance from the European continent. We simply missed out on that continent's nation-by-nation translation of social contract principles into statutes conferring a right to counsel in civil cases. Indeed in most of those countries, government guaranteed poor people free lawyers in the courts before they gave them health care or welfare or other purely social benefits. Had this country been on or near the European continent, it might well have been caught up in the movement to create statutory rights to counsel in civil cases as it spread from nation to nation.

Distance from Europe may not be the only explanation, however. We as a nation and a people also may be guilty of a bit of chauvinism about the virtues of our justice system, much of it deserved, which would tend to discourage any serious attention to what was happening in Europe. Then, once legal aid started here in 1876 as a charitable not a governmental responsibility the pattern was set—a fixed resource of salaried lawyers working in special offices dedicated solely to serving the poor and funded as private charities.

From the early chapters of this book we know legal aid started as a private charity in 1876 and became a national movement backed by the ABA in 1920 still committed to private charity as its primary source of financial support. Indeed in the 1950s those in charge of the legal aid movement strongly opposed a proposal for federal funding of civil legal aid in the United States. Coming at the height of the McCarthy era, this possibility provoked an outcry against government funding of civil legal aid from bar leaders and legal aid proponents alike— with the ABA trumpeting charitably funded legal aid societies as the "American way" to deliver justice to the poor and the NLADA president urging those societies were the primary bulwark against "socialization of the legal profession."

It took the nation's brief "War on Poverty" to awaken the federal government to the plight of the poor in our courts and the rest of our legal system—and to turn the organized bar from an opponent to a supporter of government funding of civil legal aid. With that came the OEO Legal Services Program and the first federal funding of civil legal aid. There is no reason to rehearse again the many ups and downs of that program and its successor, the Legal Services Corporation, covered in previous chapters. After all that toil and turmoil, as documented earlier, the United States remains far behind in our commitment to equal justice for the poor—whether measured against other comparable industrial democracies or our own federal government's earlier willingness to invest in civil legal aid or our nation's investment in major social program for the poor, such as Medicaid.

This low status was confirmed when our nation's level of "access to justice" was ranked by an international body the ABA itself had created for another reason. In the early years of the 21st century, under the leadership of its then president, William Neukom, the ABA began putting together a "rule of law" initiative. The primary purpose was to elevate the "rule of law" in emerging nations, former Soviet bloc countries, and other less democratic societies, and to improve the institutions essential to that goal in those countries.[45] A vital part of this endeavor was an annual "rule of law index," which ranked all nations in the world on various dimensions of their adherence to the rule of law—criminal justice, civil justice, judicial independence, and the like. This index was designed to encourage countries to move up the rankings by improving their institutions of justice.

The compilation of the "rule of law index" entailed extensive research and analysis by teams of experts. The first annual edition was not ready for publication until 2011. That first book contained a startling surprise for many in the United States, most of them lawyers, who read it. While the United States rated high on most "rule of law" measures, it ranked next to the bottom on one—"access to justice in civil cases"—when compared to 11 other Western industrial democracies, with only Italy lower.[46] No surprise, however, nearly every nation above the United States on the list has a right to counsel in civil cases.

The United States also was near the bottom when compared to a longer list of 23 high-income countries from around the world, most of them democracies but some not. The United States ranked 20th with only Italy, Poland, and Croatia below our country.[47] Among those above us besides the usual suspects such as Norway, the Netherlands, England, Sweden, Germany, and Finland, were countries such as Estonia, Hong Kong, the Czech Republic, and South Korea. Our nation's low rating on access to civil justice was no surprise to those few who knew we had long been far behind in giving poor people a right to equal justice and in our willingness to fund civil legal aid. But it was a shock, one hard to believe, for most lawyers and even some legal services lawyers.

The chief research officer for the World Justice Project, Alejandro Ponce, explained the reason for our country's low ranking, in an interview appearing in the *Huffington Post.* "In the U.S., socioeconomic level matters. Poor people are at a disadvantage. . . . Legal services are expensive or unavailable, and the gap between rich and poor individuals in terms of both actual use of and satisfaction with the civil court system is significant."[48]

This embarrassing ranking on the "access to justice in civil cases" measure certainly was a wakeup call for many lawyers in this country. But it should be a wakeup call for the rest of the U.S. population, too. Hard to feel good about "American exceptionalism" when we are exceptional by being at the bottom rather than the top. And, hard to recite the Pledge of Allegiance with a straight face when the reality is our country too often provides "justice only for those who can afford it."

Although the legal services community owes the organized bar many thanks for its strong support of the OEO Legal Services Program and the Legal Services Corporation over the years, the legal profession and those supporting civil legal aid also bear considerable responsibility for the continued low priority accorded equality before the law in the nation's funding decisions. Seldom have they sounded a loud alarm in the public arena about the millions of poor people who have to go without lawyers every year and how far we are from fulfilling the promise of our constitution "to establish justice."

Viewing and hearing our public rhetoric, one would think our nation already provides "justice for all" including the poor. We chisel "equal justice under law" over the entrance to the U.S. Supreme Court building, a guarantee seen repeatedly on television. Our Constitution purports to offer all citizens, irrespective of income, "due process," and "equal protection of the laws." And our "Law Day" and "July 4th" speeches tend to praise our legal system rather than criticizing it for its failure to provide equality before the law to many of the nation's people. Even the stories about legal aid that occasionally pop up in our nation's newspapers usually feature the success stories—the poor people legal aid lawyers managed to save from a difficult legal problem not what happens to the far greater number those lawyers lack the time to help.

This was brought home to me at a conference on "The Justice Gap and the Right to Counsel" sponsored by the San Francisco Bar Association in October 2008. The moderator was the former long-time publisher of San Francisco's daily newspaper. He listened to a series of panelists describing how few resources the United States allocates to civil legal aid, how far we are behind other countries, the statistics about unmet need, and from a legal aid lawyer telling of the pain she experienced in having to turn away the majority of the applicants who came to her office. Finally, this sophisticated and knowledgeable journalist shook his head and told the audience he had no idea about any of this. He had assumed poor people had all the civil legal aid they needed. Small wonder, given what the general public, educated or not, are told about justice in this country, from childhood on reciting a pledge of allegiance that emphasizes two values this country represents—"liberty" and "justice for all."

The San Francisco publisher felt only mildly relieved about his own ignorance on this subject when told that public opinion polls revealed nearly 70 percent of Californians[49] and 80 percent of the U.S. public believe poor people already have a right to counsel in civil cases just as they do in criminal prosecutions.[50]

From the beginning, legal aid leaders have wondered and worried about the low priority justice for the poor has enjoyed among those funding assistance for that population. Nearly every annual report of the first legal aid organization, the Legal Aid Society in New York, contained a complaint and plea from the society's iconic president, Arthur Von Briesen. Typical is what he wrote in the 1909 annual report, explaining why he believed legal aid was erroneously consigned such a low priority among charitable givers and why it deserved more.

> Another reason for the lack of financial support may be found in the fact that the nature of the suffering caused by unjust treatment, for which there is no relief, cannot be understood and appreciated by those who, when unjustly treated, have the means of securing prompt relief. . . . Physical suffering in others we all realize. Likewise the pangs of hunger, lack of shelter and of warmth in winter. Such suffering leads the benevolent to open their hands and grant relief. But one who has himself suffered injustice, yet had the means to secure justice, will rarely realize how intense the agony and how long lived, in the victim for whom there was no relief."[51]

What Von Briesen had to say about the attitude of wealthy New Yorkers over a century ago has some relevance today when the target audience is Congress, state legislators, and the voting public. In one sense, justice seems an abstract value, especially compared to concrete ones like food, health, housing, and the like. Yet as Von Briesen emphasized, the absence of justice, that is, a feeling one is the victim of injustice, especially if shared by a large number of people, destroys any loyalty to the law and threatens a nation's social stability. To ask people to obey a legal system that can only be their enemy and not their friend is neither fair nor realistic.

Equally important, but not mentioned by Von Briesen, is the fact, demonstrated repeatedly in this book, that justice is a means as well as an end. That is, it often is the means through which a person obtains concrete things such as food, health care, housing, and the like—or the money to purchase those necessities. Conversely, without the opportunity for justice this same person loses that food, health care, or housing. Moreover, as more than one Congressman pointed out during the debates over LSC's survival, unless poor people have access to justice much of the legislation enacted for their benefit will not be enforced and the lawmakers' own work will have been for naught.

If civil legal aid is to gain the status it deserves among the panoply of programs meriting public funding, the general public, the nation's legislators and other officials, its journalists, and other opinion makers will have to learn and appreciate the hard facts. What they are assuming about justice in this country is simply not true. Our justice system has a "dirty little secret" and one none of those constituencies should be allowed to ignore. We do not provide the promised "justice for all." Indeed to be fully honest, we probably don't provide justice at all to the majority of the people in the bottom one-third of the nation's population—especially when, as often happens, they have a dispute with a well-to-do individual or a corporation or the government or any other institutional party. Also, we have to admit that when it comes to equality before the law we are not guaranteeing "fair hearings" or "effective access to justice" or "equality of arms" to our lower-income population as many other comparable democracies do. Nor have we demonstrated nearly the financial commitment to equality before the law as have several other comparable industrial democracies. The public also needs to hear the tragic stories of what happens to the many poor people whom legal aid lawyers cannot represent because of the present lack of adequate resources.

On the positive side, the public should know this nation can fund a right to equal justice for a small fraction of the cost of many social programs already provided to lower-income people. They also should understand it is possible to achieve equality before the law in a cost-effective way, for instance, perhaps by revamping our justice system in ways that allow disputants from the same economic class to resolve many of their disputes with active judicial inquiry and self-help assistance rather than requiring representation by lawyers.

Until the U.S. economy fully recovers, it may not be reasonable to expect an immediate infusion of government funding for civil legal aid no matter how powerful a case is made. But that does not mean those convinced of the importance of equality before the law should hold up on efforts to build that case and spread the message, actually messages, out to the general public, the legislatures, and beyond. It usually takes a long time to overturn public misconceptions, especially comforting ones, such as the widely held assumption that the United States indeed already provides "justice for all." Likewise, it takes an even longer time to build an understanding of the critical importance of equality before the law in a democratic society and the urgency of ending our present failure to make that a reality for too many of those living in this country, those whose incomes are too low to pay the entrance fee to the justice system, a lawyer's fee.

For too many years, the *right* to equality before the law, and to counsel when needed, has been nothing but a long-term dream in this country—and even then shared by relatively few people. Only recently has that dream transformed into a goal shared by a broad coalition of legal services lawyers, academics, private law firms, and even some judges. The question is whether this goal becomes a movement and begins expanding beyond the legal profession. Frankly, it will not be a movement for the short-winded. But if the United States is ever to "establish justice" as promised in the Constitution's preamble, to make "justice for all" a reality in this country and not just a motto to mouth when reciting the Pledge of Allegiance, and to provide the nation's lower-income population true "due process" and "equal protection of the law," the right to equal justice and a lawyer when needed must become a legal guarantee. Only then and in that way can justice be established for all and thus become, as it should be, an inherent right of citizenship.

Glossary

AALS	Association of American Law Schools
ABA	American Bar Association
ALR	Action for Legal Rights
ATLA	American Trial Lawyers Association
CR	Continuing Resolution
CRLA	California Rural Legal Assistance
CSA	Community Services Administration
FY	Fiscal Year
GAO	Government Accountability Office
HEW	Department of Health Education, and Welfare
INS	Immigration and Naturalization Service
IOLTA	Interest on Lawyers' Trust Accounts
LSC	Legal Services Corporation
NAACP	National Association for the Advancement of Colored People
NAC	National Advisory Committee to the OEO Legal Services Program
NALAO	National Association of Legal Aid Organizations
NCC	National Clients' Council
NEJL	National Equal Justice Library

NLAA	National Legal Aid Association
NLADA	National Legal Aid and Defender Association
OEO	Office of Economic Opportunity
OEO-LSP	Office of Economic Opportunity Legal Services Program
OMB	Office of Management and Budget
PLEA	Poverty Lawyers for Effective Advocacy
PLF	Pacific Legal Foundation
PAG	Project Advisory Group
SCLAW	Standing Committee on Legal Aid Work
SCLAID	Standing Committee on Legal Aid and Indigent Defendants

Notes

Chapter 26: Gingrich's "Contract" Cancels Clinton's "Hope"

1. "Clinton Names 11 to Legal Services Corp.," Associated Press, AP News Archive August 6, 1993, 8:12 P.M. ET.

2. Douglas Eakeley, Telephone interview with author.

3. Douglas Eakeley, Videotaped oral history, NEJL Oral History Collection, National Equal Justice Library, Georgetown Law Center, Washington, D.C.

4. The author used the "Inflation Calculator" app on an iPad to calculate what would be required in 1993 to match the LSC's 1981"minimum access" budget. This did not include the further adjustment required to accommodate the increase in the size of the eligible poverty population during those dozen years.

5. Transcript, Meeting of Board of Directors, Legal Services Corporation (December 5, 1993), 127–31, 159.

6. *Senate Committee on Appropriations, Subcommittee on the Departments of Commerce, Justice, and State, the Judiciary, and Related Agencies, Departments of Commerce, Justice, and State, the Judiciary, and Related Agencies Appropriations for FY1993, Hearings,* 102nd Cong. 779 (1992) (testimony of Talbot D'Alemberte, President, American Bar Association). The ABA asked for slightly less than $848 million because that year there was two years less inflation to account for.

7. Antoine Singsen, Letter to the author, May 12, 2012.

8. Singsen's calculations are explained in the document, Project Advisory Group, Inc., "Equal Justice for People in Poverty: The Long-Term Goal of Legal Services" (December 1993).

9. If the United States were to reach the $3.6 billion budget level our nation would be spending $11.40 per capita on civil legal aid for our lowest-income people, while England already invests $32 per capita on civil legal aid, Scotland spends $25 per capita, and the Netherlands spends $15 per capita. These comparisons and those with several other countries are developed more thoroughly in chapter 29.

10. Project Advisory Group, Inc., "Equal Justice for People in Poverty," 13.

11. Antoine "Gerry" Singsen, Telephone interview with author.

12. Ibid.

13. Transcript, Meeting of Board of Directors, Legal Services Corporation (December 5, 1993), 161.

14. Ibid., 170.

15. Ibid., 202–03.

16. Ibid., 117–18.

17. Singsen, Telephone interview with author.

18. Douglas Eakeley, Videotaped oral history; Eakeley, Telephone interview with author.

19. Alexander Forger, Videotaped oral history, Oral History Collection, National Equal Justice Library, Georgetown Law Center, Washington, D.C.

20. Ibid.

21. Transcript, Meeting of Board of Directors, Legal Services Corporation (December 6, 1993), 5–6.

22. Martha Bergmark, Videotaped oral history, Oral History Collection, National Equal Justice Library, Georgetown Law Center, Washington, D.C.

23. Forger, Videotaped oral history.

24. Antoine "Gerry" Singsen, Videotaped oral history; Singsen, Telephone interview with author.

25. *House Committee on Appropriations, Subcommittee on the Departments of Commerce, Justice, and State, The Judiciary, and Related Agencies, Legal Services Corporation,* 103th Cong. 1674 (1994) (Statement of Douglas Eakeley, Chairman of the Board, Legal Services Corporation). In this second budget hearing Eakeley discusses the original $850 million request along with the lower figure now proposed in reaction to the sub-committee's reaction to the initial request.

26. *House Committee on Appropriations, Subcommittee on the Departments of Commerce, Justice, and State, The Judiciary, and Related Agencies, Legal Services Corporation,* 104th Cong. 1778 (1994) (Statement of Rep. Moran).

27. *House Committee on Appropriations, Subcommittee on the Departments of Commerce, Justice, and State, The Judiciary, and Related Agencies, Legal Services Corporation,* 104th Cong. 1671 (1994) (Statement of Rep. Mollohan).

28. Forger, Videotaped oral history.

29. Forger, Videotaped oral history; Alexander Forger, Telephone interview with author; Michael Kantor, Interview with author.

30. *House Committee on Appropriations, Committee Report No. 103–708 Making Appropriations For The Departments Of Commerce, Justice, And State, The Judiciary, And Related Agencies Programs For The Fiscal Year Ending September 30, 1995* (1995).

31. 138 Cong. Rec. H10910.

32. *House Committee on the Judiciary, Legal Services Reauthorization Act of 1993,* 103rd Cong. 1–257 (1993).

33. Eakeley, Videotaped oral history; Eakeley, Telephone interview with author.

34. Forger, Videotaped oral history; Forger, Telephone interview with author.

35. Forger, Videotaped oral history.

36. On the National Legal and Policy Center's website, Boehm proclaims: "NLPC makes the case for an end to taxpayer funding for the Legal Services Corporation (LSC). We also make the case for the provision of legal aid to

the poor through private voluntary efforts. NLPC is regarded as the nation's leading LSC critic."

37. Victor Fortuno, Telephone interview with author.

38. Christian Coalition, *Contract with the American Family* 31 (1995).

39. "Contract with America," Encyclopedia Brittannica, at http://www .britannica.com/EBchecked/topic/135331/Contract-with-America [describing Gingrich and the rest of the Republican candidates signing a large version of the Contract on the steps of the Capitol building].

40. Richard L. Berke, "The 1994 Elections: The Overview; G.O.P. Wins Control of Senate And Makes Big Gains in House; Pataki Denies Cuomo 4th Term," *New York Times* (November 9, 1994). Jeff Zeleny and Carl Hulse, "G.O.P. Is Poised to Seize House, if Not Senate," *New York Times* (October 23, 2010).

41. Transcript, Meeting of Board of Directors, Legal Services Corporation, January 27, 1995, 13.

42. Transcript of January 27, 1995, LSC Board Meeting, 12. http://www .britannica.com/EBchecked/topic/135331/Contract-with-America.

43. Transcript of January 27, 1995, LSC Board meeting, 29.

44. Don Saunders [NLADA Civil Director], Telephone interview with author.

45. Laurie Zelon [another SCLAID member], Interview with author.

46. Ibid.

47. Zelon, Interview with author. Some evidence of Vivero's performance at ABA is the fact that in 1998, LSC hired him as Vice President for Governmental Affairs, a position he occupied until 2003.

48. Zelon, Interview with author.

49. Ibid.

50. 141 Cong. Rec. S19864.

51. Transcript, Meeting of Board of Directors, Legal Services Corporation, April 11, 1995.

52. *House Committee on the Budget, Committee Report No. 103–428 Concurrent Resolution on the Budget—Fiscal Year 1995,* 146 (1994) (dissenting views).

53. *House Committee on the Budget, Committee Report No. 104–120 Concurrent Resolution on the Budget—Fiscal Year 1996,* 119 (1995).

54. *House Committee on the Budget, Committee Report No. 104–575 Concurrent Resolution on the Budget—Fiscal Year 1997,* 156 (1996) (the Congressional Budget Process).

55. House Judiciary Committee, Subcommittee on Commercial and Administrative Law, Hearings on the Reauthorization of Legal Service Corporation, 104th Cong (1995) (Statement of Rep. Charles Stenholm (Democrat, Texas)).

56. *House Committee on Appropriations, Subcommittee on the Departments of Commerce, Justice, and State, The Judiciary, and Related Agencies, Departments of Commerce, Justice, and State, The Judiciary, and Related Agencies Appropriations for FY 1996,* 104th Cong. 157 (1995) (Statement of Rep. Rogers).

57. Forger, Videotaped oral history.

58. "Californians for Legal Aid" performed many of the functions in support of LSC's survival that State bars did in other states, but which the California State Bar, as an "integrated bar" was not positioned to undertake. Londen saw that gap in his state and took a leading role in forming the organization and personally supplied much of the funding. It was staffed by Kathy Dreyfus

(sister of actor Richard Dreyfus) and had a large and active board that lined up support from lawyers, local bar associations, business leaders, and other interest groups, garnered articles, editorials, and other media reports, and orchestrated contacts with California congressmen and senators.

59. Hearing of the Committee on Labor and Human Resources, United States Senate, on "Examining a Wide Variety of Views on the Legal Services Corporation," 104th Cong. 1st Sess., 84 (1995) (Statement of Jack Londen).

60. Ibid., 104th Cong. 1st Sess., 85 (1995).

61. Jack Londen, Interview with author.

62. *House Committee on Appropriations, Committee Report No. 104–196, Departments of Commerce, Justice, and State, The Judiciary, and Related Agencies Appropriation Bill, 1996,* 118 (1995).

63. 141 Cong. Rec. H20605.

64. *Senate Committee on Appropriations, Committee Report No. 104–139, Departments of Commerce, Justice, and State, The Judiciary, and Related Agencies Appropriation Bill, 1996,* 6 (1995).

65. *Senate Committee on Appropriations, Committee Report No. 104–139, Departments of Commerce, Justice, and State, The Judiciary, and Related Agencies Appropriation Bill, 1996,* 6 (1995).

66. John Robb, Videotaped Oral History, in NEJL Oral History Collection, National Equal Justice Library, Georgetown Law Library, Washington, D.C.

67. Alexander Forger, "The Future of Legal Services," 25 *Fordham Urban Law Journal* 333, 335 (1998).

68. 141 Cong. Rec. S27027 (Statement of Sen. Kennedy).

69. 141 Cong. Rec. S20604.

70. Forger, Videotaped oral history.

71. Transcript, Meeting of Board of Directors, Legal Services Corporation, October 1995, 10–11.

72. John Erlenborn, Videotaped oral history, NEJL Oral History Collection, National Equal Justice Library, Georgetown Law Center, Washington, D.C.

73. Ibid.

74. Forger, Videotaped oral history.

75. *House Committee on the Budget, Committee Report No. 104–575, Concurrent Resolution on the Budget—Fiscal Year 1997,* 140, 248–49 (1996).

76. Memorandum from Diane Harrison Ogawa to Roberta Cooper Ramo, January 24, 1996 [reporting on responses from first 12 state bar presidents contacted].

77. Memorandum from Mauricio Vivero, to LSC Call Group, re LSC 1996 Gameplan, dated February 15, 1996.

78. "Examples of the Vital Work of Legal Services," attachment to memorandum from Mauricio Vivero to LSC Supporters, entitled "The 1996 LSC Campaign," dated March 12, 1996.

79. Memorandum to LSC Recipient Executive Directors, Litigation Directors and Others, from Alan W. Houseman and Linda E. Perle, entitled "Litigation Challenging Restrictions on Recipients' Non-LSC Funds," dated 28 February 1996, 2, 3, 12.

80. A revised draft of a complaint was circulated to the litigation team with a cover memorandum on April 22, 1996. Memorandum from Lou Bogard to [nine individuals on the team, including Laurie Zelon] entitled "LSC Complaint,"

dated April 22, 1996. The cover memo stated the original draft had been modified principally to incorporate changes suggested by Alan Houseman and Linda Perle, who suggested the first version "overstated a number of the restrictions."

81. Attachment to LSC UPDATE, from Mauricio Vivero to LSC Supporters, dated April 24, 1996. The letter also is described in an article in *CQ's Congressional Monitor,* dated March 22, 1996.

82. H.R, 3019, President Clinton's signing this appropriations bill into law on April 26, 1996, cited in National Immigration Law Center, "Alien Eligibility for LSC Programs: Impact of New FY 1996 Restrictions" (May 10, 1996).

83. Transcript, Meeting of Board of Directors, Legal Services Corporation, February 24, 1996, 36–41.

84. Transcript, Meeting of Board of Directors, Legal Services Corporation, March 20, 1996, 30–31.

85. Transcript, Meeting of Board of Directors, Legal Services Corporation, February 24, 1996, 32–33. McCalpin abstained from voting on the motion approving this regulation.

86. Lawrence Fox, "ABA-Beacon for Ethics," speech when accepting award from ABA, see http://www.americanbar.org/content/dam/aba/migrated/cpr/pubs/fox.authcheckdam.pdf (last visited May 12, 2012).

87. In an obviously light-hearted account of the request that his brother, Jon Fox, use his position to save LSC, Larry Fox told the LSC board, "And as you know, what we did to help save Legal Services is we . . . reminded him that he would not come to Thanksgiving dinner, if he did not . . . help us in this way." Transcript of January 6, 1997 Meeting, Board of Directors, Legal Services Corporation, 47.

88. Memorandum from Alan and Linda to Clint, Harrison, Julie, Don, Andy, Jon, Esther, Laurie, James, De, and Lynn, entitled "Legal Services Litigation," dated April 30, 1996.

89. Jonathan Weiss, E-mail message to author.

90. "Handsnet" message [an internet network for LSC grantees] entitled, "Let's Litigate Against Legal Services Restrictions from Legal Services for the Elderly," signed by Jonathan Weiss, dated May 24, 1996.

91. Memorandum from Alan W. Houseman and Linda E. Perle to Litigation Team, entitled "Interpretation Memos and LSC Regulation Process," dated May 28, 1996.

92. Proposed letter to the Honorable Harold Rogers with blank signature lines, dated May 28, 1996, attached to Memo to Key LSC Contacts from Mauricio Vivero, dated May 30, 1996.

93. Memo to Key LSC Contacts from Mauricio Vivero, dated May 30, 1996.

94. Erlenborn, Videotaped oral history.

95. *House Committee on Appropriations, Committee Report No. 104–676, Departments of Commerce, Justice, and State, The Judiciary, and Related Agencies Appropriation Bill, 1997,* 128 (1996).

96. For the full text of the Fox–Mollohan amendment which added $109 million to the $141 million the committee bill provided, as well as the entire debate on the amendment in the House of Representatives, see http://capitolwords.org/date/1996/07/23/H8149-4_departments-of-commerce-justice-and-state-the-judi/ (last visited December 2, 2012).

97. Letter from Congressmen Alan B. Mollohan, Jon D. Fox, Charles W. Stenholm, Steven Schiff, Julian C. Dixon, and David Skaggs, to "Dear Colleague," dated July 19, 1996, attachment to LSC UPDATE, from Mauricio Vivero to LSC Supporters, dated July 24, 1996.

98. The speaker responding to an earlier speaker's argument often appeared much later in the debate, rather than immediately after the original speaker. Consequently, the following account does not purport to present excerpts of speeches in the order the House members spoke, but rather is organized around the major issues discussed. Nor does this account include every member who spoke or even summarize full speeches. Rather it provides excerpts of key points the speakers made during the debate.

99. 142 Cong. Rec. H18625 (July 23, 1996) (Statement of Rep. Mollohan).

100. 142 Cong. Rec. H18626 (July 23, 1996) (Statement of Rep. Taylor).

101. 142 Cong. Rec. H18626–27 (July 23, 1996) (Statement of Rep. Fox).

102. 142 Cong. Rec. H18629 (July 23, 1996) (Statement of Rep Hunter).

103. 142 Cong. Rec. H18629 (July 23, 1996) (Statement of Rep. Skaggs).

104. 142 Cong. Rec. H18627 (July 23, 1996) (Statement of Rep. Stenholm).

105. 142 Cong. Rec. H18628–29 (July 23, 1996) (Statement of Rep. Ramstad).

106. 142 Cong. Rec. H18630–31 (July 23, 1996) (Statement of Rep Schiff).

107. 142 Cong. Rec. H18631 (July 23, 1996) (Statement of Rep. Weldon).

108. 142 Cong. Rec. H18631 (July 23, 1996) (Statement of Rep. Flake).

109. 142 Cong. Rec. H18632 (July 23, 1996) (Statement of Rep. Shays).

110. 142 Cong. Rec. H18632 (July 23, 1996) (Statement of Rep Berman).

111. 142 Cong. Rec. H18630 (July 23, 1996) (Exchange between Rep. Berman and Rep. Doolittle).

112. 142 Cong. Rec. H18632 (July 23, 1996) (Statement of Rep. Gekas).

113. 142 Cong. Rec. H18632 (July 23, 1996) (Statement of Rep. Cummings).

114. 142 Cong. Rec. H18633 (July 23, 1996) (Statement of Rep. Spratt).

115. 142 Cong. Rec. H18633 (July 23, 1996) (Statement of Rep. Dornan).

116. 142 Cong. Rec. H18634 (July 23, 1996) (Statement of Rep. Dornan).

117. The Congressman probably meant the "Community Legal Assistance Center," not the "Philadelphia Legal Assistance Center" since the Philadelphia program with a similar name is some 2,500 miles from Santa Clara.

118. 142 Cong. Rec. H18627 (July 23, 1996) (Statement of Rep. Burton).

119. 142 Cong. Rec. H18635 (July 23, 1996) (Statement of Rep. Lofgren).

120. 142 Cong. Rec. H18632–33 (July 23, 1996) (Statement of Rep. Hastings).

121. Whether the congressman's brief account of Durant's career as LSC board chair was entirely accurate, the claim he opposed LSC was clearly true—since, as described earlier, Durant advocated for a zero: LSC budget while still serving as the organization's chair.

122. 142 Cong. Rec. H18635 (July 23, 1996) (Statement of Rep. Taylor).

123. 142 Cong. Rec. H18636 (July 23, 1996) (Statement of Rep. Collins).

124. 142 Cong. Rec. H18636 (July 23, 1996) (Statement of Rep. Edwards).

125. 142 Cong. Rec. H18638 (July 23, 1996).

126. 142 Cong. Rec. H18638. (July 23, 1996).

127. David Rogers and Christopher Georges, "House Damps Bid By GOP to Cancel Legal Aid Funding," *The Wall Street Journal,* July 24, 1996.

128. *Conference Committee Report No. 104–725, Personal Responsibility And Work Opportunity Reconciliation Act Of 1996* (1996).

129. Ibid.

130. Ibid.

131. Ibid.

132. *Washington Legal Found. v. Texas Equal Access To Justice Found.*, 873 F. Supp. 1, 7 (W.D. Tex. 1995).

133. *Washington Legal Found. v. Massachusetts Bar Found.*, 993 F.2d 962, 975–76 (1st Cir. 1993); *Cone v. State Bar of Fla.*, 819 F.2d 1002, 1004 (11th Cir. 1987).

134. *Washington Legal Found. v. Texas Equal Access to Justice Found*, 94 F.3d 996, 1000 (5th Cir. 1996).

135. "Petitioners filed this action in January 1997 in U.S. District Court for the Western District of Washington, alleging that the IOLTA program violated their rights under the First and Fifth Amendments. Named as defendants were [Legal Foundation of Washington], its President, and the nine justices of the Supreme Court of Washington—sued in their official capacities only. In January 1998, the district court issued an Order and Judgment granting Respondents' motions for summary judgment and denying Petitioners' motion for summary judgment. Pet. App. 86a-96a. The district court stated that the existence of a property right in IOLTA interest was "a prerequisite to establishing either a First or Fifth Amendment claim." Id. 92a. The court held that Petitioners lacked any property rights in the IOLTA interest and accordingly, dismissed their constitutional claims. Id. 94a. The court also rejected Petitioners' alternative claim that the IOLTA program violated their Fifth Amendment rights by failing to compensate them for the use of their funds." "Proceedings Below," United States Supreme Court Petitioner's Brief, *Washington Legal Foundation, et al. v. Legal Foundation of Washington, et al.*, 01–1325 (August 22, 2002), at https://docs .google.com/viewer?a=v&q=cache:fcw8D0k7DbYJ:communityrights.org/ PDFs/Briefs/WLFPetitioners.pdf+%22Washington+Legal+Foundation+ v.+Legal+Foudation+of+Washingtong%22+%22District+court%22&hl=e n&gl=us&pid=bl&srcid=ADGEESgaaO5XWrV49aDRb1w3qxCmbEVL_ GNOaw3-4niwWn-BfTG7iMIVKYvLcFTxNSZykawg4iZD-_tR0vIgRPWVG SlZyd6ecsHHFdVuv4B9KKt9EViQ0FLQLQgIK6pvoWpkVLDwL j0M&sig=AHIEtbTJHctyiAHXqQ2gkL_Gl9H2zbGzzw (last visited December 12, 2012).

136. Editorial, "Zero to Forever," *National Review*, July 31, 1995. In this editorial, the National Review complains about the 3-year "glide path" rather than an immediate and total elimination of funding for LSC in 1995.

137. Forger, "The Future of Legal Services."

Chapter 27: Coping with the Compromise

1. "Let's Litigate Against Legal Services Restrictions from Legal Services for the Elderly," "Handsnet" message [an internet network for LSC grantees] signed by Jonathan Weiss, dated May 24, 1996.

2. Burt Neuborne's biographical entry on the NYU Las School website reads in part: "Burt Neuborne is the Inez Milholland Professor of Civil Liberties and founding legal director of the Brennan Center for Justice at NYU Law School. For 45 years, he has been one of the nation's foremost civil liberties lawyers, serving as National Legal Director of the ACLU from 1981 to 1986,

Special Counsel to the NOW Legal Defense and Education Fund from 1990 to 1996, and as a member of the New York City Human Rights Commission from 1988 to 1992. He has argued numerous Supreme Court cases, and has litigated literally hundreds of important constitutional cases in the state and federal courts. He challenged the constitutionality of the Vietnam War, pioneered the flag burning cases, worked on the Pentagon Papers case, worked with Justice Ruth Bader Ginsburg when she headed the ACLU Women's Rights Project, anchored the ACLU's legal program during the Reagan years, and defended the legal services program against unconstitutional attacks. He currently directs the legal program of the Brennan Center, especially its efforts to reinforce American democracy and secure campaign finance reform. The Brennan Center was established in 1994 to honor Justice William Brennan Jr.'s monumental contribution to American Law." http://its.law.nyu.edu/facultyprofiles/profile.cfm?section=bio&personID=20165 (last visited May 16, 2012).

3. Nina Bernstein, "Suit Challenges Accord That Bars Legal Services Class-Action Cases for Poor," *The New York Times,* August 1, 1996.

4. Alan Houseman, Videotaped Oral History, in Oral History Collection, National Equal Justice Library, Georgetown Law Library, Washington, D.C.

5. Bernstein, "Suit Challenges Accord that bars Legal Services Class-Action Cases for Poor."

6. Ibid.

7. *Varshavsky v. Perales,* 608 N.Y.S.2d 184, 185 (1994).

8. Bernstein, "Suit Challenges Accord that bars Legal Services Class-Action Cases for Poor."

9. *Varshavsky v. Geller,* No. 40767/91 (N.Y. Sup. Ct. December 24, 1996), reprinted in N.Y.L.J., December 31, 1996, t 22 (col. 2).

10. Mary Burdick, Written message to the author.

11. Ibid.

12. *Serrano v. Priest,* 20 Cal. 3d 25 (1977).

13. *Serrano v. Priest,* 18 Cal.3d 728 (1976).

14. Burdick, Written message to the author.

15. Ibid.

16. Ibid.

17. Burdick, Written message to the author. The foregoing account of the Western Center's survival was verified, and in several respects corrected, by Mary Burdick in a message to the author.

18. Lonnie Powers [Executive Director, Massachusetts Legal Assistance Corporation], E-mail message to the author.

19. This is the same Allan Rodgers who spoke vigorously on behalf of the support centers before the Reagan board in 1987 when that board tried to justify defunding those grantees.

20. Allan Rodgers, Interview with and e-mail message to the author.

21. See, biographical note on Henry Freedman, Executive Director, National Center for Law and Economic Justice (renamed Welfare Law Center), http://www.nclej.org/about-staff.php (last visited May 17, 2012).

22. Henry Freedman, Written message to the author.

23. Ibid.

24. Ibid.

25. Ibid.

26. Ibid.

27. Ibid.

28. Ibid.

29. Henry Freedman, "Reorienting and Expanding A National Advocacy Program," *Management Information Exchange,* Vol. XXIII, No. 2 (Summer 2009), 31.

30. Victor Geminiani, "Crossing the Rubicon: Why We Sued," NLADA *Cornerstone,* November, 1999, 1.

31. Ibid., 2–3.

32. Ibid., 4–5.

33. Ibid., 5.

34. Ibid., 1, asterisked footnote.

35. Ibid., 1, asterisked footnote.

36. *Velazquez v. Legal Services Corp.,* 985 F. Supp. 323 (E.D.N.Y. 1997).

37. *Legal Aid Soc. of Hawaii v. Legal Services Corp.,* 961 F. Supp. 1402 (D. Haw. 1997).

38. *House Committee on Appropriations, Subcommittee on the Departments of Commerce, Justice, and State, the Judiciary, and Related Agencies, Departments of Commerce, Justice, and State, the Judiciary, and Related Agencies Appropriations for 1998 Hearings,* 105th Cong. 28 (1997) (testimony of Douglas Eakeley, Chairman, Board of Directors, Legal Services Corporation).

39. *House Committee on Appropriations, Subcommittee on the Departments of Commerce, Justice, and State, the Judiciary, and Related Agencies, Departments of Commerce, Justice, and State, the Judiciary, and Related Agencies Appropriations for 1998 Hearings,* 105th Cong. 28 (1997) (Statement of Rep. Rogers).

40. Victor Geminiani, E-mail message to the author.

41. John McKay, Telephone interview with author.

42. Ibid.

43. Ibid.

44. *House Committee on the Judiciary, Subcommittee on Commercial and Administrative Law, Reauthorization of Legal Services Corporation,* 104th Cong. 416 (1995) (testimony of John McKay, Washington Equal Justice Coalition).

45. McKay, Telephone interview with author.

46. Ibid.

47. Ibid.

48. Ibid.

49. Ibid.

50. Ibid.

51. Mauricio Rivera, Telephone interview with author.

52. John Erlenborn, Videotaped oral history, NEJL Oral History Collection, Georgetown Law Center, Washington, D.C.

53. *Casarez v. Val Verde County,* 957 F. Supp. 847 (W.D. Tex. 1997).

54. *Casarez v. Val Verde County,* 957 F. Supp. 847, 850–51 (W.D. Tex. 1997).

55. McKay, Telephone interview with author.

56. Ibid.

57. See Tampa Tribune "Truth-o-meter" account of Gingrich's resignation at http://www.politifact.com/truth-o-meter/article/2012/jan/23/did-gingrich-leave-speakership-disgrace (last visited November 16, 2012).

58. 144 Cong. Rec. H18992 (August 5, 1998). The Conference Committee report on H.R. 2670 included $300 million for LSC. This was identical to the

FY1999 appropriation and the Administration's FY2000 budget request. Both the House and the Senate approved the Conference Committee recommendation. H.R. 2670 was vetoed by the President on October 25, 1999. In his veto message, President Clinton stated that "adequate funding for legal services is essential to ensuring that all citizens have access to the Nation's justice system" and urged Congress to fully fund the program at $340 million.

59. Legal Services Corporation, "Assessment of 1999 Case Statistical Data: Special Report to the Committee o n Appropriation (July 30, 2000), 2 Exhibit 1, 7 Exhibit 4.

60. Legal Services Corporation, "Assessment of 1999 Case Statistical Data: Special Report to the Committees on Appropriations, 8 Exhibit 5. As reflected on that same chart, using the IG's 13-percent correction, LSC would have reported 903,000 cases for 1999.

61. McKay, Telephone interview with author.

62. *United States v. American Library Assn., Inc.*, 539 U.S. 194, 210 (2003) (holding that under the unconstitutional conditions doctrine, "the government may not deny a benefit to a person on a basis that infringes his constitutionally protected . . . freedom of speech even if he has no entitlement to that benefit"); *Bd. of County Com'rs, Wabaunsee County, Kan. v. Umbehr*, 518 U.S. 668, 678–80 (1996) (finding that under the unconstitutional conditions doctrine, the First Amendment protects independent contractors from termination or prevention of automatic renewal of at-will government contracts in retaliation for their exercise of freedom of speech); *Rust v. Sullivan*, 500 U.S. 173, 192 (1991) (holding that regulations restricting abortion-related speech is an unconstitutional condition on the receipt of a federal government benefit).

63. *Legal Aid Soc. of Hawaii v. Legal Services Corp.*, 961 F. Supp. 1402, 1419 (D. Haw. 1997).

64. Ibid., 961 F. Supp. 1402, 1418 (D. Haw. 1997).

65. The new "Transfer of recipient funds" section was found in 45 C.F.R. sec. 1610.7 (1996).

66. 50 Fed. Reg. 49,276, 49,279 (November 29, 1985). The factors constituting sufficient "control" to impose LSC restrictions on the non-LSC-funded organization included, among others "an overlap of officers, directors or other managers," contractual or financial relationships or historical relationships between the two, "close identity of interest," one is a "mere conduit," or "straw party" for the other, or funds are solicited for the other entity in the name of or with the express or implicit approval of the LSC grantee.

67. *Legal Aid Soc. of Hawaii v. Legal Services Corp.*, 961 F. Supp. 1402, 1419 (D. Haw. 1997).

68. Transcript, Meeting of Board of Directors, Legal Services Corporation, March 8, 1997, 53–55.

69. Transcript, Meeting of Board of Directors, Legal Services Corporation, March 8, 1997, 58–59.

70. Ibid., 60. The interim regulations were promulgated in 62 Fed. Reg. 12,101 (1997) and expressly stated it was "intended to address constitutional challenges raised by the previous rule."

71. 45 C.F.R. sec. 1610.7.

72. *Legal Aid Soc. of Hawaii v. Legal Services Corp.*, 980 F. Supp. 1142 (D. Haw. 1997).

73. As revised in this interim regulation, the "Interrelated Organizations" prohibition read:

"If a recipient controls, is controlled by or is subject to common control with another organization, the two organizations are interrelated organizations and the [congressional restrictions] will be applied to both organizations, *unless the association between the two organizations meets the standards of program integrity in paragraph (b) of this section.*" 45 C.F.R. 1610.8(a). (Italics added.)

74. The "program integrity" standards in the interim regulation read:

[The Act's restrictions do not apply to an affiliate if it] is physically and financially separate from the organization. Mere bookkeeping separation of LSC funds from other funds is not sufficient. In order to be physically and financially separate, the recipient and the other organization must have an objective integrity and independence from one another. Factors considered to determine whether such objective integrity and independence exist shall include but are not limited to:

 (i) The existence of separate personnel;
 (ii) The existence of separate accounting and timekeeping records;
 (iii) *The existence of separate facilities;* and
 (iv) The extent to which signs and other forms of identification which distinguish the recipient from the organization are present.
 45 C.F.R. sec. 1610.8(b)(3).

75. *Velazquez v. Legal Services Corp.,* 985 F. Supp. 323, 334 (E.D.N.Y. 1997).

76. Transcript, Meeting of Board of Directors, Legal Services Corporation, May 21, 1997, 36–37.

77. *Legal Aid Soc. of Hawaii v. Legal Services Corp.,* 981 F. Supp. 1288, 1301 (D. Haw. 1997).

78. *Velazquez v. Legal Services Corp.,* 985 F. Supp. 323, 343–44 (E.D.N.Y. 1997).

79. Ibid., 985 F. Supp. 323, 335–36 (E.D.N.Y. 1997).

80. Ibid., 985 F. Supp. 323, 344 (E.D.N.Y. 1997).

81. Neil McBride [general counsel, Middle-Tennessee Legal Services], conversation with author.

82. The California Rural Legal Assistance Foundation describes its mission on its website http://www.crlaf.org/who-we-are- (last visited November 15, 2012):

"CRLAF is a statewide non-profit organization providing legal services and policy advocacy for California's rural poor. We focus on some of the most marginalized communities: the unrepresented, the unorganized and the *undocumented.* We engage in impact litigation, community education and outreach, *legislative and administrative advocacy,* and provide public policy leadership on the state and local levels in the areas of labor, housing, education, health, worker safety, pesticides, citizenship, immigration, and environmental justice. We seek to bring social justice to rural poor communities in all of California."

83. McKay, Telephone interview with author.

84. The moving force behind creation of the Beverly Hills Bar Foundation was Fred Nicholas, a public-spirited and hugely successful lawyer-businessman. He chaired the Foundation's first board and supplied much of the financial support. The author was a member of that founding board.

85. For this and additional information about Public Counsel, see http://www.publiccounsel.org/contact_us?id=0001 (last visited May 18, 2912).

86. For this and additional information about Bet Tzedek see, http://www.bettzedek.org/about-us/our-story (last visited May 18, 2012).

87. Beverly Groudine [long-time Staff Counsel, American Bar Association Commission on IOLTA], E-mail message to the author. Indiana started it IOLTA program in 1998.

88. *Washington Legal Found. v. Texas Equal Access to Justice Found.*, 106 F.3d 640 (5th Cir. 1997).

89. *Cone v. State Bar of Florida*, 819 F.2d 1002, 1007–08 (11th Cir. 1987) (concluding that Florida's IOLTA program does not commit an unconstitutional taking, reasoning that the owner of principal has no legitimate expectation of earning interest on money deposited into a Florida IOLTA account because "the use of [the client's] money had no net value, therefore there could be no property interest for the state to appropriate").

90. *Phillips v. Washington Legal Found.*, 521 U.S. 1117 (1997).

91. *Washington Legal Foundation v. Legal Foundation of Washington*, No. C97–0146C (WD Wash., Jan. 30, 1998).

92. *Phillips v. Washington Legal Found.*, 524 U.S. 156, 172 (1998).

93. Ibid.

94. *Washington Legal Found. v. Texas Equal Access to Justice Found.*, 86 F. Supp. 2d 617, 617–18 (W.D. Tex. 2000) (Hughes & Luce, L.L.P., Dallas, TX; Hale and Dorr, L.L.P., Washington, D.C.; Hale & Dorr, L.L.P., Boston, MA; Jones, Day, Reavis & Pogue, Washington, D.C.; Jones, Day, Reavis & Pogue, Washington, D.C.; Vinson & Elkins, Houston, TX; Covington & Burling, Washington, D.C.; Dow, Cogburn & Friedman, Houston, TX).

95. *Washington Legal Found. v. Texas Equal Access to Justice Found.*, 86 F. Supp. 2d 624, 637 (W.D. Tex. 2000).

96. Ibid., 86 F. Supp. 2d 624, 643 (W.D. Tex. 2000).

97. John McKay, "Federally Funded Legal Services: A New Vision of Equal Justice under Law," *Tennessee Law Review* 68 (2000): 101, 112.

98. Alan Houseman, presentation as part of panel on "The Future of Legal Services," one of the events commemorating the opening of the National Equal Justice Library, at Washington College of Law, American University, Washington, D.C., held on September 19–20, 1997. (In 2006, the National Equal Justice Library relocated to Georgetown Law Center.)

99. John McKay, Telephone interview with author.

100. Reginald Heber Smith, *Justice and the Poor* (New York: Carnegie, 1919), 206.

101. San Francisco, Oakland, Berkeley, Contra Costa county, Marin, and San Mateo all had their own LSC-funded legal services programs.

102. McKay, Telephone interview with author.

103. This statewide system is described on the website of The Alliance for Equal Justice, which is Washington state's umbrella organization for this network of funders and legal services grantees. See, http://allianceforequaljustice.org/index.php?p=Funding_for_Legal_Aid&s=209 (last visited November 16, 2012).

104. McKay, Telephone interview with author. McKay said two board members had opposed his selection as president and didn't support his consolidation strategy.

105. McKay, Telephone interview with author.

106. Ibid.

107. Ramon Arias [long-time Executive Director of Bay Area Legal Aid and former Executive Director of San Francisco Neighborhood Legal Aid Foundation], Telephone interview with author.

108. McKay, Telephone interview with author.

109. Arias, Telephone interview with author.

110. Ibid.

111. Ibid.

112. Toby Rothschild [General Counsel of the other surviving LSC grantee in Los Angeles County, Legal Aid Foundation of Los Angeles (LAFLA)], E-mail message to the author. Rothschild had been executive director of the Long Beach Legal Aid Society before it was merged into LAFLA, and as part of the negotiations became LAFLA's general counsel. A former Reggie, he was and remains a leading "statesman" in California's legal services community serving in statewide leadership roles in several organizations.

113. Rothschild, E-mail message to the author.

114. See, celebration of the result in the Ashtabula County litigation, LSC Board of Directors, Resolution #2000–06, "Recognizing and Thanking Porter, Wright, Morris & Arthur's Litigation Team of Daniel F. Gourash & Natalie Peterson for Their Outstanding and Valuable Pro Bono Representation," passed August 1, 2000.

115. McKay, Telephone interview with author.

116. John McKay, Written comment to the author.

117. McKay, Telephone interview with author.

118. Justice Laurie Zelon, Telephone interview with author.

119. McKay, Telephone interview with author.

120. For more information about SPAN, see http://lobby.la.psu.edu/ 064_Legal_Services/Organizational_Statements/NLADA/NLADA_Span_ justice_access.htm

121. Rothschild, E-mail message to the author. Rothschild participated in the state planning process in California every year it took place, in his capacity as General Counsel of the Legal Aid Foundation of Los Angeles. The last plan was filed in 2001, McKay's final year as LSC president.

122. Among the states that had early success in obtaining substantial funds from their state government were Maryland, Massachusetts, New Jersey, Pennsylvania, Ohio, Washington, and Minnesota. As a result, by 2000 several of these states were funded at two or three times the level (on a per capita basis) of states that still relied entirely on the federal government, IOLTA, and private donations to support legal services for the poor. California Commission on Access to Justice, *The Path to Equal Justice: A Five-Year Status Report on Access to Justice in California* (San Francisco: State Bar of California, 2002), 32–33, available at http://www.calbar.ca.gov (last visited November 16, 2012).

123. WSBA Report, "Access to Justice Task Force 1992–1993," 1.

124. "The now famous Ada Shen-Jaffe circle chart illustrates the many different organizations, agencies, and private attorneys involved in providing services to low and moderate income citizens." WSBA Report, Access to Justice Task Force 1992–1993, 2.

125. WSBA Report, "Access to Justice Task Force 1992–1993," 1.

126. Ibid., 8.

127. Ibid., 13–14.

128. Ibid., 11.

129. Ibid., 15–17.

130. Ibid., 19.

131. Washington Supreme Court, "Order Establishing Access to Justice Board for an Initial Evaluation Period of Two Years," May 10, 1994.

132. Memorandum to Talbot "Sandy" Delemberte, ABA President-Elect, re "National Access to Justice Commission," October 15, 1990.

133. See, Talbot "Sandy" Dalemberte's faculty biography on the Florida State Law School's website, http://www.law.fsu.edu/faculty/tdalemberte.html (last visited May 21, 2012).

134. The author served on an ABA committee chaired by Dalemberte for seven years (1976–83) and the two have remained friends and colleagues on various projects since then. The passages about Dalemberte's personality and character are based on personal observations during those experiences.

135. Access to Justice Working Group, *And Justice for All: Fulfilling the Promise of Access to Civil Justice in California* (San Francisco: State Bar of California, 1996), 45–53.

136. Ibid., 48. Recommendation 2 in the report reads: "Create the California Commission on Access to Justice to provide leadership and oversee efforts to increase funding and improve delivery methods."

137. The appointing entities and the appointees, as of 2002, are listed in California Commission on Access to Justice, *The Path to Equal Justice: A Five-Year Status Report on Access to Justice in California* (October 2002).

138. Ibid., 19–20.

139. Ibid., 21.

140. Ibid., 21.

141. Ibid., 22.

142. Robert Echols [long-time consultant, ABA Project on Access to Justice Commissions], E-mail message to the author. As of 2012, 26 states and the District of Columbia have Access to Justice Commissions (or boards, or similar entities performing the same functions).

143. Echols, E-mail message to the author.

144. *Legal Aid Soc. of Hawaii v. Legal Services Corp.,* 145 F.3d 1017, 1031 (9th Cir. 1998).

145. *Velazquez v. Legal Services Corp.,* 164 F.3d 757, 773 (2d Cir. 1999) *aff'd,* 531 U.S. 533, 121 S. Ct. 1043, 149 L. Ed. 2d 63 (2001).

146. Ibid., 164 F.3d 757, 768–69 (2d Cir. 1999) aff'd, 531 U.S. 533, 121 S. Ct. 1043, 149 L. Ed. 2d 63 (2001).

147. *Velazquez v. Legal Services Corp.,* 164 F.3d 757, 763 (2d Cir. 1999).

148. *Legal Services Corp. v. Velazquez,* 529 U.S. 1052, 120 S. Ct. 1553, 146 L. Ed. 2d 459 (2000) (granting certiorari); *Legal Services Corp. v. Velazquez,* 531 U.S. 533, 121 S. Ct. 1043, 1044, 149 L. Ed. 2d 63 (2001) (limiting review to "welfare reform" issue).

149. 146 Cong. Rec. H12034 (June 22, 2000).

150. McKay, Telephone interview with author.

151. *House Committee of Conference, Committee Report No. 106–1005, Making Appropriations for the Government of the District of Columbia and Other Activities Chargeable in Whole or in Part Against Revenues of Said District for the Fiscal Year Ending September 30, 2001, and for Other Purposes,* 143 (2000).

152. Due to inflation, $321 million in 1981 was the equivalent of $608 million in 2000. But the number of people with incomes low enough to qualify for LSC-funded services had increased nearly 20 percent during those two decades, thus requiring $728 million to match the 1981 "minimum access" target, which was based on providing something over $7.00 per eligible poor person in 1981 dollars.

Chapter 28: A Time of Respite and Risk

1. *Washington Legal Found. v. Legal Found. of Washington,* 236 F.3d 1097, 1115 (9th Cir. 2001). NO CITATION AVAILABLE FOR TRIAL COURT DECISION.
2. *Phillips v. Washington Legal Foundation,* 524 U.S. 156, 160 (1998).
3. *Washington Legal Found. v. Legal Found. of Washington,* 271 F.3d 835, 873 (9th Cir. 2001).
4. Ibid., 271 F.3d 835, 883 (9th Cir. 2001).
5. Ibid., 271 F.3d 835, 879, 884 (9th Cir. 2001).
6. John McKay, Telephone interview with author and a later review of the text by McKay.
7. CNN Politics, "Bush Picks White House Counsel for Supreme Court" (October 4, 2005) at http://articles.cnn.com/2005-10-03/politics/scotus.miers_1_dallas-bar-association-third-branch-conference-leonard-leo?_s=PM:POLITICS (last visited May 31, 2012).
8. Harriett Meier, application papers to United States Senate, Committee on the Judiciary for the Supreme Court of the United States. This document contains a comprehensive biography of Harriet Meier.
9. "Alberto Gonzalez, Former Attorney General," George W. Bush White House Archives, at http://georgewbush-whitehouse.archives.gov/government/gonzales-bio.html (last visited May 31, 2012).
10. Transcript, Meeting of the Board of Directors, Legal Services Corporation, June 30, 2001, 35.
11. *Velazquez v. Legal Services Corp.,* 164 F.3d 757, 772 (2nd Cir. 1999).
12. *Legal Services Corp. v. Velazquez,* 531 U.S. 533, 549 (2001).
13. Ibid., 531 U.S. 533, 537–46 (2001).
14. Ibid., 531 U.S. 533, 548–49 (2001).
15. McKay, Telephone interview with author.
16. 67 FR 19342 (45 CFR Part 1639); *House Committee on the Judiciary, Subcommittee on Commercial and Administrative Law, Hearing on the Legal Services Corporation,* 107th Cong. 1–71 (2002).
17. McKay, Telephone interview with author.
18. Ibid.
19. See, for example, David Bowermaster, "Gonzales: McKay's Judgment Doubted," *Seattle Times,* April 20, 2007, at http://seattletimes.com/html/localnews/2003673977_mckay20m.html (last visited November 18, 2012). This scandal ultimately led to Gonzales' resignation from the position of U.S. Attorney General. David Bowermaster and Christina Siderius, "State Democrats, McKay Hail Gonzales' Resignation," *Seattle Times,* August 27, 2007, at http://seattletimes.com/html/localnews/2003855603_webgonzdelegation27.html (last visited November 18, 2012).

20. Douglas Eakeley, Videotaped oral history, NEJL Oral History Collection, National Equal Justice Library, Georgetown Law Center, Washington, D.C.; John Erlenborn, Videotaped oral history, NEJL Oral History Collection, National Equal Justice Library, Georgetown Law Center, Washington, D.C.

21. Transcript, June 30, 2001, Meeting of LSC Board, 43–44.

22. Transcript, Meeting of the Board of Directors, Legal Services Corporation, June 30, 2001, 99.

23. *Washington Legal Found. v. Legal Found. of Washington*, 271 F.3d 835 (9th Cir. 2001). Chief Judge Schroeder along with Judges Pregerson, Tashima, Fisher, Berzon, and Rawlinson joined Judge Wardlaw in her opinion while Judge Kozinski issued a dissent that was joined by Judges Trott, Kleinfeld, and Silverman.

24. *Washington Legal Found. v. Legal Found. of Washington*, 271 F.3d 835, 861 (9th Cir. 2001).

25. Ibid., 271 F.3d 835, 861–62 (9th Cir. 2001).

26. http://www.brennancenter.org/content/elert/president_bush_announces_first_five_names_to_be_nominated_to_legal_services/. The five nominees were Professor Lilian R. BeVier from the University of Virginia Law School, Professor Robert J. Dieter of the University of Colorado Law School and Bush's college roommate, Thomas A. Fuentes of California, head of a construction firm and chair of the Orange County Republican Party, Frank B. Strickland, a lawyer and prominent Republican from Atlanta, and Michael McKay, former U.S. Attorney for Washington State, and brother of former LSC president John McKay.

27. For a critical overview of the Federalist Society, see "Federalist Society for Law and Public Policy Studies," Right Wing Watch, People for the American Way, at http://www.rightwingwatch.org/content/federalist-society (last visited November 18, 2012). According to this source, "The Federalist Society hopes to transform the American legal system by developing and promoting far-right positions and influencing who will become judges, top government officials, and decision-makers. FS is 'dedicated to reforming the current legal order.' " Among other information supplied are the Society's annual budget (over $5 million) and a partial list of judges, cabinet members, and high-ranking positions in the executive branch Federalist Society members occupied during the Bush administration. For another perspective on this organization, see the Federalist Society's own website, http://www.fed-soc.org/aboutus/ (last visited November 18, 2012). On that website, the Society is described as follows: "The Federalist Society for Law and Public Policy Studies is a group of conservatives and libertarians interested in the current state of the legal order. It is founded on the principles that the state exists to preserve freedom, that the separation of governmental powers is central to our Constitution, and that it is emphatically the province and duty of the judiciary to say what the law is, not what it should be. The Society seeks both to promote an awareness of these principles and to further their application through its activities."

28. *Washington Legal Found. v. Legal Found. of Washington*, 536 U.S. 903 (2002).

29. "United States Supreme Court Hears IOLTA Case," Senior Lawyer News, Fall 2002, at http://www.vsb.org/slc-foo/attorney/newsletterfall02/iolta.html (last visited November 18, 2012).

30. An observer who attended the oral argument reported, "As with the Supreme Court's earlier decision in *Phillips v. Washington Legal Foundation,* the Court appears sharply divided over the critical constitutional questions involved in this case. Little can be predicted about the outcome from trying to read the questioning from the various justices on the Court." "United States Supreme Court Hears IOLTA Case."

31. *Brown v. Legal Found. of Washington,* 538 U.S. 216, 240 (2003).

32. Ibid., 538 U.S. 216, 239–40 (2003).

33. Ibid., 538 U.S. 216, 235–36 (2003).

34. Ibid., 538 U.S. 216, 240–41 (2003).

35. California became the 16th state to enact a "comparability" rule, in that state via a statute. That statute "requires attorneys with IOLTA accounts to hold those accounts at financial institutions offering to pay dividends or interest rates to IOLTA customers that are "comparable" to what they pay their similarly situated customers" and "also update[s] the kinds of investment vehicles attorneys can use for their IOLTA accounts, particularly large-balance accounts, allowing IOLTA funds to be held in conservative, high-yield bank products." See, http://www.calbar.ca.gov/Attorneys/MemberServices/IOLTA/FAQ.aspx (last visited June 1, 2012).

36. Frank Strickland, Telephone interview with author.

37. Ibid.

38. Ibid.

39. Ibid.

40. Ibid.

41. Ibid.

42. Ibid.

43. Ibid.

44. Ibid.

45. Ibid.

46. Ibid.

47. Ibid.

48. Ibid.

49. Ibid.

50. Ibid.

51. "Most Outrageous: Legal Services Corp.," *Human Events,* March 10, 2003.

52. A number of law review articles appeared arguing why there was a right to counsel in civil cases under the U.S. Constitution in the years before the Supreme Court issued its *Lassiter* opinion. (See, e.g., Note, "The Right to Counsel in Civil Litigation," 66 *Colum. L. Rev.* 1322 (1966); O'Brien, "Why Not Appointed Counsel in Civil Cases? The Swiss Approach," 28 *Ohio St. L.J.* 5 (1967); Note, "The Indigent's Right to Counsel in Civil Cases," 76 *Yale L.J.* 545 (1967); Note, "The Indigent's Right ot Counsel in Civil Cases," 43 *Fordham L. Rev.* 989 (1975), Note, "The Emerging Right of Legal Assistance for the Indigent in Civil Proceedings," 9 *U.Mich. J.L. Ref.* 554 (1976), Comment, "Current Prospects for an Indigent's Right to Appointed Counsel and Free Transcript in Civil Litigation," 7 *Pac. L.J.* 149 (1976), Johnson, "Beyond Payne: The Case for a Legally Enforceable Right to Representation for Indigent California Litigants," 11 *Loyola of Los Angeles L. Rev.* 249 (1978).

53. *Gideon v. Wainwright,* 372 U.S. 335 (1963).

54. England has had a statutory right to counsel in civil cases since Parliament enacted the Statute of Henry VII in 1495, France has had such a right since 1852, Italy since 1865, Germany since 1877, and most other European countries since the late 1800s or early 1900s. These right to counsel statutes are discussed in Earl Johnson Jr., "The Right to Counsel in Civil Cases: An International Perspective," 19 *Loyola of Los Angeles Law Review* 341 (1985). Several of the foreign statutes are translated in Mauro Cappelletti, James Gordley, and Earl Johnson Jr., *Toward Equal Justice: A Comparative Study of Legal Aid in Modern Societies* (Milan/Dobbs Ferry: Giuffre/Oceana, 1975, 1981).

55. *Airey v. Ireland,* 2 Eur. Ct. H.R. (ser. A) 305 (1979). The opinion was based on language guaranteeing, "In the determination of his civil rights and obligations . . . everyone is entitled to a fair and public hearing within a reasonable time." (Convention for the Protection of Human Rights and Fundamental Freedoms, November 4, 1950, art. 6, para.1, 213 U.N.T.S. 222.) As the court then explained: "The Convention was intended to guarantee rights that were *practical and effective,* particularly in respect of the right of access to the courts, in view of its prominent place in a democratic society. . . . The possibility of appearing in person before the [trial court] did not provide an *effective* right of access. . . . [I]t is not realistic, . . . to suppose that, . . . the applicant could effectively conduct her own case, despite the assistance which, . . . the judge affords to parties acting in person." (2 Eur. Ct. H.R. (Ser. A) at p. 315, emphasis supplied.)

56. *Lassiter v. Department of Social Services of Durham County, North Carolina,* 452 U.S. 18 (1981).

57. "The [adequate and independent state grounds] rule is usually stated negatively: 'Where the decision of the state court is deemed to rest upon a non-federal ground which independently and adequately supports the state court judgment, the Supreme Court will not exercise jurisdiction to review notwithstanding the raising of federal questions upon the state court record or the decision of these questions by the state court'" Sandalow, "*Henry v. Mississippi* and the Adequate State Ground: Proposals for a Revised Doctrine," 1965 *Supreme Court Review* 187, 189 n. 9 (quoting R. Robertson Y F. Kirkham, *Jurisdiction of the Supreme Court of the United States* 163 (R. Wolfson and P. Kurland 2d ed. 1951).

58. For a brief biography, see Stephen Sachs brief biography on the website of Wilmer and Hale, the law firm where he was a partner before retiring in 1999, at http://www.wilmerhale.com/steve_sachs (last visited June 1, 2012).

59. For a brief biography, see Leonard Schroeter's entry in the website of the law firm, where he is now "of counsel" at http://www.stritmatter.com/seattle-personal-injury-trial-lawyers/schroeter (last visited June 1, 2012).

60. In 1999, the author was a member of a panel discussion on this subject at the annual "Access to Justice" conference in Washington, and in 2000, spoke on the subject at an annual legal aid dinner in Baltimore, Maryland.

61. *Frase v. Barnhart,* 379 Md. 100, 103–04 (2003). This case involved a custody dispute between Deborah Frase and Curtis and Cynthia Barnhart, a couple who, during part of an eight-week period of the Frase's incarceration, volunteered to care for Frase's child. The Barnharts then decided that

they wanted custody of the child. One issue in this civil case was Frase's denial of legal representation by the legal service agency.

62. *King v. King*, 162 Wash. 2d 378, 381–83 (2007). In a Washington dissolution of marriage dispute, a couple previously married for 10 years, Brenda and Michael King, both sought custody of their children. At trial, Brenda appeared pro se while the Michael was represented by private counsel. The court awarded custody to Michael and Brenda appealed both the denial of counsel and the decision to deny her custody of her children.

63. Deborah Gardner [Litigation Director, Public Justice Center and Chair, National Coalition for a Civil Right to Counsel], E-mail message to the author.

64. Deborah Gardner, E-mail message.

65. This coordination group is called the Civil Right to Counsel Leadership and Support Initiative (CRCLSI) and has five members, Public Justice Center (Baltimore), Northwest Justice Center (Seattle), Brennan Center on Justice (New York), Sargent Shriver Center on Law and Poverty (Chicago), and the American Bar Association's Standing Committee on Legal Aid and Indigent Defense (Chicago). Initially, it was funded by the Open Society Institute and the Ford Foundation and later by the ABA's litigation section. The chair of CRCLSI is Deborah Gardner of the Public Justice Center. Gardner, E-mail message. (The author has been a member of CRCLSI and of the National Coalition for a Civil Right to Counsel since his retirement from the bench in October, 2007 and his appointment as a member of SCLAID that same year, and thus is personally aware of most of the activities of this movement since then.)

66. From 2007 to 2009, the coordinating group was staffed by Sharon Rubenstein, and since 2009 has been staffed by John Pollock. From 2009 until 2011, Pollock was funded by the litigation section of the American Bar Association.

67. The coalition has advocated using legislative approaches as well as litigation as a way of expanding rights to counsel in certain types of cases, as well as "pilot" programs that experiment with different ways of achieving that end.

68. Some legal services lawyers have expressed reservations about the civil right to counsel movement, concerned it may divert funds from existing legal services agencies. Other legal services leaders, on the other hand, have been strong supporters. For an article about the transformation of a skeptic into a supporter of the movement, see, Catherine Carr (executive director, Community Legal Services of Philadelphia), "Right to Counsel and Legal Services: From Fear and Loathing to Love and Support," *MIE Journal,* vol. XXVI, No. 2 (Summer 2012), 37.

69. Strickland, Telephone interview with author.

70. Biography of Helaine Barnett, appointed President of the Legal Services Corporation, at http://66.35.36.177:21980/LegalDev/NLADA/DMS/Documents/1071875410.58/document_info (last visited May 31, 2012).

71. Ibid.

72. Strickland, Telephone interview with author.

73. *House Committee on the Judiciary, Subcommittee on Commercial and Administrative Law, Hearing on the Legal Services Corporation: Inquiry into the Activities*

of the California Rural Legal Assistance Program and Testimony Relating to the Merits of Client Co-Pay, 108th Cong. 13–14 (2004).

74. New American, Congressional Races, at http://www.thenewamerican. com/usnews/politics/item/2410-congressional-races (last visited November 20, 2012).

75. *House Committee on the Judiciary, Subcommittee on Commercial and Administrative Law, Hearing on the Legal Services Corporation: Inquiry into the Activities of the California Rural Legal Assistance Program and Testimony Relating to the Merits of Client Co-Pay,* 108th Cong. 13–14 (2004) (testimony of Helaine Barnett, President, Legal Services Corporation).

76. Ibid., 108th Cong. 27 (2004) (testimony of Helaine Barnett, President, Legal Services Corporation).

77. Ibid., 108th Cong. 33–34, 38 (2004) (Statements of Reps. Watt and Delahunt).

78. Ibid., 108th Cong. 20 (2004) (testimony of Jose Padilla, Executive Director, California Rural Legal Assistance, Inc.).

79. *House Committee on the Judiciary, Subcommittee on Commercial and Administrative Law, Hearing on the Legal Services Corporation: Inquiry into the Activities of the California Rural Legal Assistance Program and Testimony Relating to the Merits of Client Co-Pay,* 108th Cong. 14 (2004) (testimony of Helaine Barnett, President, Legal Services Corporation).

80. Ibid., 108th Cong. 14–15 (2004) (testimony of Helaine Barnett, President, Legal Services Corporation).

81. Ibid., 108th Cong. 14 (2004) (testimony of Helaine Barnett, President, Legal Services Corporation).

82. Ibid., 108th Cong. 33 (2004) (testimony of Rep Delahunt).

83. Ibid., 108th Cong. 18 (2004) (testimony of Jose Padilla, Executive Director, California Rural Legal Assistance, Inc.).

84. Ibid., 108th Cong. 16 (2004) (testimony of Jose Padilla, Executive Director, California Rural Legal Assistance, Inc.).

85. Ibid., 108th Cong. 17 (2004) (testimony of Jose Padilla, Executive Director, California Rural Legal Assistance, Inc.).

86. Ibid., 108th Cong. 17 (2004) (testimony of Jose Padilla, Executive Director, California Rural Legal Assistance, Inc.).

87. Ibid., 108th Cong. 23 (2004) (testimony of Jose Padilla, Executive Director, California Rural Legal Assistance, Inc.).

88. Ibid., 108th Cong. 17 (2004) (testimony of Jose Padilla, Executive Director, California Rural Legal Assistance, Inc.).

89. Statute of Henry VII, 1495, 11 Hen. 7, c. 7, 2 Statutes of the Realm 578.

90. *Frase v. Barnhart,* 379 Md. 100, 126, 840 A.2d 114, 129 (2003).

91. Ibid., 379 Md. 100, 130, 840 A.2d 114, 131–32 (2003).

92. Ibid., 379 Md. 100, 141, 840 A.2d 114, 138 (2003).

93. Ibid., 379 Md. 100, 141–42, 840 A.2d 114, 138 (2003).

94. *House Committee of Conference, Committee Report No. 108–401, Making Appropriations for Agriculture, Rural Development, Food and Drug Administration, And Related Agencies for the Fiscal Year Ending September 30, 2004,* 88 (2004) (appropriating $339 million for the LSC); *House Committee of Conference, Committee Report No. 109–272, Making Appropriations for Science, Departments of Commerce, Justice, and State, the Judiciary, and Related Agencies Appropriation*

Act, 2006, 42 (2005) (appropriating $331 million for the LSC); *Senate Committee on Appropriations, Committee Report No. 110–124, Departments of Commerce and Justice, Science, and Related Agencies Appropriations Bill, 2008* (2007) (citing $349 million as the LSC appropriation amount for FY 2007); *Senate Committee on Appropriations, Committee Report No. 110–397, Departments of Commerce and Justice, Science, and Related Agencies Appropriations Bill, 2009* (2008) (citing $350 million as the LSC appropriation amount for FY 2008).

95. Herbert Garten [LSC Board member], Interview with author.

96. McKay, Telephone interview with author.

97. Thomas Smegal [board chair of Friends of Legal Services], Telephone interview with author; Victor Fortuno [LSC's Vice President for Legal Affairs and General Counsel], E-mail message to the author.

98. Kirt West to LSC Board of Directors, "Report on the Financial Implications of the 3333 K Street Lease," April 22, 2005. The Report estimated LSC would overpay by $1.23 million over the 10 year term of the lease, using information obtained from two commercial real estate organizations. The Board commissioned its own study which disputed those estimates and concluded LSC was paying lower rent over the 10 years than it would at comparable buildings.

99. *House Committee on the Judiciary, Subcommittee on Commercial and Administrative Law, Hearing on the Legal Services Corporation: Inquiry into the Activities of the California Rural Legal Assistance Program and Testimony Relating to the Merits of Client Co-Pay,* 109th Cong. 8–47 (2005) (testimony of Thomas Smegal and Frank Strickland).

100. Gary L. Kepplinger [General Counsel, Government Accountability Office], opinion letter B-308037, to Senator Charles Grassley, Chair, Committee on Finance, U.S. Senate, September 14, 2006, 8.

101. Legal Services Corporation, "Legal Services Corporation (LSC) Response to Issues in CBS and AP news Stories," August 17, 2006.

102. The following charges were compiled in an Associated Press story, Larry Margasak, "Legal Aid Program for Poor Has Expensive Tastes," Associated Press, August 15, 2006, and LSC's responses in a press release from the Corporation, "Legal Services Corporation (LSC) Response To Issues in CBS and AP news Stories."

103. Strickland, Telephone Interview with author.

104. Ibid.

105. Professor Lillian Bevier, excerpt from oral report to LSC Board, quoted in proceedings of House subcommittee hearing, See, *Hearing before the Subcommittee on Commercial and Administrative Law of the Committee on the Judiciary, House of Representatives,* 109th Cong, 2nd Sess. On H.R. 6101 (September 26, 2006), 74.

106. *Hearing before the Subcommittee on Commercial and Administrative Law of the Committee on the Judiciary, House of Representatives,* 109th Cong, 2nd Sess. On H.R. 6101 (September 26, 2006).

107. http://www.govtrack.us/congress/bills/109/hr6101.

108. Fortuno, Telephone interview.

109. David Ingram, "Two Years After Audits, Legal Services Gets Some Praise," *The National Journal,* October 27, 2009.

110. Helaine Barnett, "Reflections on My Six Years as President of the Legal Services Corporation-January 2004-December 2009," undated, 10.

111. Susan Ragland, director of financial management and assurance at the Government Accountability Office" quoted in David Ingram, "Two Years after Audits, Legal Services Gets Some Praise."

112. Helaine Barnett, Telephone interview with author.

113. Legal Services Corporation, *Documenting the Justice Gap in America: The Current Unmet Civil Legal Needs of Low-Income Americans* (Washington, D.C.: U.S. Government Printing Office, 2005.) The three methodologies are described on page 3.

114. Strickland, Telephone interview with author.

115. Legal Services Corporation, *Documenting the Justice Gap in America*, 5–8.

116. Ibid., 9–14.

117. Ibid., 15–18.

118. In 2006, there were 965,000 lawyers in the United States. U.S. Census Bureau, *Statistical Abstract of the United States: 2008* (Washington: Government Printing Office, 2008) 389 Table 598. Many of these lawyers were serving institutional not individual clients, however, and thus were not counted in the LSC comparison of lawyers available to serve the personal legal needs of the general population and those serving the low-income segment of that population.

119. Public Law 110–161. 121 Stat 1844 (December 26, 2007).

120. Public Law 106–553, 114 Stat. 2762 (December 21, 2000).

121. Due to inflation, to match FY 1981's $321 million would have required $760 million in FY 2008, and, because of a more than 25-percent increase in the eligible client population over that quarter century, would have required an appropriation of $950 million to provide the same level of funding per eligible client.

122. Barnett, "Reflections on My Six Years as President of the Legal Services Corporation," 5.

123. Strickland, Telephone interview with author.

124. Michael Greco, E-mail message to the author.

125. Among the other Presidential Task Force members were long-time Colorado legal services director, Jon Asher, LSC president Helaine Barnett, former LSC president and Mississippi legal services director, Martha Bergmark, LSC board member David Hall, Georgia lawyer Phyllis Holmen, former Maryland AG Steve Sachs, and Lonnie Powers, who directed the Massachusetts IOLTA program.

126. The author was one of a half-dozen members of the Presidential Task Force present during the proceedings at the House of Delegates who formed a team to lobby members and react to any problems that might arise. Thus, he was a witness to those events as described in this chapter.

127. The official version of the resolution and acknowledgement it was approved by the House of Delegates appears at http://www.americanbar. org/content/dam/aba/directories/policy/2006_am_112a.authcheckdam. pdf (last visited June 1, 2012).

128. The resolution was offered by the San Francisco Bar Association and passed on October 7, 2006. See, http://www.brennancenter.org/con tent/elert/conference_of_delegates_of_california_bar_associations_passes_ resolution_ca (last visited June 1, 2012). The California resolution was

more specific and broader in proposing adoption of an amendment to the California Constitution and allowing the legislature to expand the categories of cases to which the right applies. It read:

"RESOLVED, that the Conference of Delegates of California Bar Associations recommends that legislation be sponsored to add Article 1, Section 32, of the California Constitution as follows: All people shall have a right to the assistance of counsel in cases before forums in which lawyers are permitted. Those who cannot afford such representation shall be provided counsel when needed to protect their rights to basic human needs, including sustenance, shelter, safety, health, child custody, and other categories the Legislature may identify in subsequent legislation."

129. In addition to California, New York, and Pennsylvania, other jurisdictions passing resolutions endorsing the concept of a right to counsel in civil cases included Massachusetts, Alaska, Atlanta, and Philadelphia. Shubi Deoras [consultant, ABA Civil Right to Counsel Working Group], E-mail message to the author.

130. State and metropolitan bar associations setting up committees on the right to counsel in civil cases included Alaska, Massachusetts, Minnesota, Pennsylvania, Texas, Atlanta, Boston, and San Francisco. Shubi Deoras [consultant, ABA Civil Right to Counsel Working Group], E-mail message to the author. In addition, the California Commission on Access to Justice established such a committee, of which the author was a co-chair for several years and remains a member.

131. Barnett, Telephone interview with author.

132. Barnett, "Reflections on My Six Years as President of the Legal Services Corporation," 2.

133. Ibid., 3.

134. Singleton chaired the body that drafted the new standards, which was called the Advisory Task Force on Standards Revision and Drafting. Helaine Barnett was one of the 16 members of the Task Force, and the full list of members can be found on an unnumbered page at the beginning of the report, American Bar Association, *Standards for the Provision of Civil Legal Aid* (August 2006).

135. Standard 3.2 on Legislative and Administrative Advocacy, American Bar Association, *Standards for the Provision of Civil Legal Aid* (August 2006) 105–09.

136. Legal Services Corporation: Performance Criteria (March, 2007), Acknowledgements (lists the Advisory Committee members, and the Draft Reviewers) and 1–3a, summarize the purposes and process involved in preparing the criteria; Helaine Barnett, Interview [explanation of process, including roles of Advisory Committee and Draft Reviewers].

137. "Standards for the Provision of Civil Legal Aid." The document indicates its approval by the House of Delegates in August, 2006, incidentally the same meeting at which the house approved the civil right to counsel resolution prepared by Greco's Task Force on Access to Justice.

138. Legal Services Corporation, *Performance Criteria* (March 2007).

139. Ibid., 5–12.

140. Ibid., 13–18.

141. Ibid., 19–32.

142. Ibid., 33–45.
143. Barnett, Telephone interview with author.
144. Barnett, "Reflections on My Six Years as President of the Legal Services Corporation," 5.
145. Ibid., 3.
146. Barnett, Telephone interview with author.
147. Ibid.
148. An organization named "Equal Justice Works" has compiled comprehensive information about law school LRAPs and the range and type of assistance they provide to graduates working in legal services or other public services fields. See, http://www.equaljusticeworks.org (last visited October 18, 2012).
149. The American Bar Association's Standing Committee on Legal Aid and Indigent Defendants has been promoting the expansion of LRAP for more than a decade. It's website has information about the 24 existing state LRAP programs. See, http://www.americanbar.org/ . . . /state_loan_ . . . (last visited October 18, 2012).
150. http://www.equaljusticeworks.org/ . . . term/790 (last visited October 18, 2012).

Chapter 29: How Far We Have Come, How Far Yet to Go

1. Mauricio Vivero, "From 'Renegade' Agency to Institution of Justice: The Transformation of the Legal Services Corporation," 29 *Fordham Urban Law Journal* 1323 (2001).
2. Ibid., 1340.
3. At the time of these nominations, the author was a member of the ABA committee, SCAID, that vetted all the above nominees and recommended the position the ABA president should take on each. The above background is information is a summary of what the author learned during this process.
4. This evaluation of the LSC board and the performance of its members have been confirmed by experienced LAC and NLADA staff members who have followed LSC closely for many years.
5. James J. Sandman's biography on the LSC website, see http://www.lsc.gov/about/management/president (last visited February 21, 2013). The author had the opportunity to observe Sandman's performance on several occasions, including an LSC board meeting.
6. In 2009, an attempt was made in the House of Representatives to eliminate LSC's funding which was defeated 323–105. See, http://www.vis.org/toolbox/VoteDetail.aspx?vid=11287 (last visited January 25, 2013). In 2011, after the Republicans took control of the House, another attempt in the House of Representatives to eliminate LSC funding from the FY 2012 Continuing Resolution was defeated 259 to 171. See, http://www.govtrack.us/congress/votes/112-2011/h54 (last visited January 25, 2013).
7. See Fiscal Oversight Task Force Report to the LSC Board of Directors (July 28, 2012) and Report of the Pro Bono Task Force to the LSC Board of Directors (October 2012) at LSC's website, see http://www.lsc.gov/media/reports (last visited February 21, 2013).

8. See "LSC Strategic Plan for 2012–2016" adopted October 2012, on the LSC website, http://www.lsc.gov/sites/default/files/LSC/lscgov4/LSC_Strate gic_Plan_2012-2016-Adopted_Oct_2012.pdf (last visited February 21, 2013).

9. *Supporting Justice II: A Report of the Pro Bono Work of America's Lawyers* (Chicago: American Bar Association Standing Committee of Pro Bono and Public Service, 2009) vii.

10. Ibid., 14.

11. "Law Firm Pro Bono Performance Remains Steady," at http://www .probonoinst.org/newsroom/press-releases/law-firm-pro-bono-perfor mance-remains-steady/ (last visited February 22, 2013).

12. See, AmLaw 2012 Pro Bono Report, at http://www.americanlawyer. com/PubArticleTAL.jsp?id=1202560034999&2012_Pro_Bono_Survey&slre- turn=20130126003728 (last visited February 24, 2013).

13. See 45 Code of Federal Regulations, sec. 1611 (2009), allowing LSC grantees to use non-LSC funds to serve that strata of the population in certain circumstances.

14. Legal Services Corporation, 2011 Annual Report, at http://www.lsc. gov/sites/default/files/LSC%202011%20Annual%20Report-By%20The%20 Numbers.pdf.

15. "Behind the Numbers: Noteworthy Trends and Newsmaking Firms in this Year's Am Law 100," *American Lawyer*, May 2008, 136, 138. That year, 2007, the 100 largest U.S. law firms earned $64 billion, roughly a third of the entire profession's total for the year. Id., at 137.

16. "Share of Aggregate Income Received by Each Fifth and Top 5 per- cent of Households-1970–2009" Statistical Abstract of the United States 2012 (Washington, D.C.: Government Printing Office, 2013), Table 694. The bottom fifth's share dropped 17 percent during that 30-year period.

Chapter 30: Removing the Blinders, Viewing Some Possibilities from Elsewhere in the World

1. An Act to Admit Such Persons as Are Poor to Sue in Forma Pauperis, 11 Hen. 7, c. 12 (1494), *reprinted in* 2 Statutes of the Realm 578 (1993) (spelling modernized).

2. The statute of Henry VII was finally repealed and replaced by the Stat- ute Law Revision and Civil Procedure Act, 46 and 47 Vict. c. 49 (1883). This 1883 act established a system of legal aid administered by the rules of court, which provided for the appointment of counsel. *See* Seton Pollock, *Legal Aid— The First 25 Years* (1975) 12. In 1929 parliament replaced the 1883 law with a statute creating yet another system of legal assistance. John Mahoney, "Green Forms and Legal Aid Offices: A History of Publicly Funded Legal Services in Britain and the United States," 17 *St. Louis University Public Law Review* 223, 226 (1998). In 1949, in the aftermath of World War II, England launched the comprehensive, fully funded legal aid program that caused such an uproar in United States when some lawyers in our country advocated importing that program into the United States. (See chapter 2.) Yet throughout these several changes, the right to counsel in civil cases the Statute of Henry VII first created in 1495 has remained inviolate. *See generally,* Mahoney, supra, 226–29.

3. *See, Oldfield v. Cobbett*, 41 Eng. Rep. 765 (1845), and cases cited *in* William John Jones, *The Elizabethan Court of Chancery* (London: Oxford University Press, 1967), 324–28, 501.

4. John Locke, *The Second Treatise of Government* (New York: William Benton, 1952), 65 (emphasis supplied).

5. Thomas Hobbes, *Leviathan* (London: Penguin Books, 1968) (emphasis supplied).

6. Mauro Cappelletti, James Gordley, and Earl Johnson Jr., *Toward Equal Justice: A Comparative Study of Legal Aid in Modern Societies* (Milan: Guiffre, 1975), 19 n. 57 (citing Law of Jan. 22, 1851, Arts. 1–20 (1851), Bull. Des Lois 93).

7. Ibid., 19 n. 59 (citing Law of December 6, 1865, no. 2627 [1865] Rac. Uff. 2846).

8. Ibid., 19, n. 62 (citing Zivilprozessordnung of Jan. 30, 1877 secs. 114–27 [1877].)

9. Many of these other historical statutory "right to counsel" provisions are set forth in Cappelletti, et al. *Toward Equal Justice,* 16–27.

10. *See generally* Cappelletti, et al. *Toward Equal Justice,* 19–20.

11. See U.S. Courts, History of the Defender Services for the U.S. Federal Courts, http://www.uscourts.gov/defenderservices/history.html.

12. Const. of the Swiss Federation, Art. IV, translated in Cappelletti, et al. *Toward Equal Justice,* 705.

13. Francis William O'Brien, *Why Not Appointed Counsel in Civil Cases? The Swiss Approach,* 28 *Ohio St. L. J.* 1, 5 (1967) (quoting Judgment of October 8, 1937, Arrets du Tribunal Federal [ATF] 63, I, 209 (Switz.).

14. In a 1952 decision—still filed more than a decade before the U.S. Supreme Court decided *Gideon v. Wainwright*—the Swiss Supreme Court explained the expansion of right to counsel in civil cases that had already evolved in that country.

"This Court has consistently affirmed that a party who is unable to afford the costs of a lawsuit without jeopardizing the livelihood of himself and his family and whose case is not unfounded, is entitled under the provisions of Article 4 of the Constitution (principle of equality) to a right of judicial protection. This right means that the judge must consider his case, that the indigent litigant shall not be required to pay court costs in advance nor to post security for costs, and further that he is to be granted the assistance of a lawyer (without cost) in all cases where a lawyer is required for the *adequate* protection of his interests. This right of the indigent to judicial protection embraces every action to be taken during the proceeding of the first instance [trial court] . . . and this right extends also to challenges against the judgment of the first instance [appeals].

"According to recent decisions of this Court, a case must be considered to have no probability of success only when the *probability of failure clearly prevails* or when the case must be considered capricious."

Bundesgericht (Federal Tribunal), Decision No. 27 of July 9, 1952, Entscheidungen des Schweizerischen Bundesgerichtes, Amtliche Sammlung, VOL. 78, PT. 1, pp. 193–196 (1952), *translated in* Cappelletti, et al. *Toward Equal Justice,* 704–06 (emphasis added).

15. The opinion declaring a right to counsel in civil cases also summarized the status of the right to counsel in criminal cases as of that time. "Cantonal

legislation may prescribe that an accused will be provided a lawyer only in serious cases." Schefer-Heer contre Conseil d'Etat d'Appenzell Rhodes-Exterieures, 8 Oct. 1937, Arrets du Tribunal Federal, 63, I, 209. O'Brien, supra note 32, at 5. But in 1972, the Swiss Supreme Court modified this rule, holding the cantons must grant every indigent criminal defendant a lawyer, except where his case clearly lacked merit. *"X" gegen Obergericht des Kantons Luzern,* 27 Sept. 1972, I. 340, translated in Cappelletti, et al. *Toward Equal Justice,* 706.

16. European Convention for the Protection of Human Rights and Fundamental Freedoms, November 4, 1950, 213 U.N.T.S. 222.

17. European Convention for the Protection of Human Rights and Fundamental Freedoms, Article 6, sec. 1.

18. It was not until a constitutional amendment passed by a slim margin in 1995 (15th Amendment) that Ireland became the last European nation to legalize divorce. Before that, people in failing marriages could only obtain judicial separations. Anthony Tyler Barnes, "Ireland's Divorce Bill: Traditional Irish and International Norms of Equality and Bodily Integrity at Issue in a Domestic Abuse Context," 31 *Vanderbilt Journal of Transnational Law* (1998), 643.

19. *Airey v. Ireland,* 2 eur. Ct. H.R. (Ser. A) 305 (1979).

20. Ibid., 305.

21. Ibid., 315–16.

22. "Mary Robinson biography," http: www.biography.com/search/article.do?id=9460920 (last visited March 17, 2009).

23. *Steel and Morris v. United Kingdom,* 41 EHRR 22, 414 (2005).

24. Ibid., 427 (emphasis supplied).

25. Ibid., 429–30 (emphasis supplied).

26. Ibid., 427–28.

27. Ibid., 439–40.

28. *Gideon v. Wainwright,* 372 U.S. 335, 344 (1963) (stating that "lawyers in criminal courts are necessities, not luxuries").

29. *Airey v. Ireland,* 317 (emphasis supplied).

30. The European Community maintains a website that includes extensive treatment of the Treaty of Lisbon and the dramatic changes it makes to the Community's institutions and basic arrangements. *See* EUROPA—Treaty of Lisbon, htttp://europa.eu/lisbon_treaty/indexen.htm (last visited Feb. 1, 2010). Readers visiting this website can access everything from brief overviews of the changes the Treaty achieved to the full text of the Treaty, the Charter of Fundamental Rights, and all the other associated documents.

31. *See* Charter of Fundamental Rights of the European Union art. 47, December 1, 2009, 2007 O.J. (c 303) (emphasis added), *available at* http://eur-lex.europa.eu/LexUriServ/LexUriServ.do?uri=OJ:C:2007:303:0001:0016:EN:PDF (emphasis supplied.). This provision of the Charter applies to both the Community institutions and within the member nations when Community laws are being enforced. The European Convention on Human Rights and Fundamental Freedoms as interpreted by *Airey v. Ireland* and its progeny continues to guarantee a similar right when domestic laws are involved. See supra note 31.

32. See, for example, In Germany, it is phrased as a "reasonable prospect of success" ZPO sec. 117 (formerly 114 (1) and described in Cappelletti, et al. *Toward Equal Justice*). That formulation dates back to 1931 and represented a change from a more liberal standard that allowed legal aid unless

the applicant's case was "without some prospect of success." Cappelletti, et al. *Toward Equal Justice.* A recent decision of the German Constitutional Court has liberalized the test somewhat, by declaring that legal aid cannot be denied if the prospects of success turn on a "difficult" question of law that has not been decided by the Supreme Court as yet. (Mattias Killian, "German Legal Aid by the Scruff of its Neck—or Just in a Bad Quarter of an Hour?" in International Legal Aid Group (ILAG), *Legal Aid in the Global Era* (Killarney, 2005) at 59, 61.) (This implies legal aid could not be denied on the basis the applicant's case would lack merit because of a legal interpretation made by a lower court.)

In Hong Kong, the applicant must have a "reasonable prospect for success *or of deriving some tangible benefit*" as well as having a "reasonable grounds for bringing or defending" the action. (Legal Aid Services Council, "National Report: Hong Kong Special Administrative Region of the People's Republic of China," at 2, ILAG, *Delivering Effective Legal Aid Services across Diverse Communities,* supra note, emphasis supplied.)

See also, Quebec's Legal Aid Act, supra note 67, at sec. 4.11 (1) requiring denial or withdrawal of representation if the "applicant cannot establish the *probable existence* of his right." (Emphasis supplied.)

33. In Ireland, there must be "reasonable grounds for taking or defending" the proceedings. (The Legal Aid Board, "National Report: Ireland" a ILAG, *Delivering Effective Legal Aid Services across Diverse Communities.*)

34. See accompanying text for this formulation which the Swiss Supreme Court declared and is a constitutional not just a statutory test (and thus is not subject to amendment) in that country.

It has been suggested that in Brazil the proper test to be applied by a civil "Public Defender" (a salaried lawyer representing both plaintiffs and defendants in civil cases) may be even lower than the "manifestly unreasonable" standard. "It is the Public Defender's obligation, even when there are limited chances of success, to propose suitable judicial measures. The Public Defender only will be excused from doing so when convinced of the impropriety of any measure or that the measures, . . . may reveal that they are contrary to the interests of the party." (Cleber Alves, "National Report: Brazil" at 10–11, ILAG, *Delivering Effective Legal Aid Services across Diverse Communities.*) This test is suggested, it should be added, in a legal aid system (the State of Rio) where all the services are delivered by salaried attorneys and there is no statute or regulation articulating any form of merits or significance test.

In France, the merits test is satisfied if the applicant's case is not "manifestly inadmissible or devoid of substance." (See, European Commission, European Judicial Network in Civil and Commercial Matters-Legal Aid-France, at http://www.ec.europa.eu/civiljustice/legal_aid_fra_en.htm.) But this test apparently applies only to plaintiffs who are bringing suit against someone else and not to defendants who are defending against a lawsuit brought against them by another. In that instance, no merits test is required. (Ibid.).

35. In Brazil, rules governing the legal profession preclude representation by government-funded as well as privately funded lawyers in "inconsistent or careless" (e.g., frivolous) cases. (Cleber Alves, "National Report: Brazil" at 10, ILAG, *Delivering Effective Legal Aid Services across Diverse Communities.*)

Some legal aid statutes list specific case types considered too trivial to warrant public-funded legal aid. Quebec, for instance, bars legal aid in "parking ticket" cases. (Quebec Legal Aid Act, supra note, sec. 4.12.)

36. In Scotland, for example, an applicant must satisfy a "reasonableness" test as well as financial eligibility and "probable cause" tests before receiving legal aid in civil cases. (Colin Lancaster, "National Report: Scotland" in ILAG, *Legal Aid: A New Beginning,* supra note, at 103.)

37. Quebec Legal Aid Act, supra note, at sec. 4.11 (3). Quebec makes an exception to this cost-benefit limitation, however, where the "case or remedy threatens [the applicant's] livelihood or ability to provide for . . . essential needs."

Germany denies legal aid if a case, though having sufficient prospects for success is deemed "capricious." That standard is interpreted to mean the case would not be brought by a middle-class person with the means to hire a lawyer. Z.P.O. sec. 114 (1), cited in Cappelletti, et al. *Toward Equal Justice,* at 94, fns. 32 and 35.

The Netherlands imposes both a merits and significance test. (Susanne Peters, et al., "National Report: The Netherlands" at 4, ILAG, *Delivering Effective Legal Aid Services across Diverse Communities.*

38. See, for example, Ireland excludes most real property, small claims, licensing, and group actions, as well as defamation and election contests. (The Legal Aid Board, "National Report: Ireland," at 4, ILAG, *Delivering Effective Legal Aid Services across Diverse Communities.*)

New Zealand does not exclude any categories of cases heard in the courts from potential coverage by the legal aid scheme, but does exclude some tribunals. (Legal Services Agency, "National Report: New Zealand," at 9.)

The Netherlands appears to be one of the few nations that does not exclude any case types or official forums from coverage under its legal aid program. (Susanne Peters, et al., "National Report: The Netherlands," at 1–3.)

Quebec excludes defamation, election cases, breach of promise of marriage or plaintiff in alienation of affections cases. (Legal Aid Act, Revised Statutes of Quebec, Chap. A-14, Sec. 4.8.)

39. See, Ireland. (The Legal Aid Board, "National Report: Ireland," at 4, ILAG, *Delivering Effective Legal Aid Services across Diverse Communities.*)
In Scotland legal aid is not available before tribunals except those "listed in the Legal Aid (Scotland) Act 1986." (Colin Lancaster, "National Report: Scotland" in International Legal Aid Group (ILAG), *Legal Aid: A New Beginning* (Antwerp, June 6–8, 2007) at 103.)

40. In Ireland, for example, while legal aid does not provide representation before any administrative tribunal except the Refugee Appeals Tribunal, it can give advice and assistance to those who are appearing before those tribunals. (The Legal Aid Board, "National Report: Ireland," at 4, ILAG, *Delivering Effective Legal Aid Services across Diverse Communities.*)

41. In 2007, "about 49 percent of the Dutch population [was] covered under the current Legal Aid Scheme." (Jan van Dijk, "National Facts—report on Legal Aid in the Netherlands 2007, ILAG, *Legal Aid: A New Beginning,* supra note, at 63.)

42. New Zealand requires repayment of some of the cost of legal aid—sometimes in installments—from those recipients with "disposable capital"

and/or "gross income" above a certain level. (Legal Services Agency, "National Report: New Zealand" at 9–11, ILAG, *Delivering Effective Legal Aid Services across Diverse Communities.*) Quebec province has two categories—-"gratuitous legal aid" which is given completely free of charge to those below an income level defined by regulations and "contributory legal aid" offered to those above that level but below a maximum income also set by regulation, and which requires them to contribute a portion of the cost of their representation. (Quebec Legal Aid Act, supra note, secs. 4.1 and 4.2.)

43. In Hong Kong, the independent body is the Legal Aid Services Council (LASC), with a board composed of eight members (half of them lawyers) and a chair who must be a non-lawyer, and which oversees the Legal Aid Department, a part of the executive branch of government. The latter directly administers legal aid. (Legal Aid Services Council, "National Report: Hong Kong Special Administrative Region of the People's Republic of China" at 1, ILAG, *Delivering Effective Legal Aid Services across Diverse Communities.*)

In Ireland, immediately after the European Court on Human Rights decided *Airey v. Ireland* (see footnotes—, and accompanying text), the government created an "independent body, the Legal Aid Board, . . . to administer the scheme . . . to make the services of solicitors and . . . barristers available to persons of modest means." ("National Report: Ireland" at 1.) In New Zealand, the program is administered by "The Legal Services Agency," a Crown entity established by the Legal Service Act 2000 and governed by a board the Minister of Justice appoints. (Legal Services Agency, "National Report: New Zealand" at 2.)

In the Netherlands, legal aid is administered by a Legal Aid Board with one central and five regional offices and reports both to the Minister of Justice and Parliament regarding legal aid matters. (Susanne Peters, et al., "National Report: The Netherlands" at 1–2.) In Quebec, the program is administered by the 12-member "Commission Des Services Juridiques" headed by a full-time chair who can be a judge or lawyer and a full-time vice chair who must be a lawyer, with the other commission members serving on a part-time basis. (Quebec Legal Aid Act, supra note, Division III, secs. 1–18.)

44. Hong Kong, The Netherlands, and New Zealand are examples of jurisdictions where a headquarters office administers the entire program, although often with the assistance of regional offices which have varying degrees of autonomy. In Hong Kong, the Legal Aid Department administers both the salaried and Judicare components of legal aid, but with oversight by the Legal Aid Services Council. ("National Report: Hong Kong Special Administrative Region of the People's Republic of China" at 1, ILAG, *Delivering Effective Legal Aid Services across Diverse Communities.*) In the Netherlands, the Legal Aid Board "is entrusted with all matters concerning administration, supervision and expenditure" of legal aid in that country. But the Board carries out those responsibilities through a central office and five regional offices. (Susan Peters, et al., "National Report: The Netherlands" at 1, ILAG, *Delivering Effective Legal Aid Services across Diverse Communities.*) In New Zealand, the "Legal Services Agency" has responsibility for the administration of "legal aid and related schemes." In addition to the headquarters office, the Agency has 12 regional offices and 2 "Public Defence Service Offices." (Legal Services Agency,

"National Report: New Zealand" at 2, ILAG, *Delivering Effective Legal Aid Services across Diverse Communities.*)

45. See, Mauro Cappelletti, et al. *Toward Equal Justice*, at 50–53.

46. These "bureaus" are attached to the courts and composed of members representing the legal profession and the government. After the government began paying the lawyers representing those found eligible for representation by legal aid in 1971, the composition of the bureaus was changed to increase the proportion of government representatives, presumably to protect the public treasury. (See Cappelletti, et al. *Toward Equal Justice,* at 44–46 for a description of how these bureaus and the French legal aid system function) These "bureaus" still make the eligibility determinations (see, European Commission, European Judicial Network in Civil and Commercial Matters-Legal Aid-France, at http://www.ec.europa.eu/civiljustice/legal_aid_fra_en.htm).

47. In Finland, for instance, salaried personnel at the State Legal Aid Offices decide whether legal aid is to be granted, even if the applicant originally went to a private law office that prepared an application and sent it that state office—and even if that private lawyer will be supplying the representation if the application is accepted. (Merji Muilu, "Legal Aid in Finland," in ILAG, *Legal Aid—A New Beginning*, 47–48.)

In the Netherlands, personnel at the regional Legal Aid Boards grant or deny applications for legal aid in court and administrative hearing cases, while front-line advice and brief assistance are provibded to anyone at "law counters" without requiring an approved application. (Susanne Peters, et al. "National Report: The Netherlands" 1–4, ILAG, *Delivering Effective Legal Aid Services across Diverse Communities.*)

In Quebec, the "director general" of the appropriate "regional legal aid center" is charged with making the ultimate eligibility decision, although the application is made at the "local legal aid center" closest to the applicant. (Quebec Legal Aid Act, supra note, Division VI, sec. 62, 63.

48. In New Zealand, applicants denied service can first seek reconsideration by a Legal Services Agency staff member other than the one who first denied their requests. If that fails to produce results, applicants can appeal to the Legal Aid Review Panel, an independent body appointed by the NZ attorney general and composed of lawyer and non-lawyer members that sit in panels of three considering only the paper record. In FY 2007/08 these panels reversed a third of the denials and returned 17 percent to the agency for reconsideration. (Legal Services Agency, "National Report: New Zealand" at 6–7, ILAG, *Delivering Effective Legal Aid Services across Diverse Communities.*)

49. In Quebec, for instance, applicants have 30 days to appeal a denial to a three-member "Review Committee." The decisions of this Committee are final and cannot be appealed to the courts. (Quebec Legal Aid Act, supra note, Division VI secs. 74, 78, 79.)

50. In Finland, an applicant denied legal aid by a State Legal Aid Office can appeal directly to a court for a full review and if the trial court denies relief can appeal that decision to an appellate court. (Merji Muilu, "Legal Aid in Finland "in ILAG, *Legal Aid—A New Beginning*, at 47.)

In New Zealand, either the applicant denied legal aid or the Legal Aid Agency may appeal to the High Court or the Court of Appeal from a decision of the Legal Aid Review Panel (see footnote 101, supra), but only as to a question of law. Five such appeals were brought to the courts in 2008. (Legal Services Agency, "National Report: New Zealand" at 7, ILAG, *Delivering Effective Legal Aid Services across Diverse Communities*.)

51. Currently, because of lack of resources, LSC grantees are turning away over half the applicants for their services, Documenting the Justice Gap In America: *The Current Unmet Civil Legal Needs of Low-Income Americans* (Washington, D.C.: Legal Services Corporation, 2005).

52. The Irish Legal Aid Board has set up three panels of private solicitors—one panel for "divorce and separation cases," another for "family law matters at District (local) Court level," and a third for "cases before the Refugee Appeals Tribunal." However, these panels have a limited function. "The use of private practitioners is designed to improve access to legal aid services in situations where a law centre is *not in a position to provide a timely service*." ("National Report: Ireland" at 1–2, ILAG, *Delivering Effective Legal Aid Services across Diverse Communities*)

53. Mattias Killian, "German Legal Aid by the Scruff of its Neck—Or Just in a Bad Quarter of an Hour?" in ILAG, *Legal Aid in the Global Era*, supra note, at 61. "Fees for lawyers doing legal aid work are paid (in most cases with a discount) according to . . . scales of fees [set by the government])."

54. Cappelletti, et al. *Toward Equal Justice*, 398–437. Until a new law passed in 1972, the French government did not compensate the private lawyers appointed to represent poor people. See, Law No. 72–11, of January 3, 1972, chapter V, translated in Cappelletti, et al., *Toward Equal Justice*, 403.

55. "The [Community Legal Service (CLS)—the civil legal services arm of the Legal Services Commission] funds a variety of legal services, ranging from initial advice to full representation in court. Funding for such services is delivered through contracts with solicitors and non-for-profit agencies [usually using non-lawyer staffs and limited to advice and out-of-court work]. Individual providers conduct the legal aid merits and means test for applicants for [advice and assistance short of representation, and representation in emergency cases and a limited range of family cases in the lower courts]." . . . For other levels of service, the provider will apply on the applicants behalf to the relevant regional office, where LSC staff will decide whether the application meets the criteria for CLS funding." Carolyn Regan, "Legal Services Commission England and Wales—National Report," in ILAG, *Legal Aid: A New Beginning?* at 40–41. As the English legal aid program has evolved, it has added to the basic Judicare component, first "community law centers" that use salaried lawyers who focus on "poverty law" cases and community-wide problems in their geographic areas, second, not-for-profit organizations that deliver advice and representation through non-lawyers, and more recently, Community Legal Advice Centers and Networks with staffs that provide legal advice in certain areas of the country. Carolyn Regan, "National Report: England and Wales" at 1–2, ILAG, *Delivering Effective Legal Aid Services across Diverse Communities*.)

56. "With a population of about 5.2 million, and an area of about 340,000 [square kilometers], Finland has 64 Legal Aid Offices, which are located mainly in municipalities with a district court. The Legal Aid Offices have 18 branch offices and about 100 branch clinics where clients are seen as required. . . .

The total number of employees is just 460, of which half are lawyers . . . and the other half office staff." (National Report, "Legal Aid in Finland," in ILAG, *Legal Aid: A New Beginning?* supra note, at 47, 48.)

57. Robert M. Cooper, Report on the Quebec Legal Aid System, in Cappelletti et al., *Toward Equal Justice*, 614, 614–17.

58. See, Legal Aid Ontario, "About Legal Aid Ontario: Historical Overview," http://www.legalaid.on.ca/en/about/Historical.asp (last visited March 17, 2009). Legal Aid Ontario, the independent public corporation that administers both criminal and civil legal aid in that province, reports approximately 4,000 private lawyers participate in the "Judicare" component of the mixed system. See Press Release, Attorney General announces Tariff Increase for Legal Aid Lawyers (July 18, 2007), http://www.legalaid.on.ca/ennews/july 1802007a.asp. Some private attorneys also serve as "duty counsel," staffing courtrooms and providing advice and limited assistance to people who show up without counsel. Legal Aid Ontario, About Legal Aid Ontario, http://www.legalaid.on/ca/en/about (last visited March 17, 2009).

59. See "About Legal Aid Ontario, Historical Overview." There now are 80 of these community-based legal clinics in Ontario—67 in geographic areas round the province and the rest specializing in certain subject areas or vulnerable populations. Mary Collins, Richard Ferris and Michelle Lerery, "Building the Best Teams: Naming and Nurturing the 'Fire in the Belly' in Legal Clinic Support (Sept. 2004), available at http://sss.aclco.org/f/FINALFire inthe BellySept 2004CROVERSION2withpic.pdf.

60. According to an April, 2009 report to the ILAG conference in Wellington, New Zealand, which the author attended, there are now 30 of these Legal Services Counters spread evenly across the Netherlands, putting "every Dutch citizen . . . [within] an approximately one hour journey by public transport." Each has at least six legal advisors, some of whom can be paralegals. They are designed to "look more like a shop than an office. Inside is an open space with a waiting area and three desks" and behind that a "call centre," where further information can be found via e-mail or telephone, and private rooms for consultation. The legal advisors rotate among the advice desks, the call centre and the consultation rooms. "Sophisticated computer software, specifically designed for the Legal Services Counters" helps the staff correctly and quickly answer most questions clients ask. In 2008, of 645,000 persons served at this counters, 376,000 were helped via the telephone, 149,000 at the advice counters, 87,000 required a "consultation hour," and 33,000 were helped via e-mail and the website. (Table 5) 37,000 were referred to lawyers and 13,000 to mediators for extended legal services, generally involving potential or actual litigation (Table 6).

61. "At present, the Legal Services Counters annually provide easily accessible, free legal services to over a half a million clients. The Counters are meant as a first step to receive legal aid and, if necessary, referral to a lawyer or mediator." (Susanne Peters, et al., "National Report: Netherlands," 1, in ILAG, *Delivering Effective Legal Aid Services across Diverse Communities*)

62. "Private lawyers and mediators provide subsidized legal aid in more complicated or time consuming matters." (Susanne Peters, et al., "National Report: Netherlands," 1, in ILAG, *Delivering Effective Legal Aid Services across Diverse Communities*)

"In . . . relatively simple legal problems, private lawyers are allowed to charge a standard three-hours service fee, of which the client contributes only 13.50 Euros [roughly $20]. . . . Whether or not a client is entitled to three-hour legal aid, depends on his [or her] monthly income." (National Report: Netherlands, 3.)

"If a problem is expected to take more than three hours, clients are entitled to legal aid only if they have been granted a so-called legal aid certificate. In order to obtain this, a . . . lawyer needs to make an application to the Legal Aid Board on behalf of his client [which the Board will assess] "in terms of the client's means and of the merits and significance of the problem. . . . Since April 2005 it is also possible to apply for a mediation certificate . . . to call in help from an independent mediator . . . to settle an issue between himself and another party." (National Report: Netherlands, 4.)

"As soon as the case is closed, the lawyer bills the Legal Aid Board for the services provided. The Board, however, does not pay an hourly rate but a fixed fee for different types of services . . . based on extensive analyses of legal aid cases from the past . . . correspond[ing] to an hourly rate of approximately 107 Euros (roughly $150 at current exchange rates)." (National Report: Netherlands, 13–14.)

Chapter 31: Establishing Justice for All: Possibilities and Prospects

1. Parts of this chapter have been adapted with modifications and enhancements from Earl Johnson Jr. "Equality Before the Law and the Social Contract: When Will the United States Finally Guarantee Its People the Equality Before the Law that the Social Contract Demands?" *Fordham Urban Law Journal* 37(1), 2009.

2. American Bar Association Working Group for a Civil Right to Counsel, "ABA Toolkit for a Right to Counsel in Civil Proceedings: ABA Model Access Act & ABA Basic Principles for a Right to Counsel in Civil Proceedings," 24 et.seq.

3. In a study conducted in California courts, the following statistics and statistical estimates emerged. "In family law, petitioners were pro per at the time of filing an average of 67 percent. In the large counties (with more than 50 judicial positions) that average was 72 percent . . . In dissolution, at the time of disposition the average pro per rate was 80 percent." Task Force on Self-Represented Litigants, *Statewide Action Plan for Serving Self-Represented Litigants* (San Francisco: Judicial Council of California (2004), 11.

4. In 2004, a task force of the California Judicial Council issued a report containing a series of recommendations calculated to create "operational systems that work well for the timely, cost-effective, and fair management of cases involving self-represented litigants and for improving access to justice for the public." The recommendations included a description of the characteristics of a proper self—help center. "A court-based, attorney-supervised, staffed self-help center is the optimum approach for both litigants and the court. Written instructional materials, resource guides, computer programs and websites, videos, and other materials should support self-help center staff. Without available staff assistance, these resources alone should not be

considered a self-help center. . . . Personal assistance by self-help center staff has been successfully provided through individual face-to-face assistance, workshops, teleconferencing, or telephone help lines. Services may be provided at court locations or in mobile vans, law libraries, jails, or other community locations." *Statewide Action Plan for Serving Self-Represented Litigants* Task Force on Self-Represented Litigants, 12–13.

5. California Judicial Council, Administrative Office of the Courts, *Handling Cases Involving Self-Represented Litigants: A Benchguide for Judicial Officers* (San Francisco: California Judicial Council, January, 2007).

See also, Richard Zorza, *The Self-Help Friendly Court* (Williamsburg: National Center for State Courts, 2002).

6. California Judicial Council, Administrative Office of the Courts, *Handling Cases Involving Self-Represented Litigants,* 2–2.

7. An introductory section explains the rationale for the Protocols and the *fundamental* change in judicial process they seek to implement.

"Until state and municipal legislatures enact a civil right to counsel and provide appropriations to finance it, court systems must develop mechanisms for promoting the fair, equitable and consistent treatment of unrepresented litigants. To provide a resource for the New York City Housing Courts, where 90 percent of the tenants appear without an attorney and the same percentage of landlords are represented by counsel, the New York County Lawyers' Association's (NYCLA) Task Force on the Housing Court studied the problem, reviewed court procedures and directives from the administrative judge, surveyed Housing Court judges to obtain their views about pro se litigants' experiences and produced a report, Protocols for Judges in the Settlement and Trial of Cases Involving Unrepresented Litigants in Housing Court. These Protocols provide for an active role for judges, both in approving settlements and conducting trials, so that unrepresented litigants will understand their rights, the court procedures and the results of the proceedings." (http://www.abavideonews.org/ABA496/media/pdf/hod_resolution/10b.pdf.)

8. A dozen retired state trial judges from Washington State filed a brief in 2007 based on their collective experience, pointing out: "Without assistance from attorneys, pro se litigants frequently fail to present critical facts and legal authorities that judges need to make correct and just rulings. Pro se litigants also frequently fail to object to inadmissible testimony or documents and to correct erroneous legal arguments. This makes it difficult for judges to fulfill the purpose of our judicial system—to make correct and just rulings." Brief of Retired Judges as Amicus Curiae, *King v. King,* 162 Wash. 2d 378, 174 P.3d 659 (2007).

9. H. Kritzer, *Legal Advocacy: Lawyers and Nonlawyers at Work* (Ann Arbor: University of Michigan Press, 1998). This study concluded lay advocates could achieve equivalent results as full-fledged lawyers in certain administrative hearings.

10. "Hotlines are now being used in over 148 programs in forty-nine states, Puerto Rico, and the District of Columbia." A. Houseman, op. cit. supra note 5, at 128. See also, www.legalhotlines.org.

11. R. Staudt, "Technology for Justice Customers," International Legal Aid Group, op. cit. supra note 23, 411, 415–20.

12. A link to this self-help website is prominently displayed on homepage of the California court system's main webpage (http://www.courtinfo.ca.gov) and is an integral part of that system's overall site. In 2003, this

website experienced more than 1.6 million "hits." Task Force on Self-Represented Litigants, op. cit. supra note 65, at 11.

13. Staudt, "Technology for Justice Customers," op. cit. supra note 23, at 411, 412. These state websites can be located by accessing www.lawhelp.org.

14. LSC regulations require legal service providers funded by the corporation to establish a set of priority subject areas to guide their allocation of legal resources among potential clients. 45 Code of Federal Regulations 1620—Priorities in the Use of Resources. This priority-setting process is to include non-LSC-funded services as well as services funded by LSC.

15. As of 1942 when the U.S. Supreme Court held a right to counsel for criminal defendants in federal courts, it meant the federal government was joining 35 states that already had such a right. Twenty-two states signed a brief to the court in *Gideon v. Wainwright* urging the Supreme Court to find a right to counsel in the U.S. Constitution. *Oxford* Companion to the U.S. Supreme Court: *Gideon v. Wainwright,* at http://www.answers.com/topic/gideon-v-wainwright (last visited February 24, 2013).

16. John Pollock, "Where We've Been, Where We're Going: A Look at the Status of the Civil Right to Counsel, and Current Efforts," *MIE Journal*, Vol. 26, No. 2 (Summer 2012): 30.

17. *In re Smiley,* 330 NE 2d 53 I1975).

18. *Frase v. Barnhart,* 840 A.2d 114 (Md 2003).

19. *Quail v. Municipal Court* (1985) 171 Cal.App.3d 572, 217 Cal. Rptr. 361.

20. *Lassiter v. Department of Social Services of Durham County, North Carolina,* 452 U.S. 18, 34–35 (1981).

21. Judge Robert Sweet, "Civil Gideon and Confidence in a Just Society," 17 *Yale Law & Public Policy Review* 503, 505–06. (2001).

22. *Turner v. Rogers,* 131 S. Ct. 2507 (2011).

23. Ibid., 131 S. Ct. 2512.

24. Ibid., 131 S. Ct. 2519.

25. Ibid., 131 S. Ct. 2512.

26. Ibid., 131 S. Ct. 2519.

27. Ibid., 131 S. Ct. 2519.

28. Ibid., 131 S. Ct. 2519–20.

29. Brief from Trial Judges, *King v. King,* 162 Wash.2d 378, 174 P.3d 689.

30. See, Earl Johnson Jr., "Key Features of Fifteen National Legal Aid Programs," in ILAG, *Legal Aid in the Global Era,* 157–171, which summarizes in chart form the essential elements and statistical data gleaned from the "National Reports" included in the book produced from that conference's proceedings. Exchange rates used to convert from local currency to U.S. dollars were those in effect on June 30, 2004. At that point, a Euro = $1.25, a Canadian dollar = $0.83, a New Zealand dollar = $0.72, a Hong Kong dollar = $0.13, and a British pound = $1.81. Per capita GDP figures for each country are from the World Fact Book (2004) and were based on the GDP (PPP), which is corrected for the relative purchasing power of the nation's currency. The Legal Services Commission received government grants totaling 905 million British pounds, which on June 30, 2004, at the prevailing exchange rate of $1.81 to the pound was the equivalent of $1.63 billion.

31. Mike Hope, Expenditure on Legal Services, UK Dep't for Const. Aff. (1997), http://www.dca.gov/uk/research/1997/997esfr.htm. While this in-

formation is now a dozen years old, there is no reason to expect any dramatic change in the ratio of legal aid-funded legal work to overall expenditures on lawyers since that time.

32. In 2004, an estimated $209 billion was spent on the services of lawyers in the United States, most in the form of legal fees paid to law firms by individuals, businesses, governments, and other entities, and in 2006 an estimated $236 billion was spent on such services. (Statistical Abstract of the United States (2009), Table 1247.) In the meantime, expenditures on civil legal aid from all sources, public and private, totaled roughly $1 billion in those years, less than a half percent of total expenditures on lawyers.

33. Table 2. "Public budget allocated to courts, legal aid and public prosecution in 2006, in Euros" in European Commission for the Efficiency of Justice, *European Judicial Systems* (Council of Europe Publishing, Belgium, 2008), 20–21.

34. The civil legal aid expenditure figures used to calculate the percentage comparison with the judicial budgets are the same as reflected on chart 2, supra. The judicial expenditure figures were then converted to U.S. dollars, to make the comparison possible. The figures are for 2004 while the court expenditure figures, as noted, are for 2006. However, it is unlikely a significant change occurred in civil legal aid expenditures in any of these countries between 2004 and 2006, especially an increase or decrease so large that it would distort the comparison with judicial expenditures in that same country.

35. Unfortunately, no agency compiles national expenditure figures for courts in the United States. In most states the courts are funded by a combination of state, county, and sometimes municipal governments, thus complicating the problem of aggregating budget or expenditure data. But it is possible to estimate a minimal figure of $20 billion for all U.S. courts, including the Federal courts where U.S. legal services lawyers also appear. The Federal Judicial Branch alone expended an estimated $ 5.8 billion in FY 2007 (Statistical Abstract of the United States: 2008, supra note, at Table 458). The California Judicial Branch budget for FY 2008 (which is a unified state-funded system) exceeded $3.7 billion. With a population of approximately 38 million people, California is spending nearly $100 per capita on its judicial system. (California Judicial Council, Annual Report-FY 2007–08, at 26). Assuming the rest of the country averaged even half of California's per capita level of expenditure on the courts (e.g., $50 per capita × 270 million = $13.5 billion), the combined annual state and federal expenditure level would have easily exceeded $20 billion in the 2007–08 period, and may well remain near that level even with the serious cutbacks occasioned by the recent economic crisis.

36. See 45 C.F.R. sec. 1611 (2009).

37. In the pre-recession year of 2006, the Census Bureau estimated 91,091,199 people in the United States had incomes below 200 percent of the poverty level. (U.S. Census Bureau, Poverty Status in the Past 12 Months (2006), available at https://factfinder.census.gov/serviet/STTable?-geo_id-01000US&-qr_name-ACS_2006_EST_G00_S1701&-ds_name=ACS_2006_EST_GOO.). By 2011, fully 122 million U.S. citizens, almost 40 percent of the nation's population, were at or below 200 percent of the federal poverty level. http://www.urban.org/center/liwf/index.cfm (last visited January 24, 2013.

38. A typical prepaid legal insurance co, Pre-Paid Legal Services, Inc., charges premiums in the range of $180 to $300 per year, for a rather limited range of services. See, http://www.magicdiligence.com/prepaid-legal-PPD-2010-04 (last visited January 25, 2013).

39. "Public Expenditures on Health services and Supplies." Table 128, *Statistical Abstract of the United States 2010* (Washington, D.C.: Government Printing Office, 2011) In addition to Medicaid, this figure includes most other miscellaneous health expenditures on the poor, but not expenditures Medicare may make for health services to elderly poor people.

40. In 2006, combined private and public expenditures on health care totaled $2.106 billion. ("National Health Expenditures from 1960 to 2017," Table 124, *Statistical Abstract of the United States 2010.*) The $323 billion federal and state governments allocated to health care for the poor in 2006 represented 15.33 percent of the combined health expenditures from all sources, public and private, for all U.S. citizens during that year.

41. In 2004, State and municipal governments spent $655 billion on education and $325 billion on public welfare. (Table 429, *Statistical Abstract of the United States 2010.*)

42. Reginald Heber Smith, *Justice and the Poor* (New York: Carnegie, 1919), xxvii. At the time Elihu Root wrote this Forward to Smith's book, he was a renowned and revered figure in the bar and in the nation. In the last decade of the 19th century and the first decades of the 20th century, he served as secretary of war and later secretary of state, a senator from New York, president of the American Bar Association, almost became a Republican candidate for U.S. president, and was awarded the 1912 Nobel Peace Prize. In between his stints in public service, he was one of the most successful and sought-after lawyers in New York and the nation. (*Yale Biographical Dictionary of American Law* (New Haven: Yale University Press, 2009), 467–68.

43. *Boddie v. Connecticut,* 401 U.S.371, 374–05 (1970).

44. Chief Justice Ron George, "State of the Judiciary" speech (2001).

45. As explained in the introduction to the large section devoted to this program on the ABA's main website: "The ABA Rule of Law Initiative is a public service project of the American Bar Association dedicated to promoting rule of law around the world. The ABA Rule of Law Initiative believes that rule of law promotion is the most effective long-term antidote to the pressing problems facing the world community today, including poverty, economic stagnation, and conflict." (See, http://www.abanet.org/rol/) William Neukom, the ABA president during 2006–07, launched this "Rule of Law Initiative" as his signature program and it remains as a continuing project of the association. Although it has several aspects, the most visible element of the Initiative so far was a "World Justice Forum" in Vienna, Austria, during July, 2008. This conference brought together more than 450 governmental and nongovernmental leaders from 83 nations including Asia and the Pacific, Africa, the Middle East, Europe, Latin America, and North America. Edited versions of the papers prepared for the conference were published recently as R. L. Nelson, J. Heckman, and L. Cabatingan (Editors), *Global Perspectives on the Rule of Law* (London: Routledge-Cavendish, 2009).

46. Mark David Agrast, Juan Carlos Botero and Alejandro Ponce, *WJP Rule of Law Index 2011* (Washington, D.C.: The World Justice Project, 2011), 113.

47. Mark David Agrast, Juan Carlos Botero and Alejandro Ponce, *WJP Rule of Law Index 2011*, 24 et seq.

48. Dan Froomkin, "Rule of Law Index: U.S. Ranks Low in Access to Justice Compared to Other Wealthy Nations" at http://www.huffingtonpost.com/2012/11/28/rule-of-law-index-2012_n_2200765.html (last visited January 23, 2013).

49. See, "Bar Survey Reveals Widespread Legal Illiteracy," *Cal. Lawyer* (1991): 68, 69.

50. See, poll results reported in Association of Trial Lawyers, 1991–1992 Desk Reference Supplement: Commemorating the 200th Anniversary of the Signing of the Bill of Rights (1991).

51. *Thirty-Fourth Annual Report of the President, Treasurer and Attorneys of the Legal Aid Society for the Year 1909* (New York: The Thomas Press, 1910), 6.

Index

About the Author

EARL JOHNSON JR. served as a Justice on the California Court of Appeal for a quarter of a century, retiring in 2007 for the express purpose of researching and writing this book. Now a visiting scholar at the University of Southern California and at the Western Center on Law and Poverty, he has been involved with civil legal aid as a participant, observer and writer for nearly half a century. Johnson served as the Director of the War on Poverty's OEO Legal Services Program from 1966 to 1968, leading some to call him "the architect of the modern legal services program." After leaving government, Johnson became a professor of law at the University of Southern California where he helped create and codirect the USC Clinical Semester, which gave legal help to low-income clients. He has chaired or served on the boards of half a dozen legal services organizations at the national and local levels, and co-drafted the first version of the Legal Services Corporation legislation, which, after many changes, eventually passed as the Legal Services Corporation Act in 1974.

For several years Professor Johnson directed USC's Program on Dispute Resolution Policy and was a visiting scholar at the University of Florence (Italy), codirecting an international access to justice study. Johnson's research resulted in several books and a dozen articles on the subject, including authoring *Justice and Reform: The Formative Years of the American Legal Services Program* (New York: Russell Sage, 1974/New Brunswick: Transaction Books, 1978) and coauthoring *Toward Equal Justice: A Comparative*

Study of Legal Aid in Modern Societies (Dobbs Ferry: Oceana, 1975, 1981). A review of *Justice and Reform* called Johnson "a careful historian, persuasive evangelist, and fearless prophet."

After his appointment to the bench in 1982, Johnson published several more articles on legal aid, and authored the "Access to Justice" article in Elsivier's International Encyclopedia of the Behavioral and Social Sciences. He also chaired the "Access to Justice Working Group," which in 1997 led to creation of the California Commission on Access to Justice, and in 1999 was invited to join the International Legal Aid Group (ILAG), an organization of scholars from more than a dozen countries who research and write about legal aid and related access to justice issues.

Born and raised in Watertown, South Dakota, Johnson earned his B.A. with Honors in Economics from Northwestern University, his J.D. from the University of Chicago Law School, where he was book review editor of the *University of Chicago Law Review,* and his L.L.M. in Criminal Law from Northwestern University School of Law. He lives in Channel Islands Beach, California, is married to Barbara Yanow Johnson, a former legal services lawyer, and has three children and two grandchildren.